ALSO BY JOHN HEWITT

The Model 12 Winchester As A Way of Life

All Great Retrievers Are Temperamental

John Hewitt

Hopper Creek Press
Fairbanks, Alaska

© 2017 John Hewitt

All rights reserved. No part of this book may be reproduced in any manner without prior written permission from the author and publisher:

Published 2017 by Hopper Creek Press

John Hewitt, Hopper Creek Press, 920 Amanita Rd., Fairbanks, Alaska 99712
hoppercreekpress@gmail.com • hoppercreekpress.com

First Edition

Printed in Canada

ISBN 978-0-9974691-0-3
Library of Congress Control Number 2017932700

All the stories in this book were previously published in *Gray's Sporting Journal*.

Photo opposite page from McCarthy family collection.

All other photos from Hewitt family collection, except as noted.

Illustration on page 174 by the author.

For Mary Liz (Zercher) McCarthy

Contents

INTRODUCTION xi
PREFACE xvii

1. Pilot Error 1
2. The Revenge of Ernest Hemingway 9
3. On the Cusp of Winter 17
4. The Lone Star Prufrock 27
5. Oatmeal 35
6. The Cheerleader and the Bear 41
7. All Great Retrievers Are Temperamental 49
8. Nearly Skunked Again 67
9. Russ 75
10. Pushing the Season 93
11. Raw Canadian 99
12. Montana Done Traditionally 107
13. A Duck Camp French Lesson 113
14. There's Always Tomorrow 121
15. Sugar Snow 147
16. Walking Up Lake Trout 157
17. The Last Drink in the Bottle 165
18. Cornered 199
19. Staying in Touch 207
20. Hiram's Theme Song 233
21. Maneaters of Moose Creek 241
22. Ted Zercher's Sandwiches 249
23. The Year the Swan Decoyed 257
24. Is It Alberta Yet? 285

John Hewitt

Contents, continued

25. Bwana Walker's Guaranteed Sheep Hunt 301
26. Bobwhites, Doctors, and Hunts Remembered 311
27. Walker Among the Musk Ox 315
28. Stanley Goes with the Flow 323
29. The Dharma Goose 333
30. Avoiding Zillich's Mortgage 343

Introduction
by Reed Austin

In the autumn of 1975, twenty years ago nearly to the day, a manuscript decoyed unbeckoned into what passed for the editorial ivory tower of the fledgling *Gray's Sporting Journal*. Armed with a newly minted college degree in American literature, and the vast wisdom accumulated during three months on the job as editorial grunt, I dutifully noted the following:

"Nice story, but nothing much happens."

For some reason, I bumped the story, "Sugar Snow," by some guy named John Hewitt, up to aspiring publisher Ed Gray for a second opinion. His comment, in its entirety:

"Buy it!"

Those fortunate enough to have trailed John Hewitt's stories through the succeeding twenty years of *Gray's Sporting Journal* ought to ponder what might have happened, had cluelessness won out over intuition and that rejection letter been mailed.

Having thus qualified myself as an editor, I'll turn to John as a hunter and fisherman, since the reader has enough of John's stories in hand to arrive at his or her own conclusion about John's writing abilities.

On and off for twenty years I've survived deer hunts with John (and Larry Taylor and Ed Gray), *all* the way up in Maine, where townships are known simply as T5 R6, where pack tents in deep snow and still-hunting the high ridges are the order of the week. (John claims to be the only person on earth who routinely travels from Alaska to New England to hunt big game.) We've conspired against ducks on Cape Cod's winter marshes, fly fished for killer pumpkinseeds and largemouth, and plugged boulder-strewn Buzzard's Bay surf for stripers and blues. And corresponded. Some day, if we're lucky, I may convince John to let me publish his letters, which are, in their own way, as good or better than anything you might enjoy in these pages.

It would be hard to think of a more well-rounded (have you seen him lately?) writer working in the outdoor field today. In John we have what may be the ideal blend of small- and big-game hunter, rifleman and shotgunner, fly fisherman, bait fisherman, plug caster and noodler. When supper is on the line, this is the guy you send to the creek with the how-big and how-many orders.

John is a reasonably avid ice fisherman, but worries that another hunter/gatherer might mistake him for a walrus while thus engaged, and hose him for his tusks, which he claims are Boone & Crockett class.

Getting back to the supper department, here's an item I wangled out of John years ago, after considerable prodding. It seems that he was banging nails on the roof of an outfitter's cabin in Alaska's far hunting grounds, where John was an assistant guide. A herd of caribou appeared at full lope, three hundred plus yards away. The winter meat locker being empty this early in the season, John, ever the pragmatist, exchanged his hammer for a .264 Winchester, and took four caribou on the dead run with four shots.

Another raconteur would likely be met with what might charitably be called a cocked eye. John being John, a man of exact memory and even more exacting honesty, as you'll see for yourselves in the following pages, exaggeration is not at issue here. (Actually, I suspect he might have taken six for six or better, but will only admit to four. Groceries are groceries, and it's a *long* season...)

All Great Retrievers Are Temperamental

John is a fifty-year-old former Marine officer and transplanted Kansan who has spent the last 26 years near Fairbanks, Alaska. Growing up in a family which raised bird dogs, built their own fishing boats, and hunted and fished year 'round, he found those two avocations to be natural choices for he and his twin brother, only one of whom would return from Viet Nam.

John was five when he received his first fly rod, if you don't count the telescoping steel outfit of two years prior. A BB gun at age seven, pellet gun at nine and full-sized 20 gauge at eleven were the natural progression. Pigeons, doves, ducks and prairie chickens occupied his summers and falls thereafter.

He bought his own .22 also at eleven, his family considering squirrels and cottontails much more sporting with a rifle than a shotgun, and added an eighty-year-old .45/70 when he was thirteen, and his .264 Winchester at sixteen, to use for coyotes hunted with trail hounds in Kansas through the winter.

John spent eight years guiding for big game in Alaska, did some fire fighting and commercial fishing, where he met his wife, Mary; spent years laboring on the Trans-Alaska Pipeline and in the oil fields of Prudhoe Bay, followed by fifteen years of carpentry. He prepared for these pursuits with a B.A. in English, and Purple Heart hard-earned in a rice paddy, and a Master's degree in English, in that order.

Today, as *Gray's Sporting Journal's* Senior Editor, John is an advertiser's worst nightmare. He still shoots the Remington 870 three-inch 12 gauge he bought in 1965 for $110, and fishes with the Orvis Battenkill six-weight he bought (with reel, line and aluminum tube) in 1969 for $168. These, to the best of our knowledge, are the last two items in the sporting line he actually bought, except for a few boxes of steel shot, and that took an act of Congress.

On really cold days he still wears the Duofold Operation Deepfreeze four-layer insulated long under wear he bought in 1959 with the fifty bucks his mother gave him to go downtown and buy a suit fit to graduate from junior high school in.

He bought a two-burner Coleman stove in 1969 and used it for eleven years, until his father died and he inherited the Hewitt family Coleman two-burner, vintage 1946. Now his new (?) one is in storage, to be used at such time as he wears the old one out.

John and Mary live with their six children in Fairbanks, where John raises 300 pounds of potatoes a year and shoots a moose, in order to, as much as possible avoid having to buy food at all. (For more about gardens and moose, see "Sugar Snow.")

If you've enjoyed John's stories through the years, you undoubtedly bought this volume on purpose. If not, and possibly were given this book by a friend, consider yourself lucky, because you have a good friend.

What the newcomer will discover is that John Hewitt is a consummate story-teller, with stories worth telling. But of all the compliments on both his writing and wingshooting ability, and assessments of the place he has won for himself in the world, he is most fond of quoting the drunken prostitute who, while exiting an elevator in the lobby of the poshest hotel in Houston, collided with him and, backing up and taking in his wardrobe which included his ubiquitous patched Carhartt bib overalls, exclaimed, "Whut is somebody lak *you* doin' in a place lak *this*?"

I could say more, but I wouldn't want to ruin his image.

Enjoy.

Reed Austin, 1995

All Great Retrievers Are Temperamental

Preface

How I got the money to afford my guns…

Gramps got me the shotgun, a Model 50 Winchester 20 gauge (with a 28" modified choke barrel, to which he had a Simmons ventilated rib installed in Kansas City) in 1956 for $145, minus the rib. That was a shitload of money in those days, twice what a Model 12 would cost. But, it was a semi-auto, Winchester's third attempt, and it was widely accepted that it would be the Remington 1100 of the firearms world (which it never was…). *But*, it served me well for ten years, and *never* jammed. But I kept it scrupulously clean.

My .22 was a Winchester Model 77 clip-loader (8 rounds) bought for $57.00 in 1957, at Gordon Elliot's, which had then changed owners and names to Bob Shoyer's Sporting Goods. I put a Weaver B6 scope on it, a $14.00 ¾" scope that was functional, at best. I later shitcanned the scope and got a Weaver K3 for $37.50, a 1" high-powered rifle scope which worked much better and is on it yet. It accounted for a ton of cottontails and fox squirrels the next ten years in Kansas (or, more accurately about 40 or 50 of each).

I found a couple of used-gun stores, which I visited every week (I could ride the bus downtown for a nickel), and I fell prey to a .45/70 Model 1884 Springfield trapdoor for $28.50 in 1958. When I got it home and showed it to Clyde, he said, "I could have bought one of those for $.50 when I was ten in 1914; they were selling them off… it was $4.40 for a .30/40 Krag, as surplus." Oh, well…

An admission as to jobs: they were *really* hard to get in the Fifties. So, my twin and I sold tomatoes and cucumbers door-to-door for ten cents a pound from Gramps' victory garden. We opened up bank accounts at four years of age, and put the proceeds in there to be used against college tuition. We got a dollar an hour for working in Gramps' garden, which seemed like taking Gramps for a ride, but he was determined that we would go to college. I had six hundred dollars in the account when it came time to go to college.

Tom bought a .243 from Bob Shoyer in 1958 for $75, to shoot coyotes with, a FN Mauser, ostensibly made by Colt, and had a Weaver K4 scope ($45.00) mounted on it by Bob. He killed several coyotes with it over the next ten years.

I was 16 in April of 1961, and at last, I could get a job! And I did, working in the concession stand at the Cloverleaf Drive-In Theater, where the modern-day Dillon's grocery store now stands, for $17.00 a week. But I really got more, taking over the cleaning-up of the grounds from the person who was paid to do it, which paid me an extra $6.00 a week, from July 3rd to September 1st. When I saw what my total take would be, I went down to Bob Shoyer's and ordered my .264 Winchester Magnum for $142.50, and $78.50 for my Weaver V8 variable-power scope. Which by and by proved unequal to the task and had to be replaced with a Leupold 3X-9X variable. It is still on it.

I had got into reloading at 13, for my older brother's 1903 Springfield .30/06, Jug's 8 mm Mauser and my twin's .243, so I was all set up to do it for my .264.

I went to Alaska (for good) in January of 1969, and enrolled in graduate school. On the G.I. Bill. In 1973, I took a job assistant guiding for $28.00 a day, and figured I would need a bigger rifle. A used pre-'64 Model 70 in .338 showed up on the shelves of Frontier Sporting Goods for $200, with scope, and I purchased it. And changed scopes to a Leupold 3X-9X. I guided for eight years, but the guiding was getting in the way of my duck hunting, so I quit, and never shot a thing with that .338, although it shot as well as my .264, into ¾" groups at 100 yards. And I *did* shoot a moose with the .338 in 1990. And a caribou in 1973.

Before I came to Alaska, I needed a bigger shotgun, something that would take down a goose, and I found it in 1966, from a gun dealer on campus, for $110.00, a Remington 870 Wingmaster 3" Magnum, marked down from $130.00 because the guy he sold it to originally fired it twice (1 7/8 oz. loads) and declared that it kicked too much! I've used that shotgun my whole life and it hasn't malfunctioned yet. It is light enough to be an all-purpose gun. As a matter of fact, one year before my stroke, I purchased an identical gun off the used-gun rack at Cabela's in Kansas City for $350, and it even had finish left on its stock!

And there you have it: a .22, a high-powered rifle and a shotgun. I did not acquire a great number of guns in the old days because I would rather spend cash on going hunting.

In the interim, you inherit a lot of guns just by outliving everybody. I have inherited seven Model 12s and two Model 42 Winchesters.

I had my stroke (caused by a hole in my heart, a .55 caliber one, in case you're interested), which was patched up in Swedish Memorial Hospital in Seattle using a thing like a stent, put in through my femoral artery on December 11th, 2007, and haven't been able to shoot a shotgun or cast a fly rod since. I can drive, though. So every year, I go to Kansas and up to South Dakota, and drive hunters to the ends of fields, and go around and pick them up at the other end. Sort of like old Shorty. Of course, I wasn't in WWI, and, more important, didn't let them Bohemians from Oberlin come over and kick Norcatur's ass at baseball.

Where was I? Oh yeah, guns. I have passed my .264 on to Rose (thirty now, I think…) and I have bought a couple of high-powered rifles for other family members. I bought Clyde a Model 77 Ruger .270 Winchester, left-handed, and Deborah, a Model 7 Remington in 7mm/08. She has killed a caribou with it, and Clyde has killed a Sitka black-tailed deer with the .270. In 2015, Clyde went moose hunting with Ann, but, Clyde being Clyde, the .270 was locked in a friend's cabin, and so he took the .264. And got a moose with it! One shot, from a spruce tree, 200 yards. And twelve years ago, Tom plugged a bull caribou on the North Slope with the .264 (I had the .338) at 20 feet! Two years ago, hunting with Ann, Rose laid a bull caribou down on the Taylor Highway with the .264 (at 90 yards, in the fog), the same as she did this year on the Steese Highway at 80 yards. The kids have more luck getting up close than I ever did! The average range I used to shoot caribou was 200 yards.

I have three reloaders. Two Hornaday 366's, one for 12 gauge, the other one for 20 gauge. And one RCBS Rock-chucker, with dies for .243 Winchester, .264 Winchester Magnum, .270 Winchester, 7mm/08 Remington, 7mm Remington Magnum, .30 M1 Carbine, .30/40 Krag, .308 Winchester, .30/06 Springfield, .338 Winchester Magnum, .45/70 Govt., .458 Winchester Magnum, .357 Magnum/.38 Special, .41 Remington Magnum, .45 ACP.

In spite of having done my Science Fair project on the Armalite AR-10 and AR-15 in 1959, I last fired an M16 in Vietnam in 1968, and I don't have any of the rifles on the AR-15 body. I've stuck to bolt-actions… for better or for worse.

Pilot Error

It would be inaccurate to assume Tom and I were always fast friends with Terry. In fact, when we met him in the seventh grade, we regarded him with a great deal of suspicion; he had already ignored two of the fundamental precepts in our belief system. First, he had caught a bigger bass than we had, and, second, had charged straight down to Mel Shell's Phillip's 66 station with it. Mel did the weekly Friday half-column "Outdoor Notes" for the *Topeka Daily Capital*.

He even got his picture in the paper, with the fish. And told exactly where he caught it. Never mind that it was a pond in the most public of city parks…Tom and I both knew there were bigger ones in there than anyone had ever admitted to catching, though thus far we had never landed one. The last thing we needed was some publicity hound with more luck and less brains than us, to horn in and dredge a three-and-a-half pound largemouth out of our closest fishing hole with, of all things, that Ford Fairlane 500 of lures, the Heddon River Runt Spook. We'd been using a Jitterbug and a Hawaiian Wiggler.

However…six years together in the same two public schools proved sufficient to conquer our initial animosity. Terry's indiscretions seemed minor when compared to those of the hundreds of other non-hunting and non-fishing infidels who, the minute they turned sixteen, dedicated their lives to endlessly driving around town in old Fords and Chevies, swilling illegal 3.2 beer and discussing the physical attributes of the more lavishly endowed members of the other, brain-dead gender (who didn't know a Model 12 or a Hula Popper from a watermelon). The only difference between us and the early Jesuits who sought to convert Canada's Indians to Catholicism was that the three of us never got burnt at the stake…literally, anyway. The two or three guys in our graduating class who we were sure were gay were, compared to us, mainstream.

For all that, I was perennially reluctant to go hunting with Terry and his dad, Jesse. Foremost among the gun-handling rules that had been drilled into me was one about never hunting with strangers or people not as safety conscious as oneself. Jesse was inordinately fond of bourbon. All grownups were, it seemed, excepting my mother and the more fundamentally religious and tiresome of her brothers and sisters.

But Jesse and Terry kept bird dogs. And Nebraska opened their quail and pheasant seasons *weeks* ahead of Kansas, so, for the nominal price of a nonresident hunting license and a little gasoline, one could extend one's bird season almost a month. Terry and Jess had done it for years, so eventually I agreed to go along, on a weekend when Wendell and Critchfield and one or two other dissolute members of Jesse's entourage had other things to do. Jesse, I figured, I could keep an eye on.

For food, he brought a shotgun shell case, the old wooden kind, full of potted meat products, saltine crackers and longhorn cheese.

And a red metal Coca-Cola chest full of ice and Cokes. I liked Pepsis. This wasn't *lunches*, now…it was for breakfast and supper, too.

At the motel Friday night, Terry dutifully devoured a tin or two of chopped liver (suspiciously similar in both texture and smell to the two cans of horse meat we'd just gouged into dog dishes and set before Lady and old Rock) and announced, between two of Jesse's stories, that he thought he'd take a walk and see if he could find out anything about local birds.

The main street was two or three blocks long. One story later, I made a similar excuse and headed for the service station where I'd noticed old-timers gathered. A half hour of listening politely to how much better farmers had had it under Ike than they did now under Kennedy resulted in some questions directed at me by one of the regulars, and shortly I had an invitation to hunt a half section of milo and soil bank land bristling with pheasants. Lot of birds, *if* you was willing to walk. It had always been the grownups' job to get permission, and I was surprised to discover it was so easy…it hadn't even cost me the usual pint of Glenmore and pound of Russell Stovers for the missus.

Terry was researching local bird populations at the counter of the brightly-lit, deserted diner when I found him. I slid onto the stool beside him and he glanced up from his plate.

"Don't get the shrimp dinner," he whispered, "the menu claims you get two dozen shrimp and you really get twenty-one."

"What?!" I said. "There's that many left there and you been eating for five or ten minutes."

He diminished the Coke in the large Coca-Cola glass by half with one sustained suck on his straw, burped, and said, "This is *two* shrimp dinners. You order the chicken dinner."

"Why chicken?"

"So I can see if it's any good. I may want to order one myself after I finish this. You ever see shrimp this small?"

The first field in the morning had the birds, all right, but it confirmed my suspicion that we were dead in the water on pheasants without Tom and Pete. Tom's R.O.T.C. honor society was directing traffic that Saturday at the K.U. football game, and Pete, being a Lab, was at home because it seemed pointless to bring an untried retriever along when we already had two seasoned pointing dogs who also retrieved. And Jesse was not much of a walker. His southern (Arkansas) inclination was to amble from point to point and spend the whole day on the same eighty acres, with three hours off for lunch. He had a cavalry mentality where walking was concerned. Of course, he'd been in the cavalry in the Thirties before they'd ruined it (with tanks).

We scratched around all morning to get two or three, before Terry and I saw the writing on the wall and forgot about pheasants. Quail suited Jesse's style more.

A quarter mile into one section, we were following a brushy fenceline, Jesse on my left, Terry flanking wide to my right, the dogs very birdy ahead. Thirty feet beyond the intersecting quarter-mile fence, they finally quit creeping.

"They got 'em now," I said to Terry, a shotgun range away, and just across a little draw, in plain sight.

"You stay ready while I get through this fence," Jesse instructed, and clambered through, snagging the crotch of the triple-stitched canvas hunting pants he'd had the former German P.O.W. tailor sew for him at the camp he claimed he'd commanded in the closing years of the war, over in Missouri. Once through, he prepared to deal with the covey if it flushed while I was on my way through the fence, his old dented-barrel Stevens double at high port. Jesse may have been the worst wing shot in the history of the world.

"Don't forget I'm over here," Terry cautioned. This was before blaze orange hunting caps and vests. Still, I reasoned, as I belly-crawled under the fence, gunless, Terry would never have said that if it was Tom or Clyde or me on the firing line.

The flush came while I was still on my hands and knees, and the birds swung Terry's way, as we'd both expected. Jesse's stock was not even to his shoulder when he let go with the modified barrel. Right at Terry, it looked like.

"HEY!!! Goddamn it!" Terry shouted.

"Did that hit you?" Jesse asked.

"I'm going to the car," Terry replied, and climbed back over the fence we'd all just crossed. I followed suit and joined him partway back to the road. We'd both unloaded our guns. I'd never heard him swear in front of his father, much less at him. He was still pretty pale, more scared than mad. I was so scared my hands were shaking, and so relieved when I could see he wasn't hit in the face and eyes, I almost cried.

"You want to hunt anymore?" he queried.

"No."

"Me either. Let's go home, then."

"It's only Saturday. What if Jess wants to hunt Sunday like we planned?"

"He can do it by himself."

"Where'd that shot hit you?" I asked.

"Aw, mostly below the knees," he said, stopping and raising one almost-new insulated Red Wing Irish Setter, now freckled with bird-shot gouges. "But it could just as easy been my face."

"That's what I thought it was. Are all Jesse's brothers this bad with a shotgun?"

"Don't know. He's the only one I ever hunted with."

Never again, I thought to myself. Jesse drove straight home, two and a half hours, and no one said a word the whole way.

Seven Octobers, a marriage apiece and one funeral later, Terry sounded excited to hear me, on the eve of the Kansas quail opener. It was a spur-of-the-moment trip.

"Where you at, anyway?"

"L.A. International. I caught a tanker into the local Air Force base and paid some guy ten bucks to drive me over here. I can be in Kansas City on United by nine P.M."

"Good. I'll be there. You bring your shotgun?"

"Of course."

"Oh, good. You gonna have to hunt with Jess an' me. He's been planning this one for weeks. Clyde took Pete and left at noon, he's clear out west with Jug and them."

"Man, Terry. I been shot enough lately. You know what I said in '63. No more hunting with Jess."

"Jess ain't going to shoot anyone. I been hunting with him fifteen years and he ain't shot me yet."

"Uh-huh. Your Irish Setters come from the factory with all those divots in them."

"You *seen* that. It was an accident."

"That's what worries me."

"Look...I *promise* he won't hose you tomorrow. Guarantee it. Okay?"

"Who else is going?"

"Critchfield."

"Now I *know* I'm dead."

Critchfield was actually not so bad, though of an age with Jesse, and of the same opinion as to what constituted a good day's walk. We hunted Wendell's eighty, though, and had no permission elsewhere nearby, so we might as well be thorough.

We flushed a really big covey east down the main draw fairly early, and on the second flush, they split. Jess and Critch were certain the left half had put back down in a little side draw just beyond a slight rise of unharvested milo, while Terry and I were equally convinced that the main bunch had flown straight, and that the flush was short a dozen birds. Jess and Critch headed off in their direction while Terry, I, and the dogs tromped around looking for lay birds.

As bobwhites will do when well hidden, Jess's bunch let he and Critch walk right through them in the milo, then, unbeknownst to Terry and I, flushed heading straight back the way they'd come. We heard the flush just after their two hats disappeared beyond the rise, and I momentarily forgot who we were hunting with, and watched expectantly for a stray to swing back for the main draw. Having recently seen men take 30-caliber rounds in the thigh or side or bicep and, Hollywood war movies notwithstanding, never stagger, I was startled to find myself on my back in the dirt, one eye already full of blood, the knuckles of my left hand stinging. It felt like somebody two-handed me with a tennis racket, right in the face.

"Did that hit you?" Terry called from further down the draw.

"Yeh," I hollered back, weakly.

"You all right?"

"No."

"Oh shit!" I could hear him running toward me, but Lady got to me first and began licking my bloody, closed eye. I sat up.

"Can you see?" Terry was white as a sheet this time, twice as pale as when it was him that was shot.

"Don't know. I'll see." I opened the eye and blinked. Both eyes were running the tears that always result from a hard slap or blow near the nose. Blurry at first, then clearer, in a few moments I determined that the shot was under the skin, against the bone rimming the eye socket, perhaps three-quarters of an inch left of my left eye. Where it still is.

"Shit," I said, "so much for your guarantees."

At different points later in the day (Terry pretty much shot everyone's limit, as usual), Critch and Jess approached me individually and assured me it was the other one who'd blasted me. The main indication I had of how traumatic it was for both of them was the total abstention from bourbon on the half-hour ride home. Even Terry was impressed. "Maybe it taught them both a lesson," he said later.

"You kind of hope so," I said.

My best sister-in-law went along once last summer, to operate the Trius trap while I looked over the shoulders of three of my kids as they tried to break clay pigeons with the lightweight 1100 Youth model and the cut-off .410. At home, after they were all in bed, she asked, "You went pretty ballistic on Clyde when he forgot his gun was loaded and cocked. Do you think you may be a bit too severe with them when they're shooting?"

"That, Darnel," I told her, "would be impossible."

The Revenge of
Ernest Hemingway

One of the things I was sure about where Hiram was concerned, even before I'd hunted with him the first time, was that he was a great student of Hemingway. Student, I said, not scholar. The undergraduate course which alerted him to Papa's writing must've been something to behold. By the time I met him, he was married to a girl who, though he never actually referred to her as Hadley, did not last any longer. Instead of Paris, he expatriated himself to Alaska. Instead of Lady Brett Ashley, he took up with me. Now that I think of it, *I* was the wounded veteran, though.

Because no one had run any bulls through the streets of Fairbanks in recent memory, he eventually suggested a ptarmigan hunt. My own great grace in life, then and now, is that I'm always game for such proposals, so long as they're legal. And there's a shotgun involved.

The line between where Papa left off and Hiram started was very blurry. He did little towards clearing the confusion up. I spent the rest of the week before the proposed hunt in the library, boning up -

John Hewitt

not on the characteristics, behavior and preferred food of ptarmigan, which I'd never seen before - but on Hemingway's short stories, in hopes of eventually figuring out what Papa or Hiram expected of a hunting partner. *Big* mistake. Very big. This was before the advent of the "Kids - Don't try this at home!" disclaimers. But Hiram, the only person I knew at school who both hunted and owned what passed for an automobile, was my only ticket out of the dorm on weekends, so I was determined to humor him. There were only three remaining weekends before the end of April, which was the end of bird season.

We rattled through Livengood, the defunct, 1905-vintage mining town where the one-time-only winter road, the Ice Road, the Hickel Highway, abandoned forever three weeks hence, began, and commenced looking for bird tracks beside the road. One is tempted to say, in the ditches, but, of course, there *were* no ditches, no culverts, no bridges. Hiram mainly looked for tracks, while I mentally catalogued the abandoned cabins we passed for an abode for the night. We had no tent. We preferred to believe, until such time as we could afford one, that tents were for wusses anyway.

Hiram had better luck than I did. "There's some!" he exclaimed, after a few miles. Fresh, too.

"Jesus, Hiram," I said, looking at the tracks leading downhill, "lookit all of 'em. Dozens." I'd expect a family-size covey, minus the winter mortality, maybe six. Hemingway was not a great how-to source for ptarmigan hunting.

"Take plenty of shells," Hiram instructed, wrenching our snowshoes out from under the camping gear in the back seat of the aging Volkswagen, and slipping into his army surplus parka shell. I strapped on my long, surplus snowshoes and straightened up.

"Say, Lady Brett," I inquired politely, "how many shells *are* you taking?" He finished emptying one box of #6s into a large leather purse he'd requisitioned from his wife, the long strap of which he'd just slung across his chest, bandolier fashion.

"I used to carry my shells in my pockets, too," he said. "It's fine if you like wearing your pants down around your knees." Then he tossed a second, unopened box into a large canvas rucksack and wrestled into that, too. Extracting three 16-gauge shells from his purse, he fastened the little toggle and loaded his pump.

I unscrewed my forend cap, tipped the barrel down, shook the whittled-willow-branch plug out of the magazine spring into my hand, and tossed it aside. He watched as I screwed the cap back on my 12 gauge, identical to his except, as he put it, I had the fancy one, with the rib.

"You do that a lot in Kansas?" he asked.

"Oh yeh, mainly on pheasants. Didn't you say the limit on ptarmigan was twenty?"

"Yeh."

"Well…you want me to take yours out?"

"No," he said, "I never had mine out since I bought the thing in high school. What become of the little thing in yours that's supposed to keep the spring from flying out?"

"I done this once before daylight, in waist-high brome grass. It flew about twenty feet. I was always going to get another one, but it makes putting the plug in and taking it out a lot quicker, this way."

"How many does it hold now?"

"Five."

"Like I said, take plenty of shells."

It was not the best day we ever had on ptarmigan, but it was a good one. Most important, Hiram did not seem to go to any lengths to insure he got more than I did, which probably was the one area in which the Papa/Hiram line was well defined. We had ten between us when the bunch finally gave us the slip and we elected to look for more atop a treeless dome which appeared to be a half mile away but which turned out to be more like two. We took turns breaking trail.

"Even if there's none up there," I said as we paused to blow, halfway up, "next week we'll have this approach trail all tromped down. We can maybe carry our sleeping bags up there and camp out in the last trees below timberline."

"In the snow?" he asked.

"Sure," I said. "You never camped out in the snow?" I had. Twice.

"How far you think it is now?" he replied.

"Oh, a half mile."

"That's what you said an hour ago."

There were birds up there, all right. Two. I got them both. We did a perfunctory circumnavigation of the hilltop and descended on rubbery legs, putting the finishing touches on next week's trail to Base Camp 1.

My best candidate for the present bivouac site was a smallish log cabin which, on closer inspection, had not only a caved-in roof, but a fifteen-foot spruce growing out of the middle of the floor inside. The porch was somewhat more commodious, the five-foot gable-end overhang having survived, so that the snow there was only a foot deep, as opposed to the general three feet. I stamped out a campsite with snowshoes and began hauling gear from the VW while Hiram, in the fading daylight, hiked back up the road to inspect a veritable snowshoe hare interstate he'd spotted from the car. I was pumping up the Coleman stove his father was probably still looking for in his Michigan garage when I heard three measured shots.

He returned with three white hares.

"You know how to cook these?" he asked.

"Sure," I said. I'd never seen one before. I had a favorite way to cook fox squirrels, though. He cleaned them while I made coffee and cut a bunch of spruce boughs for a bed, something I'd learned from a pal in the Marines in Virginia two Decembers previous.

The recipe was successful, but not quick, so we cleaned the birds. Before the fragrant hare was tender, the stars were out. Hiram laid down, clothed, on top of his unrolled sleeping bag, fired up his corncob pipe, sipped his coffee and looked up at the stars approvingly. It was about zero.

"When we talk about this at home," he said, "around my wife... remember to call this place the 'Starlight Motel.'"

"Why?"

"Oh, I thought I'd bring her up in a couple of weeks, and she's more likely to come along if she thinks we stay in a motel."

"Okay. Where's your dishes?"

It was a one-nighter, so the following morning, Hiram threw the whole pound of bacon in the skillet, after we'd finally faced the music, crawled out of our army surplus duckfeather mummies and gotten dressed. I had my surplus canvas mukluks on over wool pants and had run up and down the short trail to the car six times, then snapped an armful of dead, dry, pencil-sized branches off the trunks of the larger nearby spruce, sloshed some Coleman fuel on (Kids - Don't try this at home!) and touched it off.

The bacon was pretty fat because it had been pretty cheap, and we forked the crisp strips straight out of the skillet into our mouths. Hiram then cracked six eggs into the half-skillet of fat, flipped some hot grease over the yolks, and lifted them onto the two plates, which I'd warmed over the fire.

We ate the eggs without salt or pepper, because Hiram had brought none and the C-Ration accessory packets he'd scavenged from summer forest fire-fighting work had already been rifled for the good stuff. We still had an entire loaf of bread I'd appropriated from the university food service, in lieu of the meals I was missing there. I worked on the breakfast shift, usually.

"Say," I suggested, "Hemingway soaked up the bacon grease in bread and ate it, you know."

"What story was that in?"

"'The Battler.'"

"Oh. That was Nick Adams."

"Nick Adams…Hemingway…what's the difference?"

He shrugged. I opened the loaf of bread, flopped two slices into the grease, and turned the burner up a little. They sank.

"Man," I said, "that's a lot of fat."

"I see that," he observed.

After a while I turned the bread. It had not browned very well on the bottom. In fact, it was not crisp at all, as I'd expected. It was kind of soggy, oozing bacon grease like a saturated sponge.

"Mr. Adams," I offered, after a while, "would you care for some bread fried in bacon fat?"

"Not after you worked so hard cooking it. Go ahead."

So I did, while he fried a second pair of slices in the now-modest amount of fat in the skillet. His browned perfectly on both sides. Or wonderfully, as Papa would've put it. He smacked his lips while he ate it, licked the grease out of his moustache and washed it down with coffee.

Like the hunter on my favorite Winchester calendar print, I tipped the coffee pot off the stove when I bolted, but a whitetail buck bounding through camp didn't set me off, and it wasn't a lever-action .30/30 I was leaping for, either.

"Hiram," I hollered from the closest clump of small spruces, moments later, "you didn't bring any extra skivvies, did you?"

"No. You need 'em?"

"I guess not. Just throw me the roll of paper towels."

He had heated up more water and made a couple of cups of Coffee, Instant, Type II, when I got back. I emptied two packets of sugar into my canteen cup, and tried it.

"It was ham fat," he finally said.

"What?"

"In the story, it wasn't bacon fat. They used ham fat."

"They did?"

A month later, the Friday night before finals week, I boarded a plane for Battle Creek, where I bought a car of my own.

John Hewitt

On the Cusp of Winter

The poet was wrong. About April being the cruelest month, that is. In Alaska, that distinction should be reserved for November. For a duck hunter in the Interior, anyway, the high point of that month being the receiving of his *Ducks Unlimited* magazine and studying the wonderful color pictures of all the kinds of ducks which every other hunter on the continent with a Federal duck stamp is avidly and successfully pursuing. The oldest of philosophical questions, "Why am I here?" becomes a lot more than just rhetorical.

Besides the obvious mental anguish, November can inflict some real pain. Technically, it's not winter yet, and the hunter with more enthusiasm than sense can get lured out by a stretch of relative Indian summer weather, only to wake up in his tent or truck to the familiar but unsettling feeling of his nose hairs all freezing stiff as porcupine quills with every inhalation.

Back very shortly after I had just fallen off the turnip truck in Alaska, when I looked up to anyone with two winters under their belt as an old timer and role model, a recent acquaintance, whom

I shall call Hiram because that's who he was, approached me about a caribou hunt. He knew I had never killed one, was convinced life was meaningless until I passed that milestone, and had no winter meat other than two dozen mallards.

There are several highways in Alaska which the state happily abandons every October, at least as far as any form of maintenance goes. As snow builds up on these, they become less the province of the automobile and more an avenue for snowmobiles.

This was pretty much before snowmobiles, though, and Hiram's choice of partner had more to do with my then-brand-new four-wheel-drive Ford Bronco than my woodsmanship. Looking back, I have to guess that he feared that I might have been noticing the "all-time low on this date" statistic in the daily newspaper and would have had an attack of common sense at the suggestion of a four-day camp-out caribou hunt, so he sweetened his proposal with the possibility of, nay, the *certainty* of an encounter with ptarmigan in flocks numbering in the *hundreds*. Well, gosh. How many boxes of sixes you think I should bring?

His worries were unfounded – I had just completed, out of scavenged, rough-cut spruce lumber, a sort of sleeping shelf which filled the inside of the Bronco from dashboard to tailgate, and I was dying for an opportunity to try it out.

I had, for the moment, thrown in the graduate school towel while Hiram was persevering, which I know sounds backward, but it forced us into opting for a holiday weekend, and the only one available was Veteran's Day.

That gave me time to scrounge up some C-rations from forest-fire-fighting friends, check to make sure the .264 was still sighted in, and field-test my Bronco/pullman sleeping arrangement in my yard, which got me barked at by my dog.

In spite of being a by times radical campus liberal, Hiram was vastly conservative in some areas, such as wearing Sorel boots the only time he streaked the campus at twenty below (with one hand over his private parts for a windbreak and saying "Ow! Ow! Ow!") and insisting we *both* bring two-burner Coleman stoves to heat the Bronco oil pan in the event it turned off cold. If we brought two, odds were that we could get *one* of them going, at a minimum.

The weather was, of course, fine when we set out with not only high-powered rifles and shotguns, but .22 rifles, to boot. Just in case. In case of *what*, Hiram was not real specific about. Snowshoe hare uprisings, perhaps.

The first order of business upon arriving at the Promised Land was "scouting the country." This consisted of driving seventy-seven miles looking out the car windows for either caribou or, lacking actual animals, their tracks. Animals themselves were not in evidence, but the next best thing was: gut piles. There were a dozen or so, frozen, mainly in the ditches but a couple on the actual road shoulder, illustrating that typical urban Alaskan caribou hunter's willingness to ignore state law (against shooting from, on, or across a road surface).

"Told you," Hiram said, kicking at a frosty and solid coil of intestines with his streaking boot. "And, can you believe it, not a single other hunter *anywhere?*"

"Yep, pretty quiet down here, all right," I replied, missing one of my life's great opportunities to parrot the old John Wayne Indian Country line, "*Too* quiet." That there might be some reason that there were no hunters about on a four-day caribou season weekend did not occur to either of us. Graduate studies in literature, while doubtless good for something, are not a blueprint for sorting one's winter meat out of a maze of snow-covered mountain valleys sixty miles from the nearest available piece of apple pie.

To say we were undaunted, however, would be an understatement. I was secretly glad the caribou were being circumspect, as I did not want to just blast one and drive home without trying out my sleeping-shelf handiwork under actual field conditions.

As the short day waned, we backtracked to a spot we'd noted, where the wind had blown clear a sort of turnout that looked level, and turned in. It was the exact spot, coincidentally, that, twenty-odd years hence, a family of three would freeze to death by underestimating the season's deadly capabilities, further proof that, while the Good Lord may indeed look after fools and small children, once in a while He is looking the other way.

Hiram touched off his Coleman stove on the tailgate and soon had a couple of C-ration cans bouncing in a coffee can of boiling water. Out came our ever-present C-ration can openers, which Hiram persisted in calling "P-38s," which I always thought was a twin-engine, twin-tail-boomed, high-altitude, high-speed long-range WWII fighter aircraft that the then-Army Air Corps used to assassinate a ranking Japanese officer in the Pacific Theater, who had been architect of most of their successes.

Before we'd finished our repast, complete with crackers, with jam, and toasted pound cake, we had to pump up and light my two-mantle Coleman lantern. Hiram insisted on trading me his pound cake for my cheese product, which I was delighted to do, and promptly punctured the pound cake can lids with my opener, dribbled in a tablespoon or two of water, and sat the cans directly on the burner.

"Nobody ever actually eats pound cake," Hiram warned. Everything he knew about C-rations, he'd learned in one summer fighting forest fires.

"Oh, really?" I said. "That's funny. Marines will fight each other for it."

He relented far enough to observe that at least it did smell kind of good, but stopped short of sampling any.

The unavoidable design flaw in my sleeping shelf was that there was only about twenty inches of room between the boards and the ceiling, and by the time the pads were unrolled and we had wrestled out of our boots, down vests, wool pants and heavy shirts, and wriggled into our sleeping bags, there was barely room to roll over and the lantern was turning the white paint on the ceiling brown. So we shut it off.

I knew about Eddie Bauer down bags but had never invested in one, though this trip was about to change that. We both had Army surplus duck-feather mummies, available locally in mint condition for fifteen dollars, less for damaged ones. In addition, Hiram had once purchased, in a romantic moment, rectangular down bags that zipped together, to allow him unrestricted access to his blonde wife when the mood moved him, and, once in our mummies we slid, in tandem, into this second layer and zipped it up and felt as secure as I'm sure all those sailors still on the *Arizona* did.

Disregarding the predictable crude jokes, this arrangement proved quite workable, and would have been perfect if Hiram's supper selection had been anything but "Ham and Limas," although my own choice of "Wieners, with Beans," allowed me to indulge in some pretty effective counter-battery fire. The night was more or less a draw.

"Christ on a crutch, Hiram," I said thirteen hours later, as the first blush of dawn lightened the eastern horizon beyond the now-thickly-frosted windows, "what's the thermometer say?"

Hiram clicked on his flashlight and squinted at the thermometer I'd duct-taped to his side of the car.

"It must be broke," he said. "It says 28 below."

"Broke, my ass," I said. "How cold does it have to be before caribou go into hibernation?"

"Wow," he said, "look at the frost."

The ceiling was now solid frost, hanging down in some places six inches and getting broke off whenever we rolled over.

"Maybe a nice tent wouldn't have been such a bad idea," I said, knocking a pint of frost down my neck trying to pull a boot on, lying on my side.

Once dressed and outside, we opted for a couple of quarter-mile warm-up jogs to get the circulation in our hands going enough to light the stoves, one of which went, minus its lid, under the crankcase, the other under the now-frozen can of water to heat our C-ration breakfast in. Hiram gladly relinquished any claim to the "Ham and Eggs, Chopped," which was my first choice.

"You actually *like* that?" he said, dropping in a can of "Pork, Sliced, in Juices."

"'Ham and Eggs, Chopped,' is so good, Hiram, God Himself eats it in heaven every morning. St. Peter, too."

"How do you know?"

"Sergeant Banaczek said the Commandant of the Marine Corps said so. Besides, I was there briefly."

"Heaven?"

"A year ago in August when Victor Charlie lowered the boom on me."

"So, why aren't you still there?" Hiram asked, poking at his can in the boiling water with a G.I. fork and puffing on the corncob pipe he had just wasted a perfectly good kitchen match on. It was in his job description as a literature student to be curious about metaphysical matters, though his firsthand experience in that area was nil. There was already frost in his moustache.

"The limit on pheasants in Kansas was more generous," I replied.

After breakfast was eaten and our shelf boards tied back on the homemade roof rack, the six-cylinder Bronco, preheated and primed with Hiram's starting fluid, roared to life and we motored off in the direction of the gut pile crossing.

It was full light when we got there, clear and cold. My binoculars revealed, wonder of wonders, two hundred caribou just out of rifle shot on the side of the road which was, alas, a refuge. They stopped warily and began feeding, pawing at the snow with their front hooves. Before this stalemate resolved itself, Mother Nature decided to test us. Or at least muddy the waters a little. A flock of about, true to Hiram's word, two hundred ptarmigan sailed in and landed in dwarf willows halfway to the caribou, and commenced feeding, also.

"Dang, Hiram," I said.

"I know, Bobby Lee. I read the regulations pretty close, and that place is only a *big game* refuge."

"So, ptarmigan are legal?"

"And the limit's twenty apiece."

"What are we waitin' for?"

"It'd run the caribou so far back in the refuge they'd *never* come out."

"Maybe they won't, anyway. These gut piles could be their next of kin."

"Let's give it awhile to see what happens. While we're waiting we can add that extra five-gallon can of gas to the auxiliary tank."

An hour passed, while I occupied myself walking up and down the road, to stay warm and police up the .270 and .30/06 brass.

Far off back down the road and below us, I heard something and put the binoculars on it.

"Uh-oh," I said, "we got company." Which pretty much settled it.

"Snowshoes and shotguns," Hiram ordered immediately. "And we better hustle. From the location of some of these gut piles, the boys haven't been real concerned about which side of the road the caribou are on when they blast away, and for half these idiots, they're in range right now."

We split up and put a double envelopment ("Not to be used on less than a battalion-sized unit," the instructing captain in Infantry Tactics at Marine Corps Schools had pointed out, "because of the possibility of friendly ancillary casualties from ricochets.") (Hiram and I knew enough not to shoot each other, we figured.) on the scattered-out birds, preoccupied with their own breakfasts. Below us on the road, two trucks; one, a two-wheel-drive, one-ton stakebed with duals (indicative of hunters with aspirations and expectations exceeding even Hiram's) rolled to a stop a few yards in front of the Bronco, and half a dozen men rolled out, in blue jeans, of all things, only recently having breakfasted at Formica tables on real food with real coffee instead of "Coffee, Instant, Type II" ("So," Hiram never tired of asking whenever he tore open a coffee packet, "who ever had a 'Type I?'") and raised binoculars to their eyes with gloved hands, looking in our direction.

Hiram's pump gun clapped flatly three times. The snow and the great space seemed to swallow up the sound, and fifty ptarmigan swung down the mountain in my direction, as they will one time in ten when we try the double envelopment. My hands were still so cold, in cotton work gloves, that I could barely get my safely off, but I swung with the closest birds and dropped not only a bird with every shot but a couple of serendipitous (for me, not for them) strays further back in the flock. The caribou were no strangers to such fusillades and, assuming it was directed at them, broke into their unhurried trot, over the mountain and deeper into the refuge.

The long, military surplus trail snowshoes crunched loudly on the crust as I headed for my downed birds, reloading, and a single, exasperated voice echoed up the slope.

"Hey, you dumb sonsabitches!" it said. "You're scarin' the caribou!"

There was a really long pause, then Hiram's voice echoed back. "Wha-a-a-at car-r-r-riboooooooo?"

John Hewitt

The Lone Star Prufrock

While calling Hallum a weirdo might be stretching the point, or at least belaboring it, that's not to say he doesn't give you pause once in a while. His life probably peaked at thirty-odd in the teeth of a force-nine gale, piloting his three-master through the storm of the century. The masts, of course, were teaspoons in empty coffee cups, the deck a corner table in our campus student union and the gale a homemade one, created when he unwisely voiced the opinion that we'd all have been better off if Abner Doubleday had never invented football. And him from Texas, where football is the dominant religion nine months of the year and baseball, the other three.

His favorite author, hero and general role model was Jack London. This was a puzzle, perhaps due to very selective reading of both fiction and biography, because any school kid knew that London, far from eschewing sports, had, like Hemingway after him, embraced them. Some of them, anyway. Hallum was something of an athlete himself, in fact. He was a most moderate drinker and frugal to a fault, to the point that he rode a bicycle rather than indulge in that sinkhole of young men's bank accounts, an automobile. In all, though, with his moustache and prematurely gray temples, I'm sure when he looked in a mirror he saw Jack London himself looking back. The rest of the student body would've agreed he was the closest our campus could come to J. Alfred Prufrock, if you didn't count Doug White, who'd been enrolled twenty years and hadn't decided on a major yet.

Hiram was never picky when selecting friends, and when Hallum turned up one fall in the writing workshop ("*Creative* writing workshop," I can hear him correcting me, but I was there and know better) and declared himself on Hiram's side of the great fiction/poetry divide, they were immediate allies. By the time Hallum learned that Hiram was an ardent and accomplished fly fisherman, and Hiram learned that Hallum had always wanted to be one, the water had gotten too stiff on top for wading, so they had put off fly fishing for a semester and a half and occupied themselves through the dark winter shopping for tackle for Hallum, an activity many fly fishers do better than fishing.

While not absolutely necessary, a canoe would open up vast reaches of local streams presently unreachable without a great deal of work. Work, like football, Hallum disdained. The canoe question had them both stymied. Winter was at its darkest when second semester started, and the "creative writing" workshop, instead of shrinking, gained a face, albeit one with hospital pallor. The balance of power, long evenly divided, was about to tip one way or the other, and by the end of the first class meeting the new guy found himself encumbered with two new fishing buddies when he revealed that he'd probably have to go with the fiction as he'd tried writing poetry and it was too hard.

"Say," Hiram asked, as the poets filed out, muttering darkly, "you don't by any chance have a canoe, do you?"

"Well, no," the new guy said, "but by summer I will. Late summer, if I have to build it myself. Why?"

Their faces lit up. "Oh, we was just wondering," Hiram said. "Will it haul three guys?"

"If none of them are idiots." The new guy was me, and the best way I knew to keep canoes right-side-up was to keep idiots out.

One thing led to another and, because the canoe took longer than I expected, and required an automobile hardier than my old Falcon to get it back to Alaska, and I had to earn some money for gas, and Michigan was overstocked with girls of marriageable age, I didn't return with the boys' fishing platform until late summer. By then they had both buggered off to slay the wily caribou, which Hiram, his wife said, had guaranteed would be crossing the Steese Highway en masse.

Hiram had previously guaranteed me a thing or two – limits of first ptarmigan and then grayling, as I recall. We'd seen a ton of ptarmigan tracks and some pieces of water where he'd *really* caught 'em *last* spring, and the fresh air was invigorating but, like Kansas duck hunting, you apparently had to spend a lot of days just paying your dues. So I took the wife fishing and we slayed 'em. Or I did. The moose, which were wearing our winter meat, were one of the other reasons for the canoe and proved as elusive as Hiram and Hallum's caribou. Before we'd even had a chance to *discuss* a joint fishing trip, Hiram and I were fast in duck season's grip, which doesn't relax as long as there's ice-free water. It's lucky we liked shopping for leaders and such, as now we had six months of it to look forward to. For Christmas, Hallum bought himself a wicker creel.

The good thing about postponing our initial three-man grayling trip a year and a half was that the wife – mine, that is – had come with a really nifty one-burner camp stove made in Sweden or somewhere, and I'd had time to practice a little. Hiram's track record as a provider being what it was, I volunteered to pack the lunch and included a pound of bacon, butter, syrup and pancake flour. And coffee, without which we were all certain Hallum would've dropped dead and not gotten his bachelor's degree, which would've disappointed his mother. The no-degree part, anyway.

Hiram had very correctly assessed Hallum's aversion for all forms of work and thus forbade the setting up of rods until we'd towed the canoe for four sweaty hours and put behind us better water than many fly fishers see in a lifetime. Hallum complained mightily, but Hiram stayed far enough ahead of the canoe that he couldn't hear him.

Finally, he came to a hole of water that suited him: gravel bar on our side that sloped off gradually for easy wading, deeper slow water with big logs against the other bank. Rises galore. Hiram was set up and had a fish on before I'd tied on my fly. I had my second fish on when I looked to see how Hallum was doing and noticed he was fifty feet back from the water, stringing his fly line back and forth from drift log spruce root to limb, back to root and back to limb. Then he got something out of his creel and walked back and forth a dozen times, wiping his line with it. I waded up beside Hiram and inquired. He glanced over his shoulder between casts and shook his head.

"All I know is," he said, "the book he learned his fly fishing from came from that room in the library he hangs out in."

"You mean the archives?"

"Uh-huh."

"Jesus, Hiram, the newest book in there's seventy-five years old.

Don't he know you don't have to dress your line like that anymore?"

"Beats me. That I know of, he's never actually been fly fishing before for anything, except for practice a block from his house out in front of the power plant a time or two. I'd stay a long ways away once he starts casting."

The casting did not go well. I tried to help. The rod, a Shakespeare Wonder Rod, was identical to Hiram's, predictably. No problem there. The line was a light green Cortland. No problem there.

"So," I asked, "is this a level line or a weight forward?"

"Weight forward," he said.

"Hmm," I said. "Fooled me. It looks different from mine. You sure you tied the right end to the backing?"

"Backing?"

"To the reel, then."

"Hoss, do I look like an idiot?"

"Hey, I've said it before, a guy can't help being from Texas. Why don't you climb up in front of the canoe, and I'll try to poke you over a little closer to where the fish are?"

Hiram came down and held the bow rope, and we got him halfway there, perpendicular to the current, perhaps twenty feet from the other bank. Not close enough. Holding the canoe and rope was a lot of work, too.

"Hiram," I suggested, "let's drop back downstream about 15 minutes' worth in the canoe. We'll take the right channel at the head of the island instead of the left. I know a real narrow hole there that was *plugged* with 'em last moose season."

"What island?"

"You know where that little channel cuts in two bends above the bluff?"

"You mean that little tributary?"

"It only *looks* like a tributary. It leaves the main channel under a logjam a half mile above. It's made to order for Hallum."

"You sure?" Hiram was a hard sell.

"Well, it's the right channel, and Hallum voted Nixon in '68. How much better a fit are we going to find?" Hiram scowled. He'd voted against Nixon. Nine times.

"Is it deep enough there to drown him if he falls in?"

Having caught my share already, I busied myself with the little stove and the bacon while Hiram coached, once we beached the canoe on the bar I had in mind. Hallum needed six for supper, according to his wife's marching orders.

I kept track of his success by the whoops every time he hooked up, a reaction I thought more appropriate to Texans at football games or trying to get steers to cross rivers on the way to Kansas. If I'd ever dared to whoop on a creek, Ted Zercher would've risen out of his distant grave and fetched me a whack with a canoe paddle that would have done me more damage than the hand grenade.

The first pancake came out of the skillet as he reeled in number six, and he ate it, several others, and a third of the bacon with considerable relish. There was a fire, and he poured a cup of coffee from my pot and relaxed. Hiram was fishing again, in the spot Hallum had vacated, with just his leader and three feet of line out. It was a short cast, indeed.

"Hoss," Hallum quizzed, "who got you your rifle, anyway?"

"My .264?"

"Yeah."

"I got it the same way Hiram got his 12 gauge: got me a job during high school one summer and saved every dern dime until school started; bought it and the scope, both. What other way is there?"

"I got my .30/30 by running away from home."

"You *what?*"

"Run off when I was twelve. Hitch-hiking. Made two hundred miles and got so dang hungry I said to hell with it and called my mom."

"Had've been *my* mom, you'd have got your butt blistered about then."

"I think the secret is to call while they're still worried and before they get mad. All I wanted was some fried chicken, but before I'd said I wanted to go home she started bawling, and I seen I had the leverage, for once. Twelve-year-olds are a helluva lot smarter than anybody gives 'em credit for. I actually wanted a horse, too, but when she caved on the rifle I figured I'd better quit while I was ahead."

"I never knowed what a weasel you were, even for a Texan. If ever I *hint* at havin' kids, just shoot me."

"OK, Hoss, but not with the .30/30," he said. "The police'd take it away, and I don't think my mom is good for another one."

John Hewitt

John Hallum, 1973

Oatmeal

One of the reasons Ron labors under the misconception that I am not a good shot with a rifle is the oatmeal I doomed him to once, for four days, by refusing to shoot at a cow caribou. For about two hours he hated me vigorously, but over the years I somehow redeemed myself and the hate wore out, and all that is left is the vague but firm impression that I am a terrible rifle shot.

As I remember, it was the third morning out on a moose float which Ron had promised could be done in three days, easy. It was obvious that the trip, at this point, was less than half over, and that the worst was yet to come. Already, my precious homemade freight canoe was a ragged, shattered shadow of its former graceful self. And all through an error in my judgment: I'd trusted Ron's judgment.

I didn't know him well enough then to understand the lengths to which he would stretch the truth to coax me into participation in his inspired follies. If he could ever apply this blockbusting corner of his imagination to writing, he'd put Shakespeare under a bushel.

It was a drizzly morning, though, and I was up early, warming the canoe by the fire preparatory to the daily patching session, wondering what I would do for patches on the rest of the trip after I used the last of the fiberglass resin, which would be in about ten minutes. I was having absolutely no luck trying to accept the idea that I might be going to lose my wonderful duck-hunting canoe, fruit of a whole summer's labor.

My rifle was propped against a nearby log on the gravel bar, and I was mixing hardener in the resin when Ron shuffled down from the tent for morning coffee. "Caribou!" he said.

He had bought the groceries for the trip. I provided canoe, kicker, paddles, tent, pads, fuel, and an increasingly ill humor as I watched the smooth, lovingly-shaped bottom of my canoe daily raked and smashed into a lumpy conglomeration of torn fiberglass, warped spruce planking and patches. I had asked, quite civilly, when I first discovered that all he had brought was oatmeal, lard and coffee (not even sugar, and he *knew* I used sugar in my coffee), "Why didn't you bring anything to eat but oatmeal?"

"I figured we could live off the fat of the land." He had been reading some Faulkner and was quite enamored of the Snopes, a white trash family so petty and mean and without virtue that they fed off each other like hyenas. I think he thought bringing nothing but oatmeal was the sort of thing a Snopes would do. He always did have trouble keeping his distance from literature. The Snopes may have won Mr. Faulkner a Nobel Prize, but they are not the sort of people you go on a hunting trip with more than once. Ron hadn't thought of this.

The land he planned to live off the fat of was proving singularly lean, particularly with no sugar for the oatmeal, and not even butter. We tried lard but no will ever become rich or famous marketing lard as a butter substitute.

The caribou he was making me aware of was the first game we saw, and the only game we could have shot with a clear conscience. It represented two suppers of liver, tenderloin breakfasts for the remainder of the trip, skillet-fried steaks for the other suppers, and cold chops for lunches. And boiled tongue for snacks. Its demise would also prove, once and for all, the wisdom of Ron's new "live off the fat of the land" philosophy, and the viability of Snopesism as an alternative twentieth-century lifestyle.

"So it is," I replied. He'd left his rifle a hundred yards away in the tent. He probably figured one rifle at the fire was plenty.

The caribou was fording the ankle-deep riffle two hundred and fifty yards above camp. Since Ron had never seen me shoot a rifle, he had no way of knowing how simple such a shot was for me with my scoped .264 - I could drop her when and where I wanted and tell him precisely where the bullet hole would be, while we walked up to dress her out.

However, since we were moose hunting, and since Ron was paddling bow and supposed to do the shooting, I'd left the .264 at home in the closet. I'd brought instead a less-bulky open-sighted .30/06. At a hundred and fifty yards I could have killed her; beyond that, I couldn't be sure. Open sights are not my forté, and taking chancy shots at big game, or any game has never been my choice.

Ron, on the other hand, with his roots firmly in seasons of Michigan whitetail hunts, subscribed then (he's changed, since) to a different philosophy: hit them wherever you can, whenever you can. Heart or lung-shoot them if possible, break a leg or make them bleed if you can't, then trail them and finish them when you find them.

"*Shoot!*" he said. I hadn't moved towards the gun, and was watching her step out onto the little gravel ledge at the edge of the water. She walked a few steps towards us, found a less steep route up the bank, and climbed it. Once on top, she stopped, broadside, and looked downstream in our direction. Perhaps she saw the blue woodsmoke drifting from our campfire.

"Well, god*damn!* Aren't you going to shoot?" he asked. It was the only time I ever heard what I'd have to call anguish in his voice. He was really tired of oatmeal. I should be ashamed to admit it (but I never have been): I was enjoying his consternation. I'd been in a minor anguish for three days, myself, over the canoe, had four more of the same to go, and it felt good to have the shoe on the other foot, if only for a moment.

"No," I said, laying a patch on the resin I'd just poured on the worst hole, "I'm not sure enough I could kill her." She had disappeared into the spruce. "I'm not that good a shot with open sights."

"Well Jesus Christ, the *worst* you could do was *miss* her! It don't hurt to *try!* You didn't even *try!*"

"Nope," I said. "Hey, the fire's burning down. You want to get some more firewood? I've already got the resin mixed or I would." He looked at me and the canoe and the rifle and the grub box full of oatmeal and lard and up the river at where she'd been.

"Okay," he said. I've always wondered what a real Snopes would've said. I don't think it would've been, 'Okay.' He took the axe and disappeared into the woods and it didn't sound as though he were *chopping* firewood, so much as it sounded like a gutshot grizzly on a rampage. When he returned with a tremendous armload of dead spruce limbs, there wasn't an axe-blade cut on any of them: they were all snapped off. I guess he hit them against other trees to break them to length.

He went away to the tent to roll up his sleeping bag and I added wood to the fire. It blazed up and I wished a caribou would step out a hundred yards away. I was tired of oatmeal, too. It was several years before he told me that he'd only discovered, in the week preceding that trip, that his marriage was over and a separation and divorce were in the offing. By the time I learned this, I no longer had a wife, either, and we could both laugh about it. "At least I didn't rag-rip your canoe over mine," I prod him.

"Only because I don't have a canoe," he says.

Ron Rau, inspecting the canoe, 1971

John Hewitt

The Cheerleader and the Bear

Stefansson was very specific about adventures; they were always the result of poor planning, he said. The most well-planned expeditions were the dullest in that nothing occurred that had not been provided for. The Marines arrived at the same conclusion independently (I never saw one reading Stefansson) and made out of this truth, as they do of everything they deem valuable enough to remember, a mnemonic device, the infamous Seven Ps: Proper Prior Planning Prevents Piss-Poor Performance.

I know that. My excuse for what happened that day was that I never set out to shoot a bear. My wife of the moment had buggered off to co-direct a local Girl Scout camp, so I had gotten my marching orders the day before from the Cheerleader, whose husband, thank the Lord for small blessings, was even farther afield, making his annual fortune gillnetting in Bristol Bay.

Which was why I showed up for what turned out to be a tango with a grizzly armed with only a tape measure and good intentions.

The gillnetter was born grumpy; the Cheerleader, by nature

in the habit of substituting ample good looks for any intellectual shortcomings, was convinced she could cure grumpiness by doing especially nice things for her spouse. Such as fiberglassing the crude plywood camper shell he'd built for his pickup the winter before. My experience at fiberglassing things was vast compared to hers, so she had enlisted my assistance in determining how much fiberglass cloth and resin to purchase. Hence the tape measure.

I arrived at her cabin, eight miles farther from town than mine, to find her and her sister in an absolute panic. That's not quite true, though they both waxed exuberant in relating their bear story. The cabin was shipshape again, even to them having stapled the screen wire back on the porch window, through which the bear had packed their groceries.

The sister was nineteen and in recovery from missing the cut for the cheerleading squad where they had gone to high school. Which was Kodiak, which brings up the logical question: What does anyone have to cheer about in Kodiak? Good question. Not being on the Pribilofs, probably.

Though she may not have been as smart as the Cheerleader, she was a brain surgeon compared to Cleo, the Cheerleader's Irish Setter. Enough said.

My Lab of the moment, who eventually ran away with my wife, had gotten in the line for muscles twice but missed the one for brains, making him a good playmate for Cleo, whom he immediately engaged in games of eye-paw coordination, such as Not Running Into Trees.

With the sister as Greek chorus, the Cheerleader related their previous evening's activities. Upon returning late from town and my place, where I'd plied them with roast mallard and whole milk (those

The Cheerleader and the Bear

were the days - think of it – *whole* milk!), they'd discovered their cabin's interior pretty thoroughly rearranged, obviously by a bear.

They'd no sooner gotten it straightened up than the bear reappeared and treed them in the yard on top of the truck's camper shell. While they watched, he reentered the porch via the screen window and left carrying an unopened 25-pound sack of Purina Dog Chow.

"That," I sagely predicted, " is a bear that's going to be in a bad way for a drink of water."

Whereupon they'd had an epiphany, which one supposes even cheerleaders gone to seed must have once in a while. They looked at each other and said something that passed for "The hell with *this!*"

Probably to avoid helping me with the dishes, they'd bypassed my place on the way to town, where they'd spent the night on the floor of a shack occupied by an expatriate Texan who'd been exiled from the Lone Star State for failing to make the football team in the seventh grade and not registering with the Young Republicans.

"Well," I told them when they finished, "you wouldn't think a bear with a belly full of Purina would be back until he got hungry again, although," and I glanced at the surrounding spruce woods cautiously, "you'd have to figure he'd definitely be back sometime. You do, uh, have a gun around here somewhere, don't you?"

Three, it turned out: an almost new .243, a new 7mm Magnum, and a reprehensible single-shot 12 gauge. With any of which the Cheerleader was an excellent shot, according to the gillnetter husband, who had trained her himself.

So, while I measured the camper shell, the sisters repaired to the cabin, where they were in the final throes of the second major cleanup in twenty-four hours.

It is surprising how many measurements, safely filed in one's head, one can forget in an instant when one glances up from the tape measure and observes the approach of a still-hungry bear.

"Get the dogs in the cabin!" I yelled. "The bear's back!" The always-annoying voice of my better judgment was grousing, "Oh sure, leave both your 12 gauge pumps at home," and the prospect of making the front page began to loom larger: "Local Man Mauled Trying To Subdue Bear With Tape Measure."

When the bear conveniently ambled behind the cabin, I covered the forty yards to the screen porch in three seconds – with the right motivation, you could, too – and put in an order with the Cheerleader for one shotgun and hold the mayo. She had the dogs corralled and issued me the old single shot and all the shells in the house: two trap loads and one slug. Oh, fine.

While simultaneously closing the action on the one slug and thinking unkind thoughts about the gillnetter, who thought he was my friend, I became aware from the popping of new staples that the bear had dispensed with the usual formalities and, standing on the deep freeze again, was entering through the accustomed window. It was a small porch, and I had nowhere to stand but right in front of his window.

When I was four or five years old I'd had a dream – a nightmare, actually – in which a polar bear got in our back yard (in Topeka) while I was watching the birds at the feeder outside the dining room window, and started trying to climb in. This lasted a long time, but the dream bear never got through the window.

This real one was having better luck. The little voice in my head, which rarely says anything very smart, was saying, "Hey, wow! This is just like that old dream!"

The porch, as I said, was not big enough for both of us, and my instinct for ownership took over. I delivered the bear, who up till then had ignored me, a tremendous whack on the side of the schnoz with the shotgun barrel. He was only a grizzly, thank God, and not some Chesapeakes I have known, who become inured to such treatment. As a consequence, he reacted a little melodramatically, I thought, roaring and squalling and falling out the window, off the freezer and onto the ground, where he flopped around briefly like Wayne Gretzky would learn to do years later, his rookie year in the National Hockey League, any time an opposing skater passed within ten feet.

Then around the cabin he went, batting at the side of his affected nose with one paw.

"Yoo-hoo," I said through the closed door, which, by now, from the sound of things, had all the furniture in the cabin stacked against it, including the wood stove and the gillnetter's worn-out deck slippers. "I have a plan. I'm going out in the yard and load up with the bird shot and try to chase this guy off a ways, then come back to the cabin and warm him up, right in the butt. Butch Hayes says that always works."

It was a good plan, as good in theory as Churchill's first scheme to go for the "soft underbelly" via Gallipoli in WWI, and in execution proved every bit as successful, the bear being almost exactly as cooperative as the Turks in 1915. When I'd make a run at him he'd grudgingly retreat ten or fifteen feet, hold his ground and counterattack, running at me and popping his jaws like a great steel trap, throwing slobbers all over hell's half acre.

It took twenty minutes to move him the requisite forty yards from the cabin porch, and when I'd back up to get some distance between us so my birdshot wouldn't blow a roast off his rump, he stayed with me every step of the way.

Other options began to occur. Mainly one. "Got the rifle all loaded?" I asked over my shoulder.

"Five rounds," Gunga Din replied confidently.

"Okay, here's the deal. I don't want to, but I think the best thing is going to be to just shoot this surly sonofabitch. He ain't letting me get far enough away to only warm him up good."

"Okay."

"So I'm going to break this thing, put in the slug and let him have it. Be ready to use the rifle on him if anything goes wrong. Don't just shoot into the wad if he gets me down. You ready?"

"Any time!"

I held the trap loads between the fingers of my left hand against the necessity of a quick follow-up shot, like Ruark's white hunters in Africa always did, while my little voice reminded me that none of them used single shots. My little voice was getting closer and closer to a pink slip.

The front bead settled on his right eye, thirty-six inches distant, and the last thing I thought as I squeezed the trigger was, "Oh, goddammit anyway."

At the report I thumbed the operating lever to the right to reload and snatched the forend down a trifle too enthusiastically. The rocket scientists who invented double barrels and single shots sometimes put little thumb-or-finger-operated catch releases on the forends to break the gun down, and sometimes they made them spring-loaded, friction-fit.

This was one of the latter. The wooden forend detached in my hand, and the barrel fell right off on the ground a foot from the thrashing bear.

"Shit!" I said to myself three times, while snatching up the wretched gun's component parts and trying to stay clear of the enormous claws on all four of the bear's flailing paws. The technician at Fish and Game who later helped retrieve the carcass and accepted the affidavit I filled out, the bear having been killed out of season, said they were the longest grizzly claws he'd ever seen – too long, in fact, perhaps the result of this particular bear having years ago lost his mother before she'd taught him to dig out ground squirrels, the activity that keeps most bears' claws a healthy length.

When I got to the porch and the girls, I glanced back and saw the bear still on his side, hind legs kicking spasmodically in unison.

"Maybe," I said, dumping my armful of gun parts and shotgun shells on the steps, "I better go and put him out of his misery." He looked like a goner to me, but everyone you ever read when you were a kid said you ought to be damn sure on the dangerous stuff. "Dangerous stuff" sounded a little strong for this individual, though grizzlies as a species qualify; I knew that in order to ever think of this, my only grizzly, in those terms, I was going to have to forget about the Purina and what a wuss he'd been when I whacked him on the nose.

"Let me have the seven-millimeter," I said, looking back at the Cheerleader, looking her right in the eye. Our eyes sort of locked. "Wow," I thought to myself, "I never noticed she had brown eyes before." Nice ones, too.

"So?" said the little voice in the back of my head. "So did the bear, you goddamn idiot."

She handed me the rifle, safety still off, and regardless of how it might look to her, I reflexively checked to make sure it was chamber-loaded, as I do any gun anyone hands me. I kind of have to see for myself.

And that was the first time all morning I got a really big chill up my spine, and my knees got so shaky it was a question whether they

John Hewitt

were going keep holding me up.

"Carolyn," I said as steadily as I could manage, "next time we do this, make real certain not to put the .243 cartridges in the seven-millimeter, okay?"

All Great Retrievers Are Temperamental

"One for you and one for me," Mary said, and closed the mailbox. I pulled into the drive and started up the hill. "Who's this?" She held up an envelope for me to read.

"Girl I used to know. I wrote her from Cordova a month ago, before I met you, right after Miriam wrote that she was leaving. Who's the other one from?"

"My folks."

"They still think you're living with a happily married couple?"

"Yep."

I shook my head. "They're *your* folks…"

Ron was at the cabin putting patches on his ancient waders. "You guys look like niggers," he said when we came in. "Does Russ have you diggin' potatoes with your faces?"

"Just dusty and warm. Sweat a lot today. Did you quit yet?" Ron was working a short job out of the Laborers' hall in town.

"Season don't open till Tuesday. I'll work Monday."

"Nothin' like givin' 'em lots of notice," I said.

"Did you tell Russ you was goin' duck huntin' Tuesday?"

"He knows."

"Any mail?" Ron was getting mail at my address.

"None for you."

"John got a letter from an old girl friend."

I sat down to read my mail. "Oh, Jesus," I said. Ron's moustache twitched. I handed him the news. "I only wrote her one letter." He read and shook his head.

"I'd like to see that one letter. I think you've found your genre…"

"What's it say?" Mary was frying potatoes she'd gleaned for supper.

"She's coming to visit."

"When?"

"Opening day."

"Oh. In time for the hunt?"

"No. In the evening." I'd have to pick her up at the airport.

"You don't sound very excited."

"Explaining *you* to *her* ain't going to be half as easy as explaining *her* to *you*…"

"I'd give a hundred dollars for a look at that letter," Ron said.

"You ain't *got* a hundred dollars."

We put decoys out before daylight, for tradition's sake; we've never decoyed a duck on the slough we hunt only on opening morning, but we enjoy putting the decoys out. It gives us an excuse to be wading around at shooting time, so that the first flock catches us unprepared. Ron thinks this is part of the tradition, too, and we're just having fun the first day, anyway; opening day is the *hors d'oeuvre*, Minto Flats the main course, and there are many other entrées – this dinner happens once a year, lasts for one month, and is called "Sep-

All Great Retrievers Are Temperamental

tember" in Alaska.

Besides, there are too many people at the Flats opening day. We go there later in the month, to hunt it alone, as we eat in good restaurants on weekdays, to avoid the crowds. The birds have less pinfeathers later in the month, and, hopefully, the northern birds are in. But all this happened several years ago, and neither Ron nor Mary had ever hunted the Flats.

Mary had never hunted anything before. But she liked the getting up early, and liked it when the first flock caught Ron and I untangling decoy strings. There were more birds than usual flying, and all the shooting was pass shooting.

At Minto, I'd tell Ron to pass up anything but mallards; here, we shot widgeon, pintail, teal, mallards, and one accidental shoveller. We both shot well, and within two hours had our limits, six apiece. Ron's last, his best shot, was a high-overhead mallard that he calls "the old down-the-throat shot," and which pleases him more than any other when he makes it. The mallard fell a long time and splashed spectacularly.

"It's too nice here to leave. Can we pick them here?" Mary asked, after we'd picked up the decoys.

"Suits me," I said, and Ron looked at me. She was doing everything right. The right sentiment expressed in the right way at the right time. He was enjoying losing our perennial argument on the possibility of a woman ever fitting into our Septembers.

"She's a *find*," he would tell me later, which was what he said about Minto Flats later that month, and about the long canoe the first time he'd hunted out of it.

So we sat three in a row on the bank with our feet in the water and a duck apiece in our laps, and picked. Feathers stuck to our hip boots and strung out down the slough with the current, like cottonwood fluff.

Upstream, we heard the clank of wood on aluminum. "Somebody floating the slough," Ron said.

"Boom! Boom! Boom!"

"Duck!" I said as shot pattered down behind us in the willows. They were still far enough away that we wouldn't have been hurt if we *had* been hit.

A pintail was coming, flying crazily, a foot off the water. He splashed down in front of us, went under, and came up shaking his head. "Cripple," I whispered, reached for my gun, and when he'd swum far enough so that the shot wouldn't ruin him, I held on his head and finished him off. Ron retrieved him.

The clanking grew louder and the boat arrived. Ron and I had trouble keeping a straight face. Even Mary, who had no way of knowing what a properly-outfitted duck-sneaking expedition should look like, regarded them oddly.

Two young soldiers from the local Army base were paddling a ten-foot aluminum johnboat with a piece of 2 X 6 and a broken oar. They had two shotguns, no ducks, were wet from the waist down, and there were several empty shotgun shells in the bottom of their boat.

"Ducks sure are spooky," they said, "we can't get close enough. We hit one a minute ago, and he got away. Did you see him?"

"Here," I said, and tossed them Ron's shoveller, "we lowered the boom on him."

"Don't you want him?"

"We got our limit."

"Gee, thanks." They clanked away down the slough happily. Ron watched them go.

"Gee, thanks," he said when they were gone. "Do I get credit for the pintail?" We kid each other endlessly and unmercifully about who's got the most, or, if we both limit out, who got the most mallards, and if we both got all mallards, who shot the least number of shells, and if we fired the same amount, who made the hardest shots.

"You ain't *got* the shoveller, and you didn't *shoot* the pintail. I think we'll let Mary have him. Six for me, five for you and one for Mary. It was her idea to stay here. Anyhow, I think it decoyed to her; thought she was a redhead." Mary's hair was very red. Ron fingered his canvas hunting coat.

"Maybe it decoyed to me; thought I was a canvasback."

"It was a drake. Wouldn't decoy to another drake. Got to be Mary's duck."

"Okay," he conceded, "but tell us again what you're gonna say to Mary from Kansas at the airport tonight."

"Hello, Mary. Welcome to Alaska."

Which, as it turned out, was exactly what I *did* say at the airport. We stopped on the way home for drinks. I tiptoed around the news about the new Mary from Montreal for an hour and two whiskey sours, like a wise dog around his second porcupine, and filled up my share of the conversation with glowing descriptions of Ron. It was the sort of review one reads on the dust jacket of someone's second bestseller.

When I finally got down to the nitty-gritty, it took about as long as it takes to eat a maraschino cherry, which is what I was doing.

"Oh," Mary-from-Kansas said, and we drove home.

The night before having been the night-before-opening-day, none of us had slept much, and I was pretty tired. I crept to bed as unobtrusively as is possible in a fourteen-by-sixteen one-room log cabin, strained heroically to get to sleep before anyone else came to bed, and failed. The wrong Mary crawled in.

Ron and Red Mary unrolled foam pads and slept on the floor, in sleeping bags. Kansas Mary seemed quite happy to be in bed with me. I seemed to be asleep. Ron was quiet after bedtime for the first and only time in his life. He didn't even fart. The cabin has never been that quiet in the seven years I've lived in it. Finally he said, "Doan feel bad, Dilsey honey, if you goin' be de camp nigger, you gots to sleep on de pallet on de flo' wid de huntin' dawg. You gets to lak it by 'm' by."

I snored resolutely. He and Dilsey snickered.

"Is t*his* what duck hunting is like?" Mary said when Dilsey paddled me up to her and Ron on the slough. We'd been trying to get a shot for me and scare ducks down to them. No one had seen anything. Dilsey enjoyed paddling the canoe, though, and we'd put a moose out.

"Sometimes," I said.

"You ought to have been here yesterday," Ron said, but Mary had not hunted or fished enough to appreciate his use of the old cliché.

"What now," Dilsey said, adding, "Boss?"

"Let's go through town for groceries, then home for the tent and kicker and stuff, and go off on a duck hunt." The best part of owning the canoe and tent and kicker and automobile is that you always get to have your way at such times in September. Ron didn't care what we did or where we went, so long as it was duck hunting.

Anyhow, he was about broke. Dilsey was absolutely broke. If Mary had money she wasn't saying. I'd had a good summer fishing on the coast, had six thousand dollars in the bank for the first time in my life, and had worked practically without interruption for eight months, which was a world record for any of us.

"How many days, Boss?" Dilsey wanted to know. Ron and Mary were in the canoe now, behind me, everyone but me paddling.

"Three at least, more if the weather's good and we want to stay with it."

"Where?" Ron asked.

"Upstream from town. We'll paddle a day or two and hunt sloughs like we do on the Little Chena, then use the kicker for the flat water at the end."

"Lots of new country this year," Ron said, "first the river, and then Minto. I hope Minto's as good as you say."

"You'll see. And we *got* to get busy and try that spot Russ told me about off the Denali, he says the grayling in there's all sixteen-inchers."

"If we goin' *that* far, I know where there's a lake down there that *always* has ducks on it. Guarantee it, by God." The only thing Ron's guarantee meant was that he wanted to hunt it; otherwise, it was as worthless as Confederate money.

"Sounds okay to me, I guess," Mary-from-Kansas said.

"Dilsey?" Ron asked over his shoulder. She was still paddling stern.

"Goin' be a lotta work aroun' heah t' do, an' Ah know who goin' be doin' it," she drawled. She had a good drawl, for a Canadian. "Paddle dat boat! Pitch dat tent! Build dat fiah! Pick dat duck! Fry dem bacons! Boil dat coffee! Mama tole me, 'Chile,' she say, 'you fetch you on down dat rivah to New Awleans, get you a man wid a silk hat an' gold teef.' An' look at me now."

Ron turned around and peeled his lip up with his thumb to show her his gold toof. "Nawsuh," she said, "did Ah want a ol' dawg lak you, Ah'd go to de pound."

"Careful, Dilsey, he may not look like much but he's the finest retriever in the state. Take me years to train up another one."

"Yassuh, Boss. Ah's sorry, boy."

He flashed her his gold toof again.

"Turn aroun' dar an' paddle de boat," she told him.

We put in seventy-five river miles above town, and Ron gave the girls instructions on how to load the canoe.

"Carry everything down to the canoe and lay it in a row on the bank. *Don't* put anything in the canoe yourself. *Don't* make suggestions. Let him load it himself. It's his boat. This may take hours."

I puzzled over the distribution of weight, got it so it suited me and places left for three passengers besides myself, and lashed it all in with yards of rope and a dozen trimmed willows. Nothing projected above or over the gunwales, which is what I was after, and everything would stay in the boat if we dumped.

"Okay, ready to go," I said finally, seated in the stern seat, steadying her with my paddle. "Mary, if you step in, step right in the middle, over the keel. Better to grab both gunwales and then step in. Wear your life vests."

Dilsey had stepped in already, in the opening just ahead of me, without rocking the boat at all. She was very graceful in a canoe, from the first time. Mary stepped in a foot off center and we shipped a gallon of water over the offshore gunwale. I looked at Ron and he shrugged his shoulders.

We camped early, slept, arose, breakfasted and repacked the canoe without seeing a duck. The new country was fine, though.

The first duck jumped out of a tangle of tree roots ahead of us, running the gauntlet straight upstream towards us.

"Twelve o'clock! Right on the water!" I said. Ron took him twice coming, and I tumbled him 30 yards astern. We reloaded and back-paddled, while he drifted down to where Dilsey could reach him in over the side.

"How did you miss *that* one?" Mary-from-Kansas inquired of Ron. If she had a talent, it was for saying the wrong thing so eloquently that, years later, we still echo her.

"Thass jist what Ah's goin' ask mahself," Dilsey said. She turned back to me in the stern and her face was red from trying not to laugh. Her brow furrowed seriously: "What fo' we tak dat boy wid us if he cain't shoot? All he do is drink de likker an' shoot up yo' shotgun shells."

"Oh, he's an absolute terror on a blind retrieve. If I could get papers on him, he'd have his field championship in one year."

Ron humped up and growled and laid his shotgun down.

"Ah b'lieve we've riled him up."

"All great retrievers are temperamental."

We watched the banks for signs of deadwater oxbow sloughs; an avenue leading back through the spruces or birch, and a trickle of brown water running down the bank were giveaways. I spotted one and went ashore to investigate while Ron and the girls inspected the dead duck, a white-winged scoter. When I returned they'd labeled it a "U.F.O." and decided to fry it for supper.

"See anything?"

"Six. Four widgeon and two pintails. Bad spot to sneak but if we surround 'em, somebody'll get a shot."

"Where do I go?"

"Down the right side around the corner, about two hundred yards." I drew the slough in the riverbank dirt with a stick. "The girls can watch from here at the end, and I'll sneak them so that if they spook, they'll go your way."

"Awright."

They spooked. Down the slough and around the bend out of sight, Ron's pump gun banged three times.

We found him sitting on a drift log scratching his head like Harpo Marx. Two widgeon floated belly-up in the center of the slough, in deep water.

"Now I did it," he said.

"We can throw sticks out and wash them in," I suggested, broke a branch off the drift log, and threw it out beyond them. It made small waves and did not change the ducks' location appreciably. "Find some good heavy dead sticks," I told the girls, and broke off another branch. Neither girl moved.

"Dey is a limit to what a girl *will* do. Ah doan min' collectin' de fiahwood, but Ah draws de line at thowin' it in de watah. All you done for two days is brag on dat dog. Le's see de boy perform."

Ron grinned. I could see the idea snowballing behind the grin, and knew I was powerless to stop it. When he gets an idea like that, the only way to survive it is to ride it out like an avalanche. He yawned and whined and took off his hip boots.

While he undressed I explained field trial etiquette to the girls. I had to make it up, because I'd never been to one. I paced the bank and snapped my suspenders to reinforce my points. Naked except for his Jones-style hunting cap and his moustache, Ron galloped around on all fours, inspecting the log and lifting his leg on the root end of it. I had forgotten how thin he was.

"Hatchet-cheeks! Heel!" I said. He heeled. "Mark!" I said, holding one hand in front of him. He saw the ducks, obviously for the first time, whined, and broke. I kicked him soundly in the rear with a muddy hip boot. "*Heel*, goddamn you!" I said. He returned to heel with a footprint on his right cheek, cowered, and whimpered.

"Mark! I started over. He took the line. "Fetch!" He bounded toward the water, stopped short, stuck his front paw in, and recoiled, shivering. The bank suddenly became very interesting, and he inspected it loudly, sniffing and digging here and there, avoiding looking at me. The girls were delighted.

"Hey!" I hollered, snapping a branch off the drift log and brandishing it. "Whatsa matter with you? *Fetch*, you sonofabitch!" and threw the stick out beyond the ducks. His interest in the stick overruled his apprehensions about the cold water and he leaped in gleefully, and dog-paddled out.

"One of the characteristics of a dog of field champion fiber," I instructed the girls, "is that once he's committed to a retrieve, his dedication and singleness of purpose are second to none. For instance, observe yonder that this fine specimen will swerve not one degree from the shortest and most direct line between his beloved handler and the object of his intentions." In the middle of the slough, Ron paddled between the two ducks, sniffed the stick, and swam a circle around it, looking this way and that.

"Fetch!" I reiterated. He bared his teeth and sank them into the stick, splintering it.

"Lawsy," Dilsey murmured, "Ah's seen alligators wif softer moufs dan dat..."

He returned, gamboled up in front of me, shook, spit the splintered stick out on the ground, and panted, begging for attention. "Heel." He did. "Mark." He did. "Fetch!" and he was off again. This time he paddled around aimlessly, ignoring the ducks. I broke off another stick to throw, but thought better of it. Finally he spotted one. His eyes lit up and he swam up to it. As soon as he was within reach, it disappeared under the water. He panicked and swam this way and that, searching. It popped up behind him. He spotted it, lunged for it and it went under again.

"It's divin' on him, Boss!" Dilsey said, and picked up one of the guns. "Ah'll git it!" Ron saw her with the gun and howled and dove himself.

"Here. Put that down. What if you hit the dog?"

"One less mouf to feed," she said, and put the gun down. Ron surfaced up to his eyes, and eyeballed her. The duck popped up. She grabbed the gun. He howled and dove again.

The duck disappeared and he came up, searching for it.

"The very finest retrievers," I told the girls, "will actually dive after a cripple." The duck re-emerged and disappeared. Ron disappeared. When he surfaced again, he had its neck clamped firmly between his teeth.

"Dar he got 'im!" Dilsey said.

"Good dog!" Mary said.

"Fetch him here," I said. He swam ashore, climbed out, shook, and sprinted up and down the bank on all fours, flopping the duck this way and that. I took it away from him.

"Fetch!" I said, pointing to the other one. He whimpered and whined and fidgeted.

"He want de pat on de head," Dilsey said.

"How could I forget?" I patted him on the head and scratched behind one ear. He wriggled. "Now fetch!" I said. He swam back out to the other widgeon, grabbed it by the tip on one wing, and dragged it in. When he had carried it in front of me, he spit it out audibly, "Ptoo!" and panted for his pat again. I patted him and he put his clothes back on. The girls had been in intermittent hysterics.

The duck hunting was pretty scratchy; in four days we only took nineteen. The weather was fine, though, and it was the best part of the year to be unemployed in Alaska. Our camps were all relaxed, and Mary-from-Kansas was laughing at Ron's jokes.

We slept all four in the same tent, in a row, Ron and I on the outside and the girls in the middle. I had brought a fifth of blackberry brandy and a pint of peppermint schnapps. Ron brought a pint of peach brandy and a six-pack of beer. I was saving mine in case the weather turned cold. Ron and Mary-from-Kansas, on the other hand, were making the most of it.

Ron isn't good for more than a sip before dark, when we're still hunting. After the tent's pitched and a fire's built, however… There was a lot of gurgling and belching and whispering over on his side of the tent, and giggling. He and Kansas Mary seemed to be getting better acquainted.

We'd hunted seriously and not travelled much, though, and darkness of the fourth day caught us miles above town. It was colder, too. We were past the best hunting.

"Believe I'll just use the kicker and run on into town," I said.

"What about supper?"

"Oh, we'll eat once we're in town."

"Okay." Ron was agreeable. "But let's get the brandy outa the grub box. It's liable to get colder 'n hell by the time we hit the bright lights."

He took the bottles up front with him, and shared them with Kansas Mary. It was too far to pass them back to the stern. I ran at half-throttle, using the reflection of the glow of city lights to steer by, and there was a lot of laughing up front. Things were getting well forward in the foc'sle…

My hand on the throttle was bitterly cold four hours later when I eased the bow ashore below the power plant. We'd come under the town bridges and put in a block from a friend's house. It was ten o'clock and we hoped he might run us and our gear the fifteen miles to my cabin.

I waded ashore, trying to straighten my fingers out.

"Whew. By God, that almost got cold out there for a while. Me for a little nip. Where's the brandy?"

Kansas Mary giggled. Ron grinned foolishly. "I think it all got drank up."

"Oh. Okay. I'll have some schnapps, then. Better cold-weather drink, anyway."

More giggles. Ron shuffled his feet and smacked his lips. "Yeh. It sure was." Kansas Mary cracked up. Dilsey snickered.

"Well, god-*damn!*" I said. "Let's go see if Hallum's in bed."

We took the shotguns and left the camping gear, entrusting it to the darkness. Ron and Kansas Mary were all over the street.

"Next time, we gots ta keep dat white girlfrien' of yours an' dat dog outa de whiskey. Dis gwine git ex-pensive, by 'm' by."

"Tell me somethin' I don't already know…"

The two of them ran ahead and peeked in the window. Back they came. Ron was beside himself. "Hey. They're still eatin' dinner in there. One of Bobbi's high-tone deals."

Hallum's wife is from New York. When she sets out to have company for dinner, it's cut crystal, linen napkins, bone china hors d'oeuvres, and the whole nine yards.

"Well, hell, there goes our ride home. Who is it?"

"Ol' Bruce Whatchamacallit an' some A-1 good-lookin' sumbitch," Ron said. "Looks like she got loose out one of Bobbi's *Vogue* magazines. All dressed up."

"Oh, fine."

"Piss on 'em. We ain't ate since noon. Le's go. C'mon, you an' me first with the shotguns. Bobbi ain't used to that. Maybe she'll give us somethin' to eat."

"You first."

Ron led the way. He didn't even knock; kicked the kitchen door open, walked in with his shotgun (Bobbi gasped; in New York, when people kick your kitchen door open at 10 p.m. with shotguns, it's a different story) reached over the shoulder of the good-lookin' sumbitch and picked up a big handful of lasagna off her plate.

"Mmmm-mmmm!" he said, and stuffed it in his mouth. "Just like in the old country! Grab some, you guys. It's good, whatever it is." He picked up her wine glass and drained it, and belched.

"Hi, Bobbi," I said.

We all had a bite to eat and gave them four ducks. The guests left. Hallum pulled his truck down to the river and we threw our gear in. The four of us toted the canoe to his yard, where I'd pick it up later. Both girls climbed in the cab with Hallum to tell him about our fabulous retriever, while Ron and I bounced along on our duffel bags in the pickup bed, lying on our sides out of the wind with our heads near each other so we could talk. The food and the cold wind had sobered him up.

"Hell of a fine trip," he said.

"Pretty scratchy for ducks," I said.

"Yeh, but a good hunt. Good camps. Good weather."

"Yep."

"I think I got some bad news for you."

"Oh?"

"Yeh. Your pre-vious bunkie gonna be spendin' some time on the floor out to your house."

"Oh?" They must've talked it over. "Which one?"

"Kansas one."

"Well, it's like you said."

"What?"

"*Hell* of a good trip."

"You ain't mad?" He sounded relieved.

"Mad? You solved all my problems."

"Oh. Here I thought I owed you a girl friend, an' you wind up owin' me a favor."

"We'll see," I buttoned my collar button and pulled my cap over my ears. "Now that we got *that* straightened out, how about the Denali? I'm sure I can find that grayling spot Russ told me about."

"*Grayling?* I know this lake down there, no foolin', where I can ab-solutely guarantee…"

All Great Retrievers Are Temperamental

The author, Kansas Mary, Ron Rau, and Canadian Mary, 1972

John Hewitt

Nearly Skunked Again

The majority of my professors were dull fellows without lives outside academia. The schools I attended were themselves in a sort of academic wilderness where "publish or perish" was only a rumor. Why anyone would, for instance, relocate to Alaska to teach, and then neither publish nor hunt nor fish escaped me.

One of these bright lights showed promise, however. He illustrated the finer points of Skinnerian classical conditioning with anecdotes from his personal experience, and where he might have used two teenaged daughters as subjects, assuming they were not immune to being trained, he used whitetail deer. There seemed to be a vast legion of whitetail bucks in his memory banks, the majority admittedly smarter than he was.

He was maddeningly able to keep the discussion focused on his teaching points, however, no matter how diligently I tried to circle it back to the deer. Did he get it or not? This required that I trail him after class to his office where, realizing he'd been run to ground, he would reveal the fate of that day's buck, not entirely reluctantly. A hunting story without someone to hear it is in the same category as a tree falling in the forest with no ear to hear it, whether he knew it or not.

He did not appear to have shot a great many deer. He had a pet theory that the right guy, with the right rifle (in his case a Model 99 Savage in .308 Winchester with a Williams receiver sight), wearing the right boots (L.L. Bean Maine Guide Shoes with sixteen-inch tops, in his opinion), getting on the right track early enough in the morning, should be able to walk or trot a deer to exhaustion by sundown. At the end of this mythical utopian deer hunt, apparently you just walked up to the panting deer and plugged him behind the ear. Or something.

He was the right guy to do it, tall and thin and tough as good leather, but circumstances had thus far conspired against him, and his New Hampshire deer hunts generally resulted in a lot of good exercise and a prodigious appetite, in addition to a wealth of useful anecdotes. I wondered whether a more patient person, such as myself, might have had more success in the same country stump-sitting. Thirty years later, unable to take my own advice, I still have not shot anything while sitting on a stump, not counting ducks, if you call a duck blind a stump.

We were both recently enough off the boat in Alaska that we had neither established successful moose-hunting locations nor even acquired delivery systems to transport us and our rifles to them, though I was a step or two ahead of him in the latter category, having spent the previous summer building a twenty-three-foot canoe and buying an outboard.

It naturally followed that I suggested we get a moose by putting the canoe in the Yukon River at Circle and motoring upstream, not being confident that the new 6-horse would push both of us back upstream should we head downstream and shoot one there. In that direction, we'd see saltwater before we saw a bridge. Dr. Moore was more than amenable. We did not know exactly what we were looking for in terms of a moose spot but trusted that some of our whitetail expertise would transfer and we'd know it when we saw it, i.e., a forest of savaged antler-rubbing trees, a moose superhighway three feet deep up the bank, or a moose pasture/honeymoon destination with moose beds everywhere. How hard could it be when you noted some of the mental giants around campus who were perennially successful? They could barely find their way back to the student union after class for a cup of coffee.

My reservations about the canoe's propulsion capabilities proved well-founded, to the point that, where the shoreline was suitable, Dr. Moore insisted I put him out and he'd stride off upstream for a mile or two while I churned along beside him. In my boat's defense, I'd point out that his walking speed was four or five miles per hour, and I was bucking that much current.

Two things about this system were disconcerting. First, in two days of such crude cross-country travel – it made me think of emigrants on the Oregon Trail who walked beside their ox teams and Conestoga wagons – we had yet to see a moose track. Second, the outboard, run of necessity at full throttle, had used up three-fourths of our twenty-gallon fuel supply only one-third of the way through our projected six-day hunt.

Fortunately, we shared the unspoken conviction, not arrived at by the sour grapes avenue, that the weather had blessed us, and being out in the country when the leaves all went to yellow and vees of geese were constantly overhead was the main thing, and the moose, if any, would be frosting on the cake. If there was indeed anything at all to classical conditioning, a Kansas duck hunter and a New England deer chaser were uniquely well suited to being skunked.

"Did you ever," I asked the second evening, poking the supper fire with a driftwood stick, "read any of the accounts of the early days along here, during the gold rush?"

"I don't think so," he said.

"Well, it wasn't so unusual for those old prospectors to throw up a cabin for winter more with an eye to good nearby gold prospects than to the availability of game. And they starved to death."

"Really?" He shared the common hunter's conceit that he could survive anywhere, as indeed Stefansson had, if you plunked him down at random in the wilderness with a rifle and enough ammunition.

"Oh yes. And they all should've known about Sir John Franklin's whole expedition starving to death over in the territories in the last century. The Canadians didn't forget. It's why the RCMP insisted that anybody bound for Lake Bennett via the Chilkoot Pass in '97 and '98 have three-quarters of a ton of groceries with them. They were afraid all of Dawson might starve out the first winter."

"You think, then, we may have rediscovered someone's starvation spot?"

"Well, you put three feet of snow over all this and it'd take a week to come as far as we have, and an empty stomach might bring you to your knees by now."

"These C-rations of yours look better all the time."

"We're seeing a lot more protein than we're getting shots at," I said, in reference to the high-flying flocks of geese. I was not dedicated enough of a moose hunter to have brought a rifle. Why bring two to shoot one moose? My gun of choice was my father's nickel steel Model 12 with #2 short magnums in the magazine and slugs in my pocket.

"What do you see as our options now?" he asked.

"Save our last can of gas for emergencies, like if we get a moose and need to get to the landing in a hurry. Hunt on foot tomorrow morning out of camp, and stay the night if we find sign. Otherwise, load her up and paddle down whichever bank looks moosiest, looking for a location. If we snoop around a little, we'll use up two or three days that way. We're pretty much where we want to be, we just got to be patient."

The morning was as fruitless, trackwise, as the previous two days had been, so we broke camp and pushed off. This was the part I had been looking forward to. Running an outboard motor all day is not hunting. Steering a canoe quietly downstream beside a riverbank, with a paddle in your hand and a rifle or shotgun in your lap, most definitely is.

Life was working out a lot different than fifteen years of *Field and Stream* and *Outdoor Life* had led me to believe. Where were the dozen mediocre bulls all the writers passed over before whacking the real bull-of-the-woods? Moose, and everything else, were proving much fewer and farther between than in their stories. It was almost enough to make you subscribe to *Playboy*.

So, my immediate reaction upon spotting the shambling black shape at the edge of the shoulder-high willows a half mile below us as we cleared a sharp bend was, "Don't screw this up!" In the real North, the one I was fast becoming acquainted with, you rarely got first chances and never, one had to assume, got second chances.

Dr. Moore saw it about two seconds after I did. His back stiffened and his paddle froze in midstroke. Very slowly he tucked it into the empty compartment behind him.

"I think that's a bear at one o'clock," he said, paused for about ten heartbeats, and added, "but isn't it too big for a black?" Since we

Dana Moore piloting my long canoe, 1973

had no intention of shooting a grizzly, neither of us had picked up a harvest ticket for one.

"Maybe in New Hampshire," I said. "Stuff grows 'way bigger up here. It's too black for a grizzly, though."

"What do you think?"

"I think the way the wind is, we need to get outside of that island and put in below him. While I paddle, you glass him for cubs. Noise is the only thing that'll ruin it, and we got a little wind cover to help."

Once out of the canoe, it was an interesting stalk, different from anything either of us had ever undertaken. When his head was down or back turned we crept forward. When he lifted it to sniff and look around, we froze. I had the shotgun with seven slugs in one hand and the old Nikon in the other, but it quickly became evident we'd never get close enough for the 12 gauge. I was not really sure why I'd brought it at all.

Besides the possibility that we'd spook him during the stalk, we had the other likelihood hanging over our head like Damocles' sword, that he'd just give up on his shoreline rummaging and be, in three steps, safe forever from us, in the woods. It would've made a brass monkey nervous.

Dr. Moore stopped at a little over a hundred yards and whispered, "What do you think?"

"If it was my rifle, I'd be shooting," I said. I had killed a lot of coyotes back in Kansas a whole lot further away than this. "But don't shoot unless you're sure of a good hit."

He raised the rifle, sighted through the peep sight, lowered it slightly, took ten more steps, and raised it again.

The shot lifted a puff of dust off the bear's shoulder, a little high but probably okay, I could tell through my camera's viewfinder, then, just as he vanished into the willows in high gear, a second puff.

I admired Dr. Moore's long strides on the run up the shingle to where the bear's tracks disappeared, and thought that, though he was a better-than-average professor, he'd probably have made a better Marine officer.

"I don't like the looks of this," he said. "That bullet usually knocks a deer right down."

"Unless I'm greatly mistaken," I predicted, "there's not a problem. The smart money's on a dead bear at the end of these tracks, if you put even one of those where it looked like you did. But since you've got the rifle, you stand here and watch both ways at once for him to break cover, and since I've got the shotgun, I'll go back in yonder and check his vital signs."

The willows were really thick. If the hair on the back of my neck looked like it felt, I could've passed for a Rhodesian ridgeback. Finally, I heard him before I saw him, and he didn't sound well. Before I could make him out plainly I was within fifteen feet, and he was down but not quite out, lungshot, it sounded like.

"Looking at him here," I called back. "Gonna whack him again unless you want to."

"Fire away," he yelled. And I did.

After I brought the canoe up, the skinning went quickly. It was an immensely fat fall bear.

"Who would've guessed," Dr. Moore said, wiping the blade of his skinning knife on his wool trouser leg near the ankle, "how much a bear with his skin off looks like a person?"

"It's why a lot of guys only shoot one, I've heard. But wait'll you get a hindquarter roast on the table with some pan gravy. No real meat hunter would pass up a nice black bear."

"Is that what we are? Meat hunters?" he asked, grinning.

"Do we ever come across some geese in a sneakable spot, that will become perfectly clear." I'd already swapped the slugs in the 12 gauge for goose loads.

Russ

Russ can be as quiet as a cat when he wants to. I heard neither his footsteps on the porch nor the door opening. A cheap plastic champagne cork ricocheted off the ceiling in the dark cabin and cracked me, sleeping, behind the ear.

"Yahoo!" he exclaimed. Then, "*Whoops!*"

"Can you point that somewhere else?"

"What's happening?" Mary was waking up.

"Russ's here."

"Yahoo! I quit my job! You guys want a drink?"

"No. I just had some, thanks. Turn the light on."

Click. There he stood, in the middle of the floor with a roll of topographic maps under one arm, trying to look concerned about the champagne dripping from the ceiling. Two fingers were left in the bottle. He shrugged his shoulders, tipped it back, and set it empty on the table.

"Want to look at some maps?" Everybody has a weakness; Russ Wood's is maps.

"Of what?" I had been in bed two hours.

"Duncan Creek."

"Never heard of it."

"Maybe I'm going to trap there this winter."

"Oh, yeh, I remember." I climbed down the ladder, scratched, blinked at the light, and pulled on my pants and socks. Mary rolled over to face the wall and pulled the covers over her head. Quit his job? Jesus, he'd been there a year and just got a promotion and a raise. At twenty, he was making twice as much per hour as I'd ever made in my life.

"How come you quit?"

He unrolled one of his maps and sat the empty bottle on one corner, the sugar bowl on the other. "Don't you remember talking about it? You said if a person was going to do it, he ought to do it right, take a whole winter for it, instead of just trapping weekends."

"I said a person ought to buy up his traps and supplies and stuff, and save up about a thousand for a stake to carry through the winter on, and *then* quit. How much you got saved?"

He handed me one of my dishtowels. "Wipe your face off. You're dripping on the map."

"You got *any*thing saved?"

"Coupla hundred."

"Jesus."

"I'll shoot a moose for meat."

"How many traps you got?"

"Three dozen."

"Jesus."

"I *had* to quit. It's almost October. Be snowing in another week or two. Got to get a cabin built."

"And the rest just gonna take care of itself."

"That's about what I figured. See here," he traced with his dirty index finger up a small river to its headwaters, where a creek ran in from the east. "Old miner I talked to, been mining around in here since 1905, says Fred Blick had a sort of line cabin right here. Maybe I can fix it up."

"How long since he'd seen it?"

"I don't know. 1935, maybe."

"Jesus."

"It's better than nothin'."

"You ain't seen it yet."

"Gotta start somewhere."

"So what's the plan?"

"Well," he scratched his head and frowned, "time's the big thing. I was kind of thinking of leaving tomorrow morning, at the latest. Want to go?"

I looked up at the bed. "Want to make a trip with Russ?" She breathed evenly, asleep again. "Sure. Why not? Can we run a motor in the river?"

"I don't know. Maybe."

"You got a motor?"

"Mine's still busted." Russ hadn't had money for a motor that spring, when he'd bought his canoe, but he'd scrounged an old one somewhere, for free.

"We'll take mine, then."

"Which canoe?" He was still deferring to my judgment in canoes. The choice was between my longer, heavier, fiberglass-on-wood freighter, and his 19-foot aluminum squarestern.

"Yours. You got a tent?'

"Not big enough for three."

"We'll take mine. You taking a rifle?"

"My seven millimeter."

"One's enough. I'll take my pump gun and some slugs. How about a chainsaw?" I knew he didn't have one of his own.

"Maybe I can borrow my dad's…"

"It's pretty old. Might's well take my Homelite."

"I got a sack of onions," he said. Onions are half of all he usually takes with him for food. "And I'll get a sack of potatoes from Dad."

"Okay. Mary will want to take some other stuff. Let's take my rig." I didn't trust his.

"All right." Neither did he.

As usual, our early-morning start got underway at three in the afternoon.

Grouse come to the road for gravel, just at twilight. Russ spotted the first pair. "Ruffs," he said. "White meat. Let's get 'em for supper." I stopped thirty yards short of them. They watched.

"All I got's slugs," I said.

"What're these?" Russ picked up a yellow #6 off the dashboard.

"Twenty gauge. They ain't no help."

"They got shot in 'em," Russ said, fishing for his pocketknife. "Find me a couple of slugs." Mary burrowed into the pile of gear in the back end. I watched as Russ circumcised the 20-gauge load. Then he cut the crimps off the two slugs that Mary handed him, worked the slugs themselves out of the cases, and poured half of the 20-gauge load in each. "Got any ass-wipe on you?" he asked. Mary had some in her pocket. He poked a piece into each altered slug hull on top of the shot, and tipped them over. The shot stayed in.

"Look out, grouse…" I whispered, dragging the pump out and nudging the door open. "These only got a half ounce of shot in each one, not even as much poop as a .410, so don't hold your breath."

The grouse got nervous at twenty yards, and seemed on the point of flying. I took the closest one. The pattern kicked up a spare amount of dust around him and he flopped in a circle on his back. His partner flew into a roadside birch, and craned his neck. I shot him without chancing getting closer. Crippled, he flew crazily downhill through the aspens, out of sight.

"You hit him!" Russ hollered, jumping the ditch and disappearing over the bank. His sliding footsteps died away while I fetched the bird in the road. Ten minutes later he was back, carrying the grouse by the feet.

"You didn't hurt him *much*. Jumped him three times before I got close enough to clobber him with a stick."

"Be good for your appetite."

Russ is a curious kid. He doesn't have a limit. I guided a couple of seasons for sheep in the Alaska Range, in country he'd hunted and told me about. We flew in, established base camps and spike camps, climbed for sheep, and flew the meat, trophies, and hunters out. These were ten- and twenty-day hunts. Russ walked in from the road, shot his ram, and carried the meat, cape and horns, and his camp, back out. In three days.

One of the events at the North American Sled Dog Championship in Fairbanks is a snowshoe race. Years ago, Russ took his old, heavy Army surplus snowshoes down and entered, in a field of men of all ages, some who had been winning for years. He wasn't taken seriously, until he won, and then they gave the prize to the second-place finisher: it was a case of beer, and they said it would be illegal to give it to a 14-year-old boy.

It was dark when we reached the river, which turned out to be much too shallow for the motor; paddling and lining upstream would be the only practical thing. Mary built a cookfire and got the skillet out of the grub box, while Russ unloaded the car and I cleaned the grouse. I set the tent up by the river, and Russ gathered firewood. When he finished, he sat down and inspected the thin aluminum frying pan.

"You going to fry the birds?" he asked, tilting the skillet at me.

"Unless you want to."

"Nope. What I like's a good *iron* skillet."

"Me, too, except on portages."

"Going to fry potatoes, too?"

"Yep."

Mary hadn't had the experience cooking outdoors that Russ had. "How would you fix the birds, Russ?" she asked.

"Fry 'em in butter."

"Rolled in flour?"

"If I had flour."

She was slicing potatoes. "And potatoes?"

"Fry 'em in butter."

"How about eggs?"

"Fry 'em in butter."

"Do you cook *everything* that way?"

"Nope. Sometimes I boil stuff, if I don't have butter. If I ain't got a can to boil water in, I poke a green willow stick in it and roast it."

I fried potatoes first, then set them near the fire on an enameled metal plate and fried the grouse breasts. Russ boiled a can of water, poured it in three enameled cups, daubed a teabag around until all three were brown, and tossed the teabag in the fire.

Stars were out and the weather was mild. We heard geese, high. Upriver, an owl hooted. I divided the browned grouse breasts between three plates and scooped potatoes on beside them. The salt and pepper shakers made the rounds and we dug in.

"Mm-mmmmm," Mary said.

"Not bad, for an aluminum skillet," Russ said.

"If it don't get no worse than this, I'll be able to stand it," I predicted.

There was a heavy frost on the tent next morning, and we all got into our long underwear. It was wool-shirt, insulated-hip-boot weather. I lashed the gear in the canoe while Russ studied his map. When we set off, he paddled bow, Mary in the middle, and I paddled stern. The current was not strong, but we rarely paddled more than two hundred yards before climbing out to ascend a riffle.

The river level was falling, as rivers always do in the North in late fall. We lined more than we paddled. Mary had been in Alaska less than two months, and scoured the banks for berries and rosehips while Russ and I took turns lining the canoe. Autumn was in its eleventh hour. The leaves were all underfoot, moose would be beginning the rut, and bears putting on a last few pounds before seeking out their dens for winter.

Russ's town cabin, built in a week between snowstorms following harvest the year before, was not unlike a bear's den; roughly the size of a large packing crate and crammed haphazardly with his possessions, it was the sort of abode that most bears or bachelors spend lifetimes creating.

The one time he asked us over for sheep steaks, the cookstove ran out of propane halfway through cooking dinner, and he finished the job over a niggardly fire in the yard. For want of a table or chairs, we sat on stumps and ate off our laps, and at that, Mary lost her steak halfway through the meal to one of his sled dogs who, overcome by the cooking odors, snapped his tether and stampeded into the cabin dragging six feet of chain. Old Rex got his teeth into

Mary's steak about the time Russ got his hand back around his skillet handle, and he added some credibility to his opinions on the relative merits of cast-iron cookware by felling the dog with one stroke. Rex's left eye popped out, and Russ had to poke it back in before dragging him, unconscious, back to his post. Mary wouldn't accept Russ's repeated offer of the remainder of his own steak, and later allowed that she certainly didn't recall meeting fellows like him on campus in Montreal.

Towards noon, we encountered our first logjam.
"What do you think?" I said. "Over it or through it?" We'd wrestled the canoe over two collections of floating drift logs already.
"Being's we got the chainsaw handy," Russ proposed, "let's cut a hole in it. Want me to?"
"No, I will. Why don't you scout up past the bend?"
"Okay," and he was off upriver scouting, which is what he likes best. He'd be back before I was finished, with everything he'd seen filed and catalogued in a memory incapable of retaining for ten minutes the barest rudiments of spelling or grammar. A fresh mink track. A two-year-old bear scrape. A blueberry patch where all the berries were big. An oxbow slough with a beaver dam and fresh cuttings. An old trail blaze. A lightning-struck spruce. A good bald-faced bluff to climb to spot moose from. Grayling, holding behind a log below a riffle.

Russ may meet someone tomorrow who claims to have canoed his old river, and the questions will be right on the tip of his tongue, as though it had been seven days instead of seven years since he'd walked up it that once: "Are there still beavers in the slough behind the lightning-struck spruce? Did the lower logjam ever wash out?"

When he returned, typically, he didn't wait for me, but grabbed the canoe alone and began yanking it up to where I was still cutting. He danced up a bank-anchored spruce log, heaved on the rope, and jumped to the next stump. Which was a floater that I'd just cut off, and offered about as solid a footing as a beach ball. Russ went straight to the bottom in five feet of water. The only sound was his breath sucking in, which happens every time that, as he puts it, his crotch hits ice water.

He never stopped. He went straight down up to his neck and came straight back out, his one "God-*DAMN!!!*" echoing through the spruce woods over even the racket of the Homelite.

It sounded like two bull moose fighting, thirty feet back in the brush, as he snapped the dead, dry bottom limbs off the big spruce to start a fire with. Mary and I helped gather wood and he lit it, shivering spasmodically, with a match from his ever-present National Guard match safe, and stripped.

Mary brought dry clothes from one of the duffel bags, and he climbed into them. "God-damn," he said again, "about one of those a day is plenty for me."

I picked a bar to camp on at sundown, and pitched the tent while Mary and Russ unloaded the duffel and grub.

"What shall we have for supper?" Mary asked.

"Stew's okay with me," I said. We had canned stew.

"Want grayling?" Russ offered.

"You got some?"

"I think I can get some."

"I haven't seen a rise all day."

"It's too cold for bugs to hatch. All you got to do is get something down to them."

"Go ahead. My rod's in the boat yet."

He dug it out and jointed it together, strung it, and tied on a

#14 Blue Upright. The stream was narrow here, with steep brush banks and no room for back casting. Russ laid the rod aside, climbed the bank, and scouted the pool from that height, returned, and waded up the middle, hunched over, rod in one hand, fly in the other. Before he cast, he dug a big split shot out of his pocket and clinched it onto the leader a foot above the fly. Then he sling-shotted it back under an alder and worked it down, twitching the rod tip.

"I thought you told me Blue Uprights should stay on the surface after you cast," Mary said.

"I did. That's when you're fishing for fun, though. Russ is fishing for his dinner." There was a faint splash upstream, and we could see Russ in over his boot-tops again, rod arched.

His voice drifted down through the deepening evening gloom: "How many can you guys eat?"

The first logjam the next day required a two-hundred-yard portage. I was chainsawing through the second when Russ brought good news.

"I found the mouth of the creek, up about a half mile," he said, "but the cabin ain't where it's supposed to be."

"Maybe it never was."

"No, Mr. Ben said he seen it. We can look for it tomorrow. There's a good stand of spruce up there to pitch the tent in."

"No more logjams?"

"This is the last one."

He was right about the spruce stand. There was even a pair of logs, eight feet apart and parallel to each other, right in front of the tent site, to build the fire between and sit on. The fire felt good as the woods darkened and the evening chilled. A camp robber landed on top of the tent and cocked his head at us, eyeballing our groceries.

"Why don't you go lay down in the riffle for a few minutes," I said to Russ, "you don't look right, all dry and comfortable."

"Aw, I slowed down a little today," he said.

"This weather can't hold much longer."

He looked up past the tall, firelit spruce to the bright, cold stars, and agreed. "Next time it clouds up," he said, "you watch. It'll snow."

Mary woke me at first light. "John," she whispered, "something's outside the tent." I was nine-tenths asleep.

"It's only a camp robber," I said, and went the rest of the way back to sleep. Minutes passed.

"John, I unzipped the tent to look, and there's a bear eating our food," she whispered.

I looked. Ten feet from the tent door, between our seat-logs, a fat black bear was pulling a box of Ritz crackers on over his nose like a feedbag. "Holy shit!"

To shoot the bear, or not to shoot the bear. If I *didn't* shoot him, he'd be a problem, having tasted the forbidden fruit. If I *did* shoot him, he represented two hundred pounds of sausage for the winter. End of deliberation.

The old Model 12 beside me was plugged, so it contained two rifled slugs in the magazine. At ten feet, that was enough for two bears. The action wouldn't open.

Two days at close hand in the canoe had exposed it to some splashing, and the freezing temperatures had set up the water that had dripped into the receiver. I clamped it coldly under my arm to thaw it, and watched the bear inhale Ritz crackers.

When the slide finally freed, the shell wouldn't feed into the chamber because of droplets frozen there, also. After checking the barrel, I blew into the chamber and reamed it with my index finger.

A slug chambered.

"Russ. Don't get excited. I'm going to shoot a bear."

"Yup," he said, asleep. He's anything but a light sleeper.

"Don't let him suffer," Mary said.

"Pssst!" I said, to the bear. He pulled his muzzle out of the crackers, holding the box between his paws, and regarded the tent quizzically. The bead was steady on his eye when the hammer fell.

"Hey," Russ said, waking up, "what's going on?"

"Just a bear."

"Get him?"

"Yep."

"Good. Bear stew," he said, and was asleep again.

A curling wisp of smoke rose from the carcass. Mary sniffed. "Something's burning," she said. I ran barefooted to the bear and heaved his hindquarters out of the grey fly-ash of our cookfire. There had been live coals under the ashes, and a spot as big as a washtub was singed hairless on his rump. We hadn't planned to save the hide, anyhow.

Russ and I gutted him, propped him open to cool, and ate breakfast. "Let's look for that cabin this morning, and skin and quarter him this afternoon," Russ said, over coffee.

"Sounds good."

We scoured the woods upstream for two hours, and found the cabin only after we'd abandoned the search and were trooping back to camp. "Oh, *that*," Mary said, "I saw *that* an hour ago. I thought we were looking for a *cabin*."

It was different from any cabin we'd ever seen, simply a crib of three-inch-thick spruce poles within a larger crib, the two-foot space between filled with sphagnum moss. The sod roof had long since fallen in, and the whole thing was moldering back to the soil. Russ wedged himself through the skewed doorframe and crawled around the edges of the dark five-foot by eight-foot interior.

"Hey, look here," he said, and crawled out with two old enamel plates and a rusty butcher knife.

"Why, shoot," I said, "a few shingles on the roof, new coat of paint and it'll be fit for a king. Even got enough tableware for company." The cabin was totally beyond repair.

"It ain't much, is it?"

"What do you mean? Puts me in mind of your place in town. Got that same 'lived-in' feeling to it. I'd think you'd be right at home here. When you going to move in?"

"At least I keep my knives sharp," he said, fingering the rusted edge of his new one.

Mary fried bannock for lunch, and Russ and I drank tea and looked at the bear a few feet from the fire. It had clouded over while we looked for the cabin, and a fine, grainy snow was falling.

"Termination dust," I said.

"What's that?" Mary asked.

"That's the first skifter of snow that ends the construction season, when everybody with any sense closes down their jobs and shags it into Fairbanks and reads newspapers in hotel lobbies all winter."

"Oh."

"I guess now we got to use Plan Two," Russ said.

"What's that?"

"Build a new cabin."

"I was afraid that's what it was."

"Got to have *somewhere* to live this winter."

"Where you want to put it?"

He looked around at the spruce we'd pitched camp in. "That's a good stand of spruce upstream, but the ground's a little higher here.

There's plenty of cabin logs right here, and the chainsaw's already here."

"Pick a spot."

"That's a pretty fair spot right where the bear lays."

"Want to move him first or build around him and use him for a kitchen table?"

"Only way I want to see that bear this winter is in pieces, peekin' out from between two potatoes and a carrot, or fried next to a stack of hotcakes. Inch-thick hotcakes."

The cabin took a week and a half, and when the last of the sod went on the roof, we were working in six inches of snow. The door and two windows would come later, when Russ returned with his traps and provisions, dog team and a little lumber. For now, we rough-framed them, chainsawed holes the right size, and called it finished.

Those parts of the bear which had not been stewed for our dinners we loaded into the canoe, with the paddles and Mary's and my gear. Russ left his in the cabin, along with the tent, skillet, coffeepot and silverware. We wanted the canoe as light as possible for the portage.

We had almost waited too long to get the canoe out that year: the still parts of the river were solid skim ice, thick enough at worst that Mary in the bow had to break it ahead of us with her paddle before we could force a path with the boat. Usually, we'd hit it going as fast as we could paddle, and crunch through, biting holes in it with each stroke.

Russ stayed with us until the portage, and as soon as we had the canoe loaded again, left to walk out alone and scout himself an overland trail, to get the lay of the land for the walk back in with his dogs. Mary and I canoed out, and it was a pleasure to be handling a light paddle instead of heavy, green cabin logs. We had pushed the season, and winter had arrived. The ridges were white, and the hares we saw were almost completely turned. Once, we raced a beaver towing the season's last willow down a riffle, before he slapped his tail and disappeared in the deeper water below.

"I get the feeling we should have been out of here a week ago," Mary said, as we neared the bridge where Russ would be waiting.

"We should've. We just lucked out, was all. This is the end of it. It got down to ten above before breakfast, and the ice is getting thicker the farther we go. I don't think we'd have made it tomorrow."

At the bridge, Russ had a tin can full of coffee made, and we shared it before loading the canoe, listening, in the silence of the winter evening, to the popping of the spruce limbs in the fire, and the riffle nearby, wishing to hear once more the wolves we'd heard twice on other nights.

We stopped, late and nearly home, at the Fox Roadhouse for supper. After two weeks outdoors, it was a peculiar sensation to be in a heated room again. Mary and I washed up in the restrooms, while Russ placed our orders, and then he went off to the restroom himself. The smells of roast beef and gravy and clam chowder hung heavy in the air. On his way back through the adjoining bar, Russ stopped and put a dime in the jukebox. Mary laughed when "North to Alaska" began.

When he returned to the table and sat down, he brought the fresh, distinctive smell of woodsmoke with him. It was in his clothes from the many hours of warming up and drying off that he'd spent beside the fire, and it cut cleanly through the cooking smells. He looked neither tired nor worn after the two weeks of hard work and the long day's walk; rather, he looked refreshed.

"Say," he said, interrupting himself singing along with the jukebox, "you guys want to go trapping with me this winter?"

"Sure," I said, "why not?"

"Good. I know where I can get a good little Yukon stove, all we'll need is about twenty dozen more traps. Mary, did you ever sew dog harnesses?"

I think of Russ every time I smell woodsmoke in a wool shirt.

Russ at potato harvest, 1972

John Hewitt

Pushing the Season

Snowshoes are not a part of my fly fishing paraphernalia anymore. There was a time, before I sprang for a gas-powered ice auger, that April Fool's Day (appropriately) signaled that six months had passed since I'd wet a line. The temptation to push the season was irresistible. Only the temptation was irresistible: the season itself was often not.

On one memorable occasion twenty-five years ago, Mary and I drove to our usual parking spot, minus the canoe, strapped on snowshoes, shouldered pack frames with cased fly rods lashed fast, and ascended our favorite stream stoically. It had been a pretty good snow year, and we only rarely saw patches of ice beneath it on our hike. Mostly it was snow from cutbank to cutbank, and only the higher parts of the gravel bars, with their covering of moose-nibbled willows, were apparent, and them under two feet of snow.

The snow, at least, was crusted from a succession of thawing afternoons and a good cold night, and we sank in not at all. So it wasn't the slog it could have been. After three miles, however, I selected a conveniently located drift log and sat down.

"Dern," I said, "I was certain we'd find a little open water *somewhere*!"

"If we find any today," Mary replied, "it's going to have to be a hot springs. Want some lunch?" She had packed three sandwiches, a Pepsi and an apple juice.

The car was fifteen road miles shy of a genuine, developed hot springs with both inside and outside pools where, for a reasonable sum, one could soak for hours. They even had loaner trunks and towels.

"Now that," I said, congratulating myself for such a marvelous idea, "reminds me, there *is* a hot springs on another fork of this river. And I haven't been in it in over a year. Want to go?"

"Sure. But don't you want to give this plan another couple of miles?"

"Not considering the hot springs alternative. I guess I just misremembered the date I got on open water here two years ago. Or it was a warmer March."

What it was, was, I got the day right and the month wrong.

For one thing, when I'd found open water in the past, anywhere a stray leaf had fallen on the snow, it'd melted its way eight or more inches down into the snowpack as the direct sun of succeeding middays warmed it. I'd seen no such signs this day.

The river ran open from underneath the snow for patches of fifty or a hundred yards then, a black strip of icy water from two to ten feet across, exposed and steaming in the cold air. I had mistrusted the ice near the open water, particularly with a 56-inch snowshoe on each foot, and rarely had got closer than eight feet.

The casting had been pretty rudimentary, more dapping than anything else, and it was one of the few times I ever tried a dropper on grayling. A weighted black #6 Woolly Worm was my main choice, with a #12 Hairwing Coachman on the dropper, for no other reason than that it was the most different-looking fly in my fly box from the Woolly Worm.

I wish I could say the rig was so successful that I often had a pair on at once. Actually, it was so unsuccessful that I generally had nothing on at all, and when I did get a hit, the fish were not that big. Ten inches, say.

But the sun was high above the spruce and warm on your face, you didn't need gloves, you were standing on the threshold of the *real* fishing months, and the quick pull of *any* fish on the line was an overdue reconnection to a host of seasons gone by, of the first explorations of this same stream, and grayling taken from wonderful holes in tight bends that twenty-five years later no longer existed, as the river changed channels, and the friends we fished those holes with went on to other things.

The Woolly Worm, as I expected, caught all the fish, which was a half dozen. I kept none. It was still twenty years until Fish & Game would unequivocally designate that a catch-and-release stream, and I'd have kept some if they had been larger or more numerous, but in that place and at that time, the reluctant and diminutive grayling there seemed more like wood ducks in the Midwest in the Fifties before their miraculous comeback. We didn't shoot them, either.

Some of the stretches of open water held no fish, or at least none I could catch, which I attributed to their shallowness.

Lynx tracks, distinctive pug marks melted much larger than the paw that made them, sometimes paralleled the open water. Snowshoe hares were high in their cycle, and the cats hunted them for a living and fished, I guessed, for sport. Like me. There was never any evidence that they had even the little success that I did, but when you found the larger impression in the snow that indicated they'd hunkered on their haunches, or laid down to peer over the edge into the dark water for an extended period, you wanted to double your efforts, because they had been looking at fish.

"I think," Mary said, after she finished her sandwich and we'd decided to switch to Plan B, soaking in the hot springs, "I'll give it a try." She unscrewed the top of her short aluminum rod tube and began putting her new-that-month rod together.

"The nearest open water is below the outfall at the power plant forty miles away," I said. Mary was a relatively new entity in my life then, and I had not broken myself of expecting the things she did would make sense.

"So? Is this a fishing trip, or what?"

In retrospect, I imagine she just wanted to try the new rod out. She never tied a fly on her leader, anyway. The rod, a four-piece fiberglass pack rod that caught most of her fish for the next twenty years, laid line out well enough, and before we headed back I gave it a try myself. It felt a little stupid, but it also felt like as close as we'd come to fishing for another month, with the pull of the line straightening out behind as you completed the final false cast and shot a few feet of line to see if you could reach the other bank.

We were down to our T-shirts by the time we got back to the car, and Mary was even starting to sunburn a little, with no cap and the glare coming off the snow. The indoor pool at the hot springs was refreshing and the hotter one, outdoors, relaxing. We were the only ones in it.

The fog surrounding us, rising from the warm water, was quite dense, and burdened every nearby birch branch and spruce needle with an incredible load of hoar frost. Mary's red hair, the individual stray hairs, anyhow, quickly froze, and her eyelashes frosted up.

"I think I remember what I was doing on this day last year," I said.

"Fishing?"

"No. That would've been next month. I borrowed some dogs and a sled and went in to a cabin I know of off the road and hunted ptarmigan."

"Get any?"

"One. In two days. It was a total fiasco. Damn dogs got in a big fight and I got bit. And I snowshoed almost one whole day and never saw a single ptarmigan, except the one, and he was in a willow outside the cabin when I went out in the morning to pee."

"You're making fly fishing on snowshoes with no water and no fly sound better all the time."

"Oh, I've had a bunch of worse days than today. A bunch. Other than a small miscalculation on when the river first opens up enough to fish, nothing major went wrong."

"Today has one big thing going for it," she said, ducking her face in the water to melt the frost in her hair, "that none of those other days had. Do you know what?"

"Well..." I thought. And thought. "Uh, the cheeseburgers I was about to offer to buy at the lodge here?" She laughed.

"You're on the right track. I was going to say that today's advantage is that it's not over yet."

"Yeh," I said, "maybe they'll have onion rings here."

Raw Canadian

After twenty years of marriage, preceded by seven years of sparring over who, assuming we ever *got* married, was going to be the bull goose and not have to do the dishes, it has occurred to me that the wife and I may no longer be in love. For one thing, she spends a lot more time with our three dogs than she does with me, and cooks better meals for them. For another thing, I have not bought her flowers in, oh, roughly twenty years.

I have my reasons. Buying flowers is what one does for a girlfriend. It's like calling in artillery fire before an infantry attack. After the objective is overrun and the casualties bandaged up, what possible good could result from calling in more artillery? A more appropriate request would be a pallet of C-rations. Therefore, once the knot was tied and her hand was won (or my hand, if you choose to believe her version) I turned my attention toward providing her with the finer things in life. Such as wild duck to eat and, when ducks were not in season, wild fish.

Not that that had not been part of the courtship process. Galled even then by the necessity for spending money on things as pointless and transitory as flowers, I bought her a very nice pack rod which she became quite fond of. I liked it myself, well enough to use it every time I've needed a pack rod for the last twenty-five years.

Previous to all this, back in Kansas in about '66, Terry and I had invented a formula for instant wilderness. All you needed was the usual camping gear, which consisted of a cheap sleeping bag and air mattress, and some kind of boat. You went to the lake, passed up the campground with its brick barbecue pits and picnic tables, launched the boat, threw all the camping and fishing gear in it, parked the car, and motored, paddled or rowed either to the farthest point on the lake from the campground or any point at least two miles distant, picked out a spot on shore, and camped.

This formula transferred well to the north, where locals use campgrounds to hold all-night beer-drinking campaigns. Nothing spoils a fishing trip more thoroughly than having to use the shotgun one brought for the bears on the locals. The resulting paperwork is a killer.

Mary was as enthusiastic about this scheme as Terry had been, if for different reasons. The occasional romantic interlude that people our age considered almost mandatory was not enhanced by someone else's children tripping over the tent pegs during their interminable games of hide-and-seek and fox-and-goose.

We happened on such a lake with such a campground on the coast one long-ago summer, which had the additional advantage of a stream running into the lake at the far end where, I predicted, the Dolly Varden had never seen a fly and would fight each other for a spot in our skillet.

That was before the bigger outboards, so all we had on the long canoe was the six-horse. And we didn't even start that until the return trip two days later when there was a headwind. The lake, when we launched, had lain flat calm, and after we'd paddled into deep enough water for the outboard, we just kept paddling.

The stream mouth we were headed for, which Mary estimated to be a half mile distant and I figured was at least two turned out to be almost four, so it was a very nice paddle, with a family of otters coming out to check on us halfway down. A vocal loon pair promised to be a more pleasant midnight racket than drunks. At that time of spring, what passes for night is more accurately a brief twilight, and then it's the next day. The main question that the alert camper must address is, where exactly will the sun pop over the mountains and where can the tent be located to take advantage of the longest-lasting shade? When the sun hits the tent, the night's over, at least the sleeping part of it.

The options were not great, so we settled for some evening shade and an early get-up, say, 3 or 4 A.M. Since the Dolly fishing I have done has not, like trout or grayling, usually depended on the presence of a hatch, being turned out of the tent at such an hour was not a great drawback. It makes for a pretty long day, admittedly, but nothing two lunches four or five hours apart won't fix.

"Where," Mary inquired the next morning after nosing through the ice chest, "is the bacon, anyway?"

"Well, hey," I replied, sawing campfire-sized sections off a drift log with a bow saw, "has it occurred to your little pea brain where we are?"

"The coast."

"Where lives what?"

"Dolly Varden."

"Besides that."

"Uh…what?"

"Large bears."

"Oh. So, the possibility of seeing a bear, which hasn't happened before, has turned you into a Buddhist monk?"

"I was thinking rabbi. But why go looking for trouble? Your own father, not to mention most good Scots, has oatmeal every morning, and how many Scots did you ever hear of getting eaten by brown bears during breakfast?"

"Correct me if I'm wrong, but don't you carry the shotgun in case of these things? Didn't you blast a bear into the next life not two years ago for sampling our comestibles?"

"That was late fall, we needed the meat, and the bear was a black not appreciably bigger than I am. This is the spring, the season is closed, we don't need the meat and it's arguably not good to eat anyway, plus there might be a cub involved, plus the bears are a lot bigger than me. More the size of our car. I only know from hearsay that a 12 gauge will even kill one."

"Whatever."

"In the interests of travelling light, I didn't bring the shotgun anyhow. So we are, as they say, going bare here."

"Ha," she said, not much amused. "My boyfriend the comedian. Oatmeal it is. Just so I know, what's today's plan if we *do* see a bear?"

"We Uncle Tom it: 'Yassuh, ole beah, dis a nice spot you got heah but us got to be runnin' along now. Y'awl see anything yuh wants, just he'p yoselfs.'"

The oatmeal was fine, since I had remembered the brown sugar, and the fishing was good, if not terribly productive. At least until we finally found the right lie, and we had to ferry across from camp with the canoe to locate it. It was more like fishing for salmon than trout: we used streamers and you only got the right drift about every thirtieth cast, but the Dollies kept moving into the lie all morning, so we

Mary at Chilkoot Lake, 1973

never seemed to fish it out.

Once we had enough for supper and started releasing, Mary eyed the tent across the water and yawned.

"I'll bet it's a sauna in that thing," she said. "Watch me find a better spot for a nap right back in the sphagnum moss somewhere."

"Suit yourself," I said, "but while the bite is on I think I'll keep my line wet."

"Chacun à son gout," she replied. I know about the same amount of French as my Chesapeake Bay retriever, but I knew she meant "To each his own," as I had been once acquainted with a girl from Toronto who used the same expression, though she always appended it with "...said the old lady as she kissed the cow."

So Mary went off to have her nap beside the trail in the woods that only get that big on the coast, towering trees four and five feet through at the stump that always make me think of Longfellow's line from *Evangeline*, "In the forest primeval."

I cast, mended my line, caught another couple of fish, checked my knot, and had the usual forty or fifty feet of line out when I heard her behind me.

"Short nap," I offered. "You stand in the wrong place back there and you'll get a hook in your ear."

She did not reply. I thought over the last thing she'd said, wondering if there might have been a message in there I'd missed. Maybe. I dropped the fly in what I hoped was the sweet spot and glanced over my shoulder. While I might be accused of a lack of expertise in divining the nuances of certain foreign languages, I rarely misinterpreted a "come-hither" look.

It was not a "come-hither" look, nor even a "Your turn to do the dishes, buster" look. It was a look of simple curiosity, perhaps a little perplexed. But it brought up goose bumps on me nevertheless, gracing as it did the countenance of the largest bear I had seen or imagined up until that time. Standing precisely where I'd last seen Mary.

Suffice to say, several thoughts occurred to me more or less simultaneously, one of which was, what exactly happened to Mary? But the only one I acted on was the conviction that I was much too close to a bear for whom I felt no romantic attachment, which was six or eight or ten times larger than my redheaded girlfriend, wherever she might be. So I increased the distance between us as inconspicuously as possible, not even pausing when the ice-cold water enveloped my private parts and, eventually, the fountain pen in my shirt pocket. I had been in over my hip boots a few times before, but never in water that chilly or deep. I stopped approximately in the only Dolly Varden lie we'd found all day and, what's more, didn't care if I spooked it or not. The four fish on the cord stringer, knotted to my downstream bait loop, must've looked around at their old digs and thought, "Now what?"

I did feel a lot better about the bear at this new distance, though I was vaguely concerned about how to retrieve my bamboo rod if I had to ditch it and swim for it. "Raw Kansan, in Levis" must not have been the special at the River Café that day, as the bear more or less shrugged and ambled on upstream, hoping for a dead salmon. And I eased quietly back into the shallow water, laid on my back on the grassy bank and raised my feet straight up to empty my boots. Then I stood my rod against a streamside alder, and backtracked down what probably had not occurred to Mary was a bear trail.

She was still asleep on the moss with her rod beside her, ten feet off the trail and a hundred feet from where the bear had observed me. The bear's unswerving pawprints in the wet trail indicated an equal lack of interest in "Raw Canadian, in Carhartts." She did not initially believe the bear story, but the lack of any other explanation for the fresh pawprints, my overall moistness, and the amount of time it took my goose bumps to go down eventually convinced her.

I cleaned the fish on the grassy bank and left the heads and guts there beside the trail for the bear. We grilled them instead of frying them, then sank the grill in the river overnight. When the sun next morning hit the bank across the river where I'd left the heads, they were long gone.

"Probably," Mary said when she awoke and got her binoculars focused through the mosquito netting, "just a mink."

"Probably," I said.

Montana Done Traditionally

In the event I live to be as old as Charley Waterman, I predict my primary conversational topic will be "Things aren't what they used to be." It seems kind of obvious, though, like saying the sky is blue.

Charley, probably overly sensitive to sounding like an Old Guy, avoids the subject entirely. But he *does* make observations about the present state of things and lets his listeners draw their own conclusions.

Such as the last time he was in a well-known West Yellowstone fly shop. He says there were no longer any Pflueger Medalists among the reels for sale. When he inquired, he was told the new fly fisherman did not want to pay less than $200 for a reel – or maybe it was $300 – and rather than insult anyone, the store had quit stocking Medalists.

As my father would've said, "Yow!"

I didn't tell Charley that I haven't spent $200 on fly reels in my life, nor that my old, semi-retired Medalist, that Remington 870 of reels, is the top end of my own stable of a dozen. Three of the ten screws that hold the Medalist together have been missing since before I inherited it twenty-four years ago, its two former owners more concerned with hunting ducks and cottontails in the winter than reel maintenance.

Being a pretty philosophical Aging Individual, Charley would never refer to a brother of the angle as a philistine. But I would. Particularly if I encounter him standing where I had hoped to stand in a stream, casting to a fish I had hoped to catch...even if he actually *is* my brother, as often used to be. A philistine is a philistine.

Still, one must mention in passing that Charley sold his house in Livingston some time ago.

Could it be that the highest purpose Montana serves is, like golf courses and stock-car tracks and spectator sports, to provide the rank and file with recreational opportunities somewhere besides their own favorite duck marshes or bass ponds? Speaking for myself, I got way ahead of the curve by concluding Montana was ruint the first time I fished it, in 1955.

Tom and I were ten then and we thrashed with level line and 10-pound test leaders every piece of roadside water we could badger our Oregon-bound parents into stopping near. To no avail. The locals appeared to have caught and kept all the trout and thrown all the rest, such as suckers, up the bank to rot. In addition to being fishless, Montana streams smelled bad.

"In Kansas," Tom said at one point, "at least you'd catch *something*." The even-then-fabled Henry's Fork skunked us in the end also, though our lack of any kind of wading gear and inability to cast more than twenty-five feet may have been factors. We ran out of patience with the trout pretty much the same time our folks ran out of patience and we all plunged farther west into Idaho. The secret there, which might have worked in Montana had we discovered it earlier, was not pattern and not presentation, but walking a mile off the road up a trickle too small to have been littered with empty bait containers and beer cans.

There was a beaver dam up there, with no footprints in the pond-bottom muck near shore, and trout of other than the rainbow persuasion, the only kind we could identify with certainty. We ran the entire mile back to the road with a skilletful of 10-inchers in a wet gunnysack.

Because Montana was a scenic and unpopulated state and because all those pilot-fish outdoor writers never stopped singing its praises, I always resolved to give it a second chance someday. Funny how many of that generation of writers lived in Idaho, though, about which they seldom wrote. There may be a lesson in there somewhere.

My wife, Mary, cooked for a horse outfit in the Anvil Range north of the Pelly River in the Yukon in '74 and arrived back at the trailhead on the road in a snowstorm the fifth of October. She'd gone in the first of July. If we drove through Calgary to see her folks, it was practically impossible to get to Kansas for birds without traversing Montana.

After noticing a stream with what any *Esquire* writer would've termed drop-dead good looks, had it been a woman, we bought fishing licenses. Even twenty years ago, we discovered, finding a stream and getting permission to fish were two entirely different things. Jay Hammond, the then-future governor of Alaska, would later articulate this realization for us in answer to often-voiced complaints (*complaints!*) that less than one percent of Alaska land was privately owned. Private ownership is the ultimate lockup.

Late the next day, we found what appeared to be an old logging road up one side of a pretty-good-sized river, a road achievable only by four-wheel drive (which we had). We pitched our small tent where, we guessed, no tent had ever been pitched before and, upon exploring the river, discovered two dandies holding half of a short cast from our bank. While we rigged up, another guy, Charley probably (we knew it wasn't Debie, as he/she didn't catch anything), waded out from the other bank (which appeared to have a regular road along it, with pull-offs and paths to the water) and covered our fish with casts the likes of which I'd never seen.

When he waded on, Mary tied on one of her three favorite flies, which she did not know the name of (an Adams), and prepared to cast.

"What's the matter?" she asked, noting that I wasn't tying anything on myself. "Lost your jam?"

"Hey," I said, "if a sonofabitch in a get-up like that, who can cast like that guy, can't catch anything, you think either of those boogers wants a look at *my* Royal Coachman?"

"Okay for you," she said, and proceeded not to catch either one of them for two hours. She did get them to discreetly shy away by the time she was using a wooly worm and a split shot.

I was digging worms under a rotten log with my tire iron when she gave up.

"Boy," she said, "Montana trout are sure snooty."

I waited till very near full dark before snatching the closest one out on the last two feet of my leader butt, a #6 Eagle Claw, and an earthworm I must've hooked under the log on a backcast. I had bitten off the sporting section of the leader in deference to the emptiness of the skillet and proximity of the dinner hour.

It was a rainbow of the size warranting filleting and had once been caught either by an otter or the water filter at a hatchery. Or had polio. None of which proved a handicap in the skillet. Mary ate her fillet with her fingers, then licked them by firelight.

"That's more like it," she said. "But are you sure that wasn't catch-and-release water?"

"I think there'd be signs," I said. "Look at it this way: I've been fishing Montana every chance I've had for nineteen years and this is the first one I've kept. Can Ted Trueblood say that?"

"Ted who?"

"A *Field & Stream* staffer. Besides, while you were fishing, a kingfisher caught six, all under six inches, and kept every one."

Now, I wonder…how many times did Debie Waterman catch that rainbow before Mary and I ate it?

John Hewitt

A Duck Camp French Lesson

In his younger days, Terry was a recipe for disaster. Watching him negotiate the path to duck camp in the late afternoon with fifty pounds of groceries balanced on his head in a cardboard box and a two-year-old Lab at heel on a short leash, I felt the ingredients were all there, and the pot about to boil.

Mary was three steps behind him and not recognizable as a Canadian or a recent college graduate or even a human being under her load of four army duffel bags stuffed with sleeping bags and other necessities.

I grunted along with a bale of cased guns – four 12 gauges and two .22 rifles with scopes – and could hear old Clyde behind me with his own cargo, an ice chest and two brown paper bags from the liquor store. My own Lab, Pete, was at loose heel, which is to say, usually within sight, or at least within hearing. Terry was thirty feet from the decoy shack and campfire pit, which were the only appointments that distinguished duck camp from any other stretch of riverbank cottonwood-and-willow second growth, when Pete started the squirrel.

It was a large and particularly rapacious fox squirrel, a boar, we imagined, who had single-handedly forced us, in just two duck seasons, to replace all dozen of our gunnysack decoy bags by nibbling swatches of burlap out of them to line his nest with. His nest, Terry believed, must be second only to Hugh Hefner's Playboy mansion for sumptuousness.

Pete was eleven, going on twelve, and even in his youth had always lacked a step or two of ever catching a squirrel, so chasing this one was more a salutatory gesture than an act fraught with any expectation of success. Which isn't to say there wasn't an element of outrage in his bark when he discovered the trespasser violating yet another decoy bag.

Tar, the young Lab, would have had a fair chance but for his fetter, which even then weighed close to two hundred pounds if you didn't count the box of groceries. There is probably a formula from high school physics that I've forgotten, to calculate Terry's rate of acceleration when the sixty-pound dog hit the end of the three-foot leash at roughly forty miles per hour, but suffice to say anything not fastened to his body with buttons, straps or buckles served as proof of the First Law of Inertia, that objects at rest tend to stay at rest, especially if they're Terry. Thus, not only the box of groceries, but his eyeglasses, Jones-style hunting cap and both loose-fitting rubber camp boots separated from his person and left him semi-undressed, plowing a furrow in the new-fallen leaves with his bald head and bellowing, "Whoa, goddamn it! Whoa!"

One of his several problems was that "Whoa!" was a command left over from training his first dog, a very steady little Brittany named Lady, and not one he had ever acquainted his present Lab with.

"Git him, boys! Git him! I said, helpfully.

"Yonder he goes!" Clyde hollered.

Mary caught up to Terry where the dog had fetched him up against a cottonwood bole and yanked back on Tar's collar to put enough slack in the leash that Terry could get his wrist out of its loop, whereupon she released him and he dashed off downriver after Pete.

Clyde stopped beside the overturned box and surveyed the dozen ears of corn, cans of beans, ketchup, mustard and relish bottles, baking potatoes, packages wrapped in white butcher paper, and bottles of Coca-Cola scattered across the path.

"Just put them groceries down here anywhere," he said.

"Damn the dog," Terry said, rubbing the top of his head, which looked like cottonwood bark in reverse.

"What was the squirrel doing in the shack, anyway?" Mary asked.

"Aw," Terry said, getting up and brushing leaves and twigs off his shirt and Levis, "that's where we keep the skillets. The boy was just checkin' to see if he fit one yet."

"On other topics," I said, kneeling and returning loose and unshucked ears of sweet corn to their sack, "what exactly are we supposed to do with *this much* food?" It was my understanding that we were staying one night, opening the prairie chicken season in the morning, and going home again.

"Eat it," Terry said. "I figured if there was lots of chickens we'd want to stay another night. Or two."

"What if there's no chickens?" Clyde asked. We hunted prairie chickens by getting up early and hiding in the dark along a fencerow between their prairie roosting grounds and their river-bottom cornfield feeding grounds, and it was always a crap shoot whether they crossed where we were hid, or somewhere east or west of us.

"Well, then we can hunt ducks."

"But," I said, "the flight birds aren't down yet."

"Then we can hunt squirrels. We know the place is workin' alive with squirrels. Sounds like old Pete's got one treed right now. And I got some fresh chicken livers in this box somewhere so we can put out some limb lines for catfish. In case we get tired of steaks and hot dogs and wild game."

"I can't cook squirrels without plenty of bacon fat and some flour," I said.

"Right here in the box."

"And I'd need barbecue sauce and fresh onions for the prairie chicken."

"Kansas City Masterpiece, two bottles, and three pounds of Vidalias."

"What if it gets cold?" Mary asked.

"Then," Terry said, pulling a large brown paper bag out from under Clyde's arm and sliding out a half-gallon bottle of Hiram Walker Peppermint Schnapps with a built-in handle on one side, "we'll have a snort of this."

"Terry," Mary said, somewhat astonished, "a *half-gallon?*"

Terry grinned and patted his jug conspiratorially. "You never know when it'll turn off warm and the snakes'll come out, and we'll need the rest for snakebite."

"If they're nice big snakes, I'll fry them up, too, if somebody'll clean 'em."

"Is there anything out here you guys *won't* eat?" Mary asked. Four undergraduate years in Montreal had had the effect of turning her into a vegetarian, but two winters of moose steaks and black bear sausage had swung the dietary pendulum back the other way, though squirrels might be getting near the edge of her comfort zone.

"Yeah," Terry said, "and he lives over yonder under the johnboat. We draw the line at packrats."

Terry's failings as a soldier, a husband and a wing shot may be a matter of public record, but no one ever said he couldn't cook or call ducks. Clyde wisely relinquished his duck-calling duties the first time Terry tuned up his trusty Lohman, and I handed over the spatula years before for good when he got the potatoes baked in the coals without incinerating the tinfoil, the skin and outside half-inch of potato. So he and Mary, who was a world-class cook, had something in common.

Like a pack of wolves, or maybe hoboes, we each chose our beds after supper and unrolled our sleeping bags by lantern light. Clyde, the oldest and most conservative, chose the decoy shack. Terry had a small tarp he stretched between willows for he and Tar, Mary propped up one end of the johnboat and rearranged the packrat's leaves, and I raked a couple of bushels of leaves into a long pile among the cottonwoods and used the stars for a roof.

I sat the lantern within reach on the ground, climbed into my down bag and shut the valve on the two-mantle Coleman off. We contemplated the star-studded November night sky.

"Oh yeah," Terry remembered, " I was supposed to tell you two Kay wants you to go out to dinner with us next week at a new place she found in Lawrence."

"Lawrence?" I said. That would be the university town downriver twenty-three miles from Topeka where new ideas, such as marijuana and cocaine, arrived first in Kansas from the coasts.

"New place?" Mary said.

"They have, uh, different food there," Terry explained.

"You mean, no T-bones?" Mary replied.

"Or even rib-eyes or New York strips, either. But you got to go there with an empty mind."

"You mean, 'open mind'?"

"Uh-huh, and you won't be able to read the menu but Kay can explain it."

"You remember what any of the entrées were?"

"Stuff like quinches and creeps."

"You mean, quiches and crêpes?"

"I guess so. A creep is like an extra-thin pancake with strawberries on it, and a quinch is – I know this sounds awful, but it's really pretty good – a kind of pie made out of bacon and eggs, mostly."

"And onions and cheese?" I asked.

"That's it. Did you eat one before?"

"Mary makes them all the time."

"Quiche Lorraine," Mary said.

"You'll like the salad bar too, Mary. There's boogoos of salad makings."

"Boogoos?"

"You know, lots of different stuff."

"Oh. Beaucoup."

"Exactly."

"How snotty are the waiters?" I asked.

"It's all waitresses. Nice ones, too. College girls, I'd guess."

"Oh well, a fake French restaurant is better than none at all."

"Say," Clyde said to Mary and I, "where're you two going in the morning?"

"Top of Rutschmann's hill," I said. "That way, if we don't get a shot, we'll at least get to *see* some prairie chickens."

"Don't forget to check that little pond in the draw south of the fence. Terry and I got into the ducks pretty good there two years ago."

"Okay."

"What size shot should I use?" Mary asked. Her Model 1100 had been in the rack in a Topeka gun emporium three days previous.

"Sixes," Terry replied.

"Fives," Clyde said.

"Fours," I added. "But half the time it don't make any difference. Chickens can be the least cooperative birds in Kansas when they want to be."

"Oh, the prairie chickens will be there," she said confidently. "Boogoos of 'em."

The author, Terry and Clyde, 1979

John Hewitt

There's Always Tomorrow

I was in the basement picking a mallard when the phone rang upstairs. Mary answered it. The door at the head of the stairs opened. "It's for you! It's Ron Rau. He's in a truckstop in Billings, Montana." I brushed most of the feathers off and went upstairs to see if his pickup was broke down and he needed bus fare, or if he was just checking in. Billings, Montana. He had the Alcan, the length of Alberta, and a good share of Montana behind him. Just Wyoming and Colorado left.

The pickup is ten years old and if it quits he calls me to come help fix it, unless it's only out of gas.

I picked up the phone. "Yeh." Didn't want to sound *too* excited that he was finally going to make a Kansas pheasant hunt.

"Lieutenant?" Well. He must've called Denver already and confirmed that John Zillich could make the hunt, too. He only calls me "Lieutenant" when there's another John around.

"Yeh." Now he would either try to say something tremendously funny, or would inquire about the outlook for opening day.

"Where's the pheasants?"

"Road ditches. Tumbleweed draws. Stubble fields. Windbreaks. Creek bottoms. One that I know of is in the ice box."

"*Ice box?*" He bit. Whatever else he isn't, he's a totally ethical bird hunter. As am I except when I slip a little to bait him now and then. I expect he cheats on his income tax, and I *know* what a hopeless rascal he is where women are concerned, but all he has to do is *suspect* I've ground-sluiced something, or overshot my limit, and he takes off like a spinster lady with a carload of high-school kids necking in the driveway.

"Yeh. Road kill. I seen him in the ditch when I drove in last week and he was pretty stiff but he didn't smell when I gutted him. Ought to be all right. Have him baked in sour cream tomorrow night."

"But is there lots of pheasants?" I'd avoided his first question.

"It's supposed to be the worst year in ten or fifteen." I'm always pessimistic about the outlook when hunting with Ron. He *guarantees* me limits of everything when the hunt is *his* idea. He'd promise me an ice cream cone in hell if he didn't want to make the trip alone. "I'm serious. The bird population is down quite a bit."

"Is that *bad?*" He was trying a little to be funny, but was also a little serious. Ron had nothing in his experience to relate to where a Kansas pheasant hunt was concerned. Years and years of pheasants in Michigan, growing up, where the limit had been two per day, eight per season, and a box of shells might last two years, was all. Seven years gone since his last ringneck. He questioned me eagerly every year when I returned north from my annual trip back to the pheasant hunts I'd grown up with, but moving to Alaska had meant the end of pheasant hunting for Ron. Until this year.

"Well, it means there's 16 percent fewer birds statewide than a year ago. And last year was bad. If we're lucky, it means that a lot of people that'd be out after pheasants normally are going to be out after quail or prairie chicken, or home watching football on TV. They pay a lot of attention to these fish and game forecasts down here."

"Can *we* get birds?"

"Hell, *I* don't know. Maybe it'll be like that day at Minto Flats it turned so cold and everyone left but us - you remember - it snowed and the snot ran out of our noses and you had your six mallards in less than an hour. That was a good old-fashioned snot-nosed day. Maybe it'll be a good old snot-nosed year on pheasants."

"But how do we get 'em when there *ain't* any?"

"Hunt like hell. Walk our asses off. I hope all this driving ain't got you out of shape. We're recuperated." Mary and I had made the same drive two weeks earlier — four thousand miles of dirt road and pavement and half the breadth of the continent, to look at another cock pheasant down a shotgun barrel.

"Eight weeks of hard labor on the North Slope buildin' the Pipeline, ab-staining from my worst habits (women and liquor) and you want to know if I'm in *shape*? Is a violin string in shape?"

"You better leave the cripples to the dogs."

"Ah, yes, dogs. How many is there so far?"

"Two Labs. Terry's Tar and my Pete. Last year for old Pete, probably. Why?"

"John Zillich's got two Labs. Want to bring one?"

"Can he handle them?"

"He says they're field-trial trained."

"Can he handle them, though?"

"I *think* so."

"Bring 'em both."

"Both?"

"Need all we can get, *if* they mind."

"Oh they won't mind. They'll probably be glad to."

"Hey, I'm pretty busy. I got a mallard half-picked downstairs and I ain't cleaned my gun yet. You're sure about Zillich?" I'd never met Ron's old Michigan hunting partner, and he knows how careful I am about who I invite along.

"He's all right. Almost as bad as you are. Hey, I got a waitress waiting, and my gun ain't been cleaned yet, either. How do I find you in western Kansas?"

"It ain't the only small town in Kansas, but it'll be the only one with a green Bronco in it with Alaska tags. Just use the map I drew you. Is this a collect call?"

"Of course. Put it on my bill."

"Say hi to the waitress."

"I already did." Click.

The backyard of the big frame house on the corner was empty when Mary and I pulled in, got out, and stretched. Shorty and Peg used to live in a tiny place five blocks away on the other edge of town, fifteen years before, when I'd first made the hunt with Dad and Jug and the old gang. Peg had had eight double beds and a couch for us, and cooked tremendous meals for the hunters, opening weekend. Shorty and she were both born north of town, of homesteader parents, just before the turn of the century.

They'd moved into town in the Thirties, where Shorty got work at the grain elevator, and he'd been down at the store or service station one November afternoon after the war when Jug and some hunters, talking within his hearing, said they couldn't find any pheasants. "Hell, *I* know where there's some pheasants," he'd said, and with him giving directions, they'd filled their limits that same afternoon. Then he brought them home and Peg fed them and they spent the night, and the tradition was begun.

She saw us through the kitchen window, yelled into another room for Shorty, and met us at the door, grinning. She always remembers me the way I'd come ten years before, a month late for one of the only pheasant seasons I ever missed, worn out from eight days and nights on the road, hitch-hiking back from my first stay in Alaska. "Come on in, come on in."

Shorty was right behind her in the door, blinking at the light like an owl. "Shorty! How's it look this year?"

"Hell, *I* know where there's some pheasants!" We laughed and filed into the kitchen. "Old Mary come back for another try. Gonna get you one this year?"

Mary contorted her face diabolically. "Got a new gun this year, Shorty. They'll never know what hit 'em."

Peg got four clean cups out of the cupboard and poured coffee, set out sugar, cream and spoons for us, wiped her hands on her apron, and sat down. "Lord, there hasn't been so many hunters comin' out since I quit cooking for the boys ten years ago. It was just you and your Dad and Tom there for awhile. If our own kids and grandkids wasn't coming home we could put you up in the house. But you can stay in the basement if you like. If you don't mind the boxelder bugs."

Shorty scowled. "Them god*damn* boxelder bugs."

The box elder bugs looked pretty thick, so Mary swept out the basement for a kitchen and mess hall, while I swept out the garage. Shorty took all this in skeptically. "Freeze your asses off out there," he allowed.

My older brother and his boy were next. They elected to put up with the boxelder bugs in the warmer basement, and went down to make their bedrolls up. Soon Dad and Mom and old Pete arrived, in their camper.

Dad climbed out and went around and let Pete out of the camper. It would be Pete's twelfth season on pheasants. He got out, stretched and yawned, and walked stiffly to the corner of the garage, where he hoisted one hind leg and watched the chickens scratching in the dust in the next yard. He glanced at me. "No," I told him. He went back and looked in the garage door at our bedrolls on the floor, and looked at me again. "No," I repeated. Dad got the leash and tied him to the trailer hitch on the Bronco.

Peg and Shorty Roe, 1975

Jug showed up an hour later. It'd been ten years since his heart attack when he had quit coming out, but he came this year "Just to see if I can still hit one," he said.

When I first made the hunt, Jug had been coming the longest – since just after the war – was the strongest walker, best shot, and had the best dog. He used to sort of run the hunt. Now he pulled into the unfamiliar yard, rolled down his truck window, spit snoose and fixed me with a baleful look. "Drove around town three times lookin' for your canoe."

I pointed to the bow of my freight canoe sticking our from behind the garage where Dad, Mary and I had unloaded it. "Oh. See any birds on the way out?" he asked.

"Nope. Seen some going east two weeks ago, though."

"Old Pete sure scared me layin' there." Pete had rolled in the dust and fallen asleep stretched out on his side, his flanks rising and falling with his breathing.

"Why?"

"I figured he was dead when I drove up, and just now he moved." Pete's feet were twitching in some pheasant dream he was having. "You better wake him up so's he don't wear himself out before opening day." Jug and Jim Whelan both laughed and went in to see Shorty and Peg. Jim hadn't been out for fifteen years, and Peg didn't recognize him.

Tar was whining in the dog box when Terry pulled in after dark. It was the dog's first long trip, and he was ready to get out. Terry readied the leash, cracked the dog box door and snared him on the way out. Once on the ground, he circled Terry at the end of the leash like a model airplane on a string. At the command "Sit!" he sat reluctantly, like a cocked pistol.

Pete had raised his head and was watching. Tar spotted him and leaned forward. Terry repeated the command, "Sit!" and he eased back on his haunches. Pete yawned and laid his chin on his paws.

We turned in early, about nine-thirty. At least we crawled in our sleeping bags. No one slept. Terry, Mary and I had made our beds up in a row in the garage, with room beyond Mary for Ron and John when they got in from Denver. Terry had set up his new cot and admired it like a raccoon with a cob of field corn, tested it and unrolled a foam mattress and sleeping bag on it and finally laid down, grunting like he'd just done a day's work. His down bag was rated "Comfortable" by the manufacturer at 30 below, and though the temperature was 40 above, he still wore his long johns to bed and zipped the bag up to his chin.

Mary poked me and when I looked at her she knit her eyebrows quizzically and inclined her head towards Terry. I shrugged my shoulders. "Been like this ever since I've known him," I whispered, just loud enough for him to hear.

He rolled over onto his side on the cot and eyed us stretched out beside him in our bags, on ensolite pads on the floor. Tar was curled up on his gunnysack at our feet, tied to the bumper of Shorty's Mercury. "Nobody but a low-cut or a dog would sleep on a concrete floor," he said, and patted the cot. The top of his bald head gleamed in the Coleman lantern light.

"I better put out a light for Ron," I said, and crawled out of my warm bed to fire up the other lantern. I found a piece of baling wire in the corner and hung the lantern from the eave, just outside the door. "There," and came back to bed. Terry farted, unzipped his bag halfway, and fanned it.

"Nobody but a low-cut would fart and then fan his bag," Mary said. The mist falling outside hissed on the lantern under the eave, and wet a half-circle of garage floor in front of the open door.

The conversation had pretty much run its course by midnight, with Terry and I recounting our favorite stories of hunts past, when headlights lit up the trucks in the yard, blinked out, and an engine died. "Told you he'd make it," I said.

"Well, there goes the neighborhood," Mary predicted.

"I got one all saved up for the boy," Terry said.

"Watch now, he'll either try and say something he thinks is funny as hell or he'll ask about the pheasants."

Ron shambled through the door and stood on the wet half-circle inside, in his rumpled wool shirt and dirty down vest, a new hunting cap pulled down to his ears, his hands in his pockets, and his shoulders hunched against the chill. The accumulated weariness of seven days behind the wheel showed in his eyes, but the rest of his face was grinning. He'd made it. The lantern behind him glistened on the mist on his shirt and vest.

"Where's-the-pheasants?" he wanted to know. John Zillich stood behind him in the doorway under the lantern and looked in to see what Ron had gotten him into this time.

We shook hands all around and Terry cut his fart. Ron eased back to the fresh air at the door. Tar was wagging his tail. John petted him and looked him over.

"How's he done so far?" Ron asked.

"He's just a pup and never seen a pheasant…" Terry started, apologizing in advance, and I interrupted.

"Comes from a disadvantaged background. Never hunted with no one but Terry so he thinks the shot is a signal that the bird got away."

"…but he does okay on ducks and doves," Terry glared at me.

"He's a good-*looking* dog," John Zillich remarked.

"Just like *me*," Terry beamed. Mary yawned loudly.

Ron leaned against Shorty's Mercury for forty-five minutes while we caught up on hunting gossip. Finally Terry said, "Hell, don't stand there all night. Get your bedrolls and pull up a piece of floor with these other low-cuts. If the dog bothers you, just slap him up aside of the head once," and let a long slow fart that sounded like canvas ripping.

"Don't mind if I do," John said.

"Think I'll sleep on my front seat," Ron said. "Wake me up when it's time. When we gettin' up anyway?"

"Four-thirty," I replied, and rolled over, finally sleepy enough to sleep, with three-and-a-half hours of night left. "Shut the lanterns off whenever you get squared away, John."

My watch said ten minutes till four when I awoke, so I got up, climbed into my long johns and lit both lanterns. I carried one outside and stood in the dirt yard among the naked elms and looked up at the mist falling into the circle of lantern light. The air smelled heavy of wet leaves, like a damp morning in the squirrel woods or on a deer stand.

Two more hours. The weeks of waiting, the days of driving, the gathering of hunters, the retelling of all the old stories, and now it was finally here. Nothing left but breakfast.

In the basement, I lit the stove and put a pot of water on to heat for coffee. Brother Ron and Mike woke up and stirred in their bags. I hung the lantern from a nail in the floor joist overhead and went back to get the folks up. Dad was already up and dressed, standing behind the truck in the mist, watching Pete explore the yard.

Molly and Luke, John's two Labs, whined in the back of his Bronco, which Ron had towed from Denver, and watched Pete make his rounds. We collected in the basement, standing up because there were no chairs, while Mom cracked eggs into her skillets and stirred in ham she'd diced the night before. She scrambled it all together with a fork, and poured steaming cups of coffee.

The scrambled-eggs-and-ham got scooped onto toasted hamburger buns, and we all stood around in our hunting clothes with her sandwiches in one hand and cups of coffee in the other, and wondered aloud what the dampness would do for us and the birds and the dogs, and whether to wear rain gear or not, and glanced frequently at our watches.

An hour before sunrise, a half hour before shooting time, we all straggled out to the yard and decided which trucks to take and who would ride where. Terry and Jug took their trucks, John and I our Broncos, and when everyone was aboard, I pulled out and headed east of town, day not yet breaking and headlights probing into the gentle mist, with the others strung out up the county road behind me.

I'd been out and checked on one good draw the evening before, but the farmer who owned it had people coming in from Denver, and said he'd like to hit it first thing in the morning. So I'd settled on Shorty's old home place, the Homestead Draw. It always produced, and I wanted to hunt it before other groups of hunters tried.

One of the perennial opening-day problems in western Kansas is finding places that haven't been walked already by mid-morning. For at least this one weekend, hunting supersedes football as Kansas' favorite autumn pastime, and the whole pheasant-populated half of the state is alive with hunters. Motels all show "No Vacancy" signs, and mealtimes pack the cafés and truckstops to beyond their capacities.

Day was barely breaking under the low clouds when we pulled up a half-mile from the draw I planned to walk. It was still too dark to see the abandoned two-story house in the draw, but my watch said it was shooting time. Practically everything this year was wheat stubble. The cover in the draws was not too heavy; it must have been a dry spring.

I got out and walked back to the other trucks, explaining how we'd walk it. Everyone got into rain pants and scattered out down the road.

The shells in my vest pocket were left over from the duck hunt Mary and I had made the morning before, but they were sixes, my choice for jump-shooting mallards or opening-day pheasants, either one. I'd unplugged my pump gun the night before, and now thumbed five red shells into it, and waved my hand forward over my head in the old "Move out" signal. We stepped into the field to the sound of other pump guns and automatics being loaded up and down the line.

Pete was with us, and Luke. Molly and Tar were in the trucks in reserve. As we walked and the sky lightened by degrees, my apprehensions about John and his dogs disappeared. I was on higher ground and could see he and Ron and Luke out on our left flank, and I hadn't seen a dog handled that well in fifteen years, since Jug used to bring old Ben out. Never out of range, no hollering at the dog, Luke hunting entirely for John and not for himself, his movements in the field a perfect projection of the hunter's will.

Pete, on the other hand, ranged the length of the line as it suited him, moving to where the cover looked likeliest and too old now to spoil a shot by outdistancing the hunters and flushing birds wild. His youth and excess energy had all been spent in the same fields, and now his movements were slower and more purposeful.

Pete and I were young together there, and then I'd gone to Alaska and left him to Dad and the duck blinds on the Kansas River, and now he and Dad were growing old together. But this morning, as always, neither were less keen than ever. Or less keen than Ron and Terry and I, or young Luke or Molly or Tar. Dad and Pete just didn't waste steps anymore.

Pete's nose was tight to the ground and Dad's 12 gauge was at high port across his chest, ready for the flush, his eyes searching the sparse cover for tracks or droppings.

Flush! Ahead of Luke and John. "He-e-en!" echoed down the line. We watched her disappear into the larger draw ahead of us. Luke dashed this way and that, casting for more scent. Pete watched the hen out of sight, ears cocked, tail wagging slowly, and renewed his own methodical search of the moist wheat stubble.

End of the field. The old tenseness building. Now or never. Within five seconds now, if at all. Nothing. Tenseness subsiding. Watch Terry, though - he's still in good cover. Maybe...Flush! No one yells "Cock!" this time. Terry and I are the only ones in range, and for us there can be no mistaking. Flushed under his feet, a straightaway shot for him, quartering towards me. A good shot for us both. First cock of the year. Gun's up, on him, ride him out. Terry's letting him get out a little so he doesn't rag-rip him at point-blank range. Wait for Terry. It's his bird. The old unwritten rules are still in control, our eagerness notwithstanding. The shot. Perfect. The ringneck, at speed now and leveled off towards the far hillside wheatfield, tumbled in a small explosion of his own brilliant plumage.

A cock pheasant is all show. When he struts at daybreak or dusk on a green wheat field he is a prima donna. Nothing in all a cock pheasant's universe is gaudier than he himself, and they all seem to know.

A cock pheasant flushing is an extravaganza, a heart-stopping burst of noise and color and indignancy. The shotgun takes care of itself and finds one's shoulder, and it's just the bird and you and the gun, but mostly just the bird and you, and it's worth every day you had to fly or drive, every mile you had to walk, to see it again. A cock pheasant shot, the mid-air halt, the final cessation of all energy and noise and motion of the flush, is no less a show than a cock pheasant doing anything else.

Pheasant hunters often remark that it's a shame to shoot anything so beautiful. But for all its color the pheasant is no more wonderful nor perfect than anything else one ever shoots, and, by one's own standards, perhaps somewhat less. He's a rascal where hens are concerned; rampantly polygamous, and no cock ever turned and flew back into the guns when a hen was shot, as a Canada goose often does when its mate goes down.

You never hear a cock pheasant passing in the November night, high overhead, two weeks out of Southampton Island with a craw full of Iowa corn, bound for the Gulf coast. But for whatever mystery he lacks, you can't take away from a cock pheasant that he has no equal for show, in a hunter's world. Or his own.

"Dead bird!" I yelled. You can usually tell if a bird is crippled or dead before it hits the ground. Terry had this one dead to rights, or so it had looked. "Pete! Come!" Pete had been up the line with Dad, but the command was superfluous; he was coming to the shot, and passed me at his aged, stiff-legged lope, headed for the spot where the bird had disappeared into the tumbleweeds in the draw. No dead bird. And he couldn't pick up a trail.

As I had expected, Ron and John broke the brow of the hill with Luke, on the left flank, and we lost sight of each other. Halfway down the wheat stubble field, following a hillside terrace, sky quite gray now, I heard the faraway flush, the clatter of wings. It sounded like a cock. Shot. "Dead bird! Dead bird!" Pete passed me again, loping toward the shot.

At the end of the long draw, Dad climbed up out of the deep road ditch and walked onto the bridge where we were waiting for Ron and John. "Just like every year," he grinned, "flubbin' our dub already. Next field we gotta *bear down on 'em*!" He always says we gotta bear down on 'em.

Ron and John showed up grinning, too. They'd knocked down one cock, failed to find it, then Pete took a trail that turned out to be a hen, but at the end of the field a cock flushed and Ron got him. They were both excited.

"Michigan was *never* like this!" Ron exclaimed.

"Neither was Kansas," I said.

"Good, huh?" John asked,

"Good? This is the *worst* I ever seen. Ten hunters hunt an hour and what do we got? *One* bird. And *lost two*."

"What's good, then?"

"Twenty-five or fifty birds in one flush at the end of the field, everybody gets a shot and we get six or eight at once."

By noon, the two pheasants I most wanted hadn't jumped yet. They would be Dad's first for the year (he'd never gotten a fair shot the year before) and Mary's first for the year. She'd had three shots the year before but hadn't connected. Her first this year would be her first pheasant ever.

I guess I wanted Dad's a little the worst. Mary was enjoying everything - the men, the dogs, the walking, the outdoors, how well her boots fit, her new gun, how good her body felt and how well it was holding up to the walking. She didn't *need* to shoot a pheasant.

But Dad…Dad's like me, keen for the shot. Just one shot. After one shot, feathers in the air, the warm bird in hand, all the other shots and birds are gravy. Frosting on the cake. He wanted a bird badly. Ron had his already. Dad and I hadn't had our first shot yet.

I was below him on the hill, so that he was silhouetted against the gray sky, when his shot finally came. Pete was tired, so we'd left him in the car. Elsewhere in the line, Tar and Luke hunted near their masters, but Dad was hunting his share of the wheat stubble alone.

The cover was good, so I was watching for it when the bird came up.

Cock! In the noise and color and hurry of the flush, time stops. Dad is past seventy, real age – but in that moment (as the gun mounts with all the smoothness it ever did) the clock spins back and back past the myriad flushes of the Sixties, the Fifties, to the Forties or Thirties, Nebraska or the Dakotas, pre-dawn of that first day of the first hunt after the all-day-before drive north in the old '28 Ford behind him in the snapshots taken that afternoon, and he's in his 30s or 40s again, and that first cock (how many times have we heard the story?) is up, and down the barrel the cock, long tail out behind, cackling, rising, leveling out, shock of recoil unfelt, arrested motion, feathers, falling down, down, down, thump! in the cornfield and Dad running toward where it fell.

Holding up the first pheasant of his seventy-first year for us to see, too far away for me to tell his expression but his voice happy and satisfied, "There's one that won't get away, John." Good, good. Now I don't care what happens the rest of the hunt.

John Zillich was the only one of us to get his limit of four that first day. Everyone was glad, as he had to leave at noon the second day to be back to his job in Denver, Monday.

For supper opening day evening, since Peg had given up her cooking chores and the cafés in nearby towns were always full, we'd taken to walking over to the basement of one of the local churches, where an annual dinner was prepared, ostensibly for pheasant hunters, but in fact more for a local get-together, one of a few evenings of the year when the people who choose to spend their lives in the houses behind the windbreaks that dot the horizon, and on the tractors one sees in every farmyard, can come to town and sit down together to eat a sumptuous meal and wear string ties and fingernail polish, to join in the conversation that souls starve for in the wide-openness and far-apartness of the flat plains landscape and way of life.

Mary and I finished the meal first, and left John and Ron still working on theirs, sitting on folding chairs at one of many long folding tables between a tiny, white-haired man with wire-rimmed spectacles and tanned, gnarled hands on one side, and someone else's gray-haired grandmother on the other, she talking happily with John, who remarked on her print dress, which was new (she beamed), while Ron was eating and watching everyone and listening. John is a gentleman and Ron, at least, a hearty eater; both types are well-accepted at small-town western Kansas get-togethers. A lady at the next table was watching Ron intently. He noticed her, smiled with his mouth full, and winked. She blushed.

"Like that meatloaf?" she asked.

He nodded his head, yes.

"I made it." She smiled. He went back for two more pieces.

Terry was somewhere else with Mom and Dad, eating lustily, as he always eats, as though he only has five minutes and knows it's his last chance at food in this life. You had to look close to pick out Mom and Dad from the crowd; their clothes and their age blended so well with the rest that it was easiest to find them by picking out Terry's bald head, bobbing towards his plate to meet his mashed potatoes and gravy halfway, then looking beside him for Mom, and beside her, for Dad.

The pheasants were skinned, gutted, washed and put on ice in short order in Shorty's basement, with so many hands at work and only twelve birds to clean. But we'd averaged two birds apiece, much better than anyone else we'd overheard or talked to at supper. Most hunters had been discouraged, and were heading home Sunday. The

Terry, Mary, Ron Rau, the author, and Clyde, 1975

secret of our success, such as it had been, as always, was the walking. We walked. And walked. And walked. On the average, some one of us had to walk five miles for each bird we took.

Once the pheasants were on ice, there was a mutual move towards our bedrolls. Nine o'clock found the garage floor full of pheasant hunters; Terry and I and Mary and Ron and John, all in a row in our sleeping bags, relaxing, feeling the fields we'd walked and the ditches we'd crossed in our calves and thighs and groins, savoring the comfort of just stretching out on a soft pad in a warm bag, listening to the wind, low in the trees in the yard, stomachs full and everyone content.

Terry's breathing was regular, Ron was snoring intermittent-

ly, Mary was sound asleep, and even Tar was dead to the world.
"John...?" It was John Zillich.

"Yeh."

"How's it been? Not so good as other years, huh?"

"There ain't been as many birds, is all, John. Not as much shooting. Mary hasn't got one yet. Or Jug. But no, it ain't a bad year. We've had to work hard for our birds, so we've appreciated the shots we've got. There's such a thing as too many birds, too easy of a hunt. You watch, I bet next year, you can tell me about every bird you got today, everything."

"Yes...yes."

"There's shots I made in the Fifties I can tell you about, which field we were in and how the bird came up and who was next to me in the field and everything. Some of them you just never forget. When you made that high overhead shot today, you weren't fifty feet from where Tom was when he made a double in 1962 with his 20 gauge, and one of the birds jumped behind him going straight back. Ask Dad some time about his first pheasant – he can tell you every single thing and that's been thirty or forty years. No, it's looking like a *real* good year to me. What do *you* think of it so far?"

No answer. John was asleep with the rest.

"Don't worry about me." Mary was awake now. "There's always tomorrow." She reached over and kissed me in the dark. Within a minute she was asleep again, weary from the hunt and the little sleep the night before and the two nights before that, getting up early to hunt ducks. Ron had quit snoring and the only sound was the wind outside, in the trees.

Mary was right. First field, second morning, me on the swing end, trotting for the end of the field to cut in and help block, when he flushed behind me near her, cutting straight across, too far for me, all hers or not at all. She knew her slowness was her greatest failing, hurried her first shot, and missed. Range increasing. One more shot, perhaps. Missing the first shot tends to calm Mary down, to get her over the momentary chaos of the flush. She settled into her 12 gauge and the second shot was perfect.

I ran for her bird and took it to her where she stood, reloading, rooted to the spot as Tom had been nineteen years before on the river when I'd brought him his first goose.

"*Good* shot," I said, and handed her the bird. She didn't say anything. I took her new gun so she could put the pheasant in her vest's game pouch. The breeze riffled her red hair, and she was a long time holding the bird and looking at all his colors. Her eyes were brimming.

"Feel bad?" I asked.

"He's so pretty, is all," she said, and slid him gently in the front opening of her game pouch. She took her gun back, and cradled it in her arm, and smiled. "Don't get so far away next time," she said. "He almost got away."

Terry walked a good part of the second morning without getting a shot. "I'm wearin' my shells out puttin' 'em in and takin' 'em outa my gun between fields," he grumbled.

After lunch, we walked another field near the highway and his chance came. A cock sat tight until he and Tar mutually stepped on it, and erupted with a tremendous clattering of wings and cackling. The whole hunt stopped in its tracks to watch Terry in his moment. He stood on a rise, with the line of walkers below him like an orchestra watching the conductor raise his baton. The sound of his shots carried down the line with the rapid constancy of a carpenter pounding nails. Bang-Bang-Bang. Silence. The cock sailed into a draw far ahead, untouched.

If Terry had been getting shooting and hitting birds, as I had, and then missed such a shot, he'd have been in for a ribbing. No one said a word. He reloaded in silence, and the dark cloud of his straightaway miss was with him the rest of the day.

At the end of the field, Dad approached me, unloading. He glanced over his shoulder at Terry shuffling up the road towards us, looking studiously at his frayed trouser cuffs, and confided, "I'll try to stay closer to old Terry. He does that at least once a year, and we need the birds."

Barely into the next field, a cock got up, under Dad's feet this time, gun up like always, waiting, waiting, visibly yanking the trigger, Terry beyond him, too far for a shot. He lowered his pump gun from his shoulder and looked at it. He sounded betrayed when he spoke. "Forgot the safety..." and at the end of the field, unloaded and climbed into a truck with a vacant look on his face.

Terry stopped as I was putting my gun in the car. "Look," he said quietly, "Clyde does that *every* year. I just wasn't close enough. I'll try to cover for him from now on."

Three walkers and two dogs had to leave the second afternoon. As Ron put it, we were getting down to the hardcore.

Evening of the second day. Everyone but Pete was holding up well. The first day had stiffened him up considerably, and the years were taking their toll. The only thing left was the old desire. He seemed ashamed at having to be lifted into the back of the truck. If I came around to see if he wanted to hunt another field without letting him rest up for at least one field, he wouldn't look at me.

So when I chose the field to walk that second afternoon, I chose it for him, knowing it would probably be his last, ever. There were no draws or steep hills or thick cover there to hinder him. Just a nice, gently sloping wheat stubble field with terraces we could walk around. I didn't want to remember him as he had finished other, thicker fields that day…following in my footsteps, head and tail down and not hunting anymore.

I got out where Pete and I always belonged, on the swing end of the line, and we started in. He quartered and cast about ahead of me, stiffly, close in, not covering the ground he used to, but hunting as he always had, with all his heart. I'd hoped for a bird, before, for Dad, and then for Mary, and they'd all had their birds. Now I hoped for one for Pete: one last great green-headed rooster to make his feet twitch in his dreams, at home on the rug in the winter, with all his hunts behind him.

As I watched, unwilling to really believe it, the tempo of his hunting increased. His tail worked faster and his snuffing became louder and more excited. *He was on birds.* "Pete's on birds!" I shouted to the rest of the hunt, for the last time.

He had the trail figured out and lined out on it down the terrace, nose down tight to the ground and me trotting to stay with him, once again and forever as it had been so many times when we were both young with Tom and Terry and Jug and Dad and the old gang. "Let it be a cock," I was saying over and over to myself as the others watched him in his stiff, hobby-horse gallop, puffing ahead of me like a small black steam locomotive, ears flopping.

It *was* a cock. It was *two* cocks, and when Pete got too close they were in the air separating, one northwest and the other northeast, and Pete's first share of the old drama was over. Now it was my turn; to try and bring down one of these of Pete's last two pheasants so he could write his own last page to his last chapter, and finish it as it was meant to be finished.

All things happened much faster than I can ever tell it, but the flush resolved itself, as it sometimes does, from the first wingbeat, into slow motion for me, stopping left foot forward carrying my weight to pivot on, all concentration on the leftmost bird quartering away and the stock firm in my shoulder, not waiting him out – shooting as soon as the barrel was out in front of him, all in slow motion and intensely aware of the necessity to take my time, left hand unconsciously pumping the slide, and attention swinging to the second bird now almost out of range, swinging from the first bird falling away now from the gun barrel amidst his own feathers, satisfied that he's a dead bird and coming onto the other one farther out, needing more lead, gun jarring in my hands and bird falling head out still trying to fly but no legs hanging down and no time to shoot again before he's down and Pete halfway to him. Let Pete have him, one dead bird and one running cripple, and I'm standing over the dead bird before I've even reloaded, while Pete's onto the scent of the second bird with no hesitation or mistakes born of haste or inexperience, on the trail and sorting all the scents he must be able to smell for the one true hot scent of his cripple. Then the shoulders coiling and straightening out in the lunge and scuffle; satisfied that he's got him firmly enough, Pete turns to look for me through the beating wing of the bird in his mouth.

He trotted heavily to where I stood putting the first bird in my game pocket, stopped before me, sides heaving, and I took his bird and wrung its neck. "Good Pete. Good boy. Good old boy."

Later, at the end of the field, he accepted the petting and ear scratching of everyone who saw him, and Ron said it all: "Ain't he *somethin'* when he's on birds?"

Ron was as good to have on the hunt as I had hoped. He left the choosing of the fields to me, and walked where I told him. If I said, "Ron, take the swing end this time while I work the draw with Pete," he wouldn't ask why or grouse about having to walk the furthest. He'd grin and hustle off out there, take his place and then walk zig-zag fashion, covering half again as much ground as some of the rest of us.

He was very intense, while walking. He concentrated. He *hunted* every minute he was in the field, watching the cover ahead of him, working it thoroughly, like a good dog, staying in the thickest weeds where walking was most difficult, and going out of his way to kick individual clumps of tumbleweeds here and there, as I did. It paid off.

And he didn't miss, that year. Once or twice, perhaps, but he was the most dependable shooter in the field. His intensity did not stop with the flush – it carried on through the shot, and it seemed that even if he *had* missed, he'd have *willed* his target back to earth for the dogs to find. He made all the easy shots, most of the hard ones, and threw in one or two impossible ones for the two of us to take north and remember, and to have to retell on the sleepless nights before other opening days, in Shorty's garage or upstairs, weaving the bright thread of these shots into the thirty-year-old fabric of the pheasant hunt tradition, and assuring him of a place in all our memories: "Hey, you 'member that shot Ron made out northeast of – hey, goddamnit, are you asleep?"

"Northeast of where?"

"The cemetery. The big high one came straight back over his head…"

"Yeh, yeh, I remember. Man! How'd you ever hit him, Ron…? Hey, you asleep, or what?"

"Yeh. No. Aw, it was easy; Terry'd just missed that straightaway bird and I'd watched him, so on the high one I just done everything ex-actly the opposite."

"Haw-haw-haw!"

"All right for *you*, low-cut. Somebody around here lettin' their mouth overrun their asshole."

"Haw! 'Ex-actly the opposite.' Haw-haw-haw!"

On the morning of the third or fourth day, down to just five of us, four walking and Dad circling around to block, we separated, Mary and I on one side of a long draw, walking one stubble strip, Terry and Ron and Tar on the other, doing the same. We'd join up at the end and walk a third field back to Dad.

Two-thirds of the way down the strips and no flushes yet, I stopped to watch Ron, several hundred yards away now, work through some heavy sunflowers in the curve of his terrace. It was an ideal spot, and I could tell he knew it, working it so thoroughly. The sun was east, beyond him. He was too distant for us to hear the noise he made, walking, or the flush, when it came.

Two hens, first, ahead of him, and his gun came partway to his shoulder instinctively, and then the third bird, the cock, coming out behind him and beyond him, flying east towards the sun, tops of its wings winking reflected sunlight across to Mary and I as Ron spun, gun mounting, all in one fluid motion, leaning into it and simultaneously, the backlighted puff of smoke at his muzzle, the puff of dust and feathers from the bird, and him breaking into a run towards where it came down before the small "whump" of his shot carried to us. A tiny figure, isolated by the action, walking, stopping, whirling, shooting, and running soundlessly across the valley, one of many birds and not even a difficult shot, unframed by any glorious sunrise or long afternoon shadows, but the single image fixed more securely in my mind than any other from the hunt.

"How was the hunt?" friends would ask, when I got back to Alaska. And the image of Ron on that faraway hillside, locked into the timeless hunter's ritual with that one cock, consummating it with the silent puff of powder smoke, dust and feathers, plays itself through my memory, and the answer is always the same.

"Perfect. It was just perfect."

Sugar Snow

The first snow fell the twelfth of October this year, in the evening while I was repairing the garden fence. Two moose had been munching the broccoli stalks in the little patch when I'd got home from work, and they'd taken off up the hill with thirty feet of chicken wire between them, like kids seining minnows.

They watched and cropped willows while I set new posts, stretched and stapled and snipped new wire, and removed the gate to make their next visit less destructive. In a half hour they were back in the garden, and before darkness hid them, their backs were white with snow, like cattle or horses sleeping out a storm.

The first snow means grouse. Rather, it means Ron will be around before daylight to coax me into a grouse hunt.

"Sugar snow!" he always exclaims, after he's got me out of bed. He builds a fire in the stove while I put coffee water on. "We got 'em now. All you gotta do is find a track, and you got a bird. Just follow it a ways, and you'll jump him."

So I left the moose to their supper and went inside to make

preparations. This would be the sixth season we've hunted grouse together. It is a pleasant ritual, a rite of passage of sorts, giving autumn over to winter, and I always anticipate the day. The anticipation is the best of it. In six years, I've yet to fire my gun.

But I sort among the guns in the closet, weighing their merits as though the decision really bears weight, and always settle on the modified 20 that I started hunting with twenty years ago.

It was a bumper year for the garden, and I had to root through the ranks of pint jars crowding my ammunition cabinet to find my grouse loads. They are #7 ½ shot, and I found them behind the zucchini relish, between the raspberry jam and the rose hip catsup. After five years, the box is about worn out, and the writing has worn off the individual shells. Their brass heads are polished from being carried in my jacket pockets.

My L.L. Bean boots were under my desk, so I dragged them out and put the insoles in. They are the only authentic grouse-hunting gear I own. Proper grouse hunters live in New England, shoot over Gordon or Llewellyn setters, carry open-choked side-by-side or superposed double guns, wear L.L. Bean boots and pronounce Portland "Patland." I knew one once.

He loaned me his skeet-choked Browning over/under to shoot the fourth round of skeet I ever shot, when I was an officer candidate at Quantico, Virginia in 1966. I broke 25 straight with that gun, tying a colonel who called me a liar because I said I was new at skeet. I finally beat him on the second set of doubles from the number four station. The shoot-off was his idea. I won $1.25, and dropped out of competitive skeet forever. The grouse hunter thought I would make a hell of a grouse shot.

Which I might, if I ever corner twenty-five grouse in two plywood shacks and scare them out one or two at a time by hollering

"Pull!" and "Mark!" at them. Most of the grouse I've met have been more narrow-minded, however, and have lurked in alder swales, thick birch and poplar stands, and sometimes in spruce. Consequently, I shoot grouse about as well as I'd shoot skeet through a picket fence.

Ron wouldn't know a Llewellyn setter from a Cornish game hen. His grouse gun is a rusty 12-gauge pump with a broken plastic butt plate, half of which is lost. It is the only shotgun he owns. His grouse jacket is a brown wool plaid shirt with the backs of both sleeve seams at the shoulders torn out by a bartender in Dawson Creek who dragged him over the bar by the lapels. He wears wool trousers with a sewn-in crease, purchased at a Salvation Army store in Michigan for fifty cents. At least his cap is a little more traditional: a camouflage Jones-style that really belongs in a duck blind.

In the field he looks like a hobo with a stolen shotgun, except for his concentration. He prowls the birch woods watching the new snow for tracks like an Olympic-class mushroom hunter. In spite of his appearance, he's twice the grouse hunter I am; he's hunted them almost all his life, while I've come to them only in the last ten years. Ron doesn't even have enough grouse-hunting class to know that he doesn't have any class.

After hiding my gear behind the fly rod cases in the closet, so he wouldn't suspect that I'd anticipated his pre-dawn arrival, I thawed out and fried up a dozen ptarmigan breast halves, to make sandwiches for lunch. I could excuse this preparation by saying I'd planned to take them to work to eat for lunch. I put cookies, a jar of sweet pickles, potato chips, cheese, hardboiled eggs, a salt shaker, some apples, four candy bars, two beers for Ron and Dr. Peppers for me in a canvas satchel with a shoulder strap. I could make the sandwiches in the morning while the coffee boiled.

When I went outside the cabin to relieve myself before bed,

the ground was white and the moose had bedded down in the dark among the wilted squash vines. One belched while I was getting an armful of split birch off the woodpile to carry inside. Once in bed, I listened to a mouse or shrew chewing to enlarge the crack above the base log so he could get inside. In the still night he sounded like a crocodile. Winter was at hand.

I awoke to Ron's headlights on the logs at the foot of the bed as he wheeled into the yard, spinning his wheels and sliding sideways in two-wheel drive. Now the headlights must be on the garden. I heard the squeak of the fence stretching like a screen-door spring, and staples pinging out of posts. The engine died and the lights went out. His footsteps crossed the porch and he came in without knocking.

"Hey! It snowed!" he said.

"Bullshit."

"No! Really! *Sugar snow!* Let's go grouse hunting."

"I got to go to work."

"You been working two weeks. You need a day off."

"It'll cost me a hundred dollars."

"You'll have your limit by noon."

"That's what you said last year."

"Yeh, but the cycle was low. It ought to 've started back up again by now, just like when I lived on Steele Creek Road."

"Uh-huh. Were the moose in the garden yet?"

"Nope," he lied. He didn't want me to discover the fence and have an excuse to stay home. "C'mon, get up." He turned on the light and put my Gene Autry album on and set the needle down at the beginning of "Back In the Saddle Again." Then he built a fire in the stove and I had to get up to keep him from making the coffee. He never gets the grounds to settle.

Sugar Snow

I dressed and fried bacon and eggs, for myself. Ron never eats breakfast. "Cup of coffee is enough for me," he says, and starts vulturizing the lunch satchel by nine in the morning if I let him carry it.

"Some day you'll want me to want you…" Ron and Gene Autry sang as he scrutinized the enlargement of himself shooting a ptarmigan, hanging on the wall.

"That'll be the day," I said.

The east was getting gray when I locked the cabin and carried the satchel and shotgun to Ron's truck. The moose were at the top of the clearing in the willows. Ron saw them but didn't say anything. The back garden fence was gone and the posts flattened again. I pretended not to notice.

"Where we goin' this year?" I asked, bouncing out my driveway in the passenger's seat, watching for rabbit tracks in the headlights.

"Ester Dome. Above Happy Road off of Henderson Road." We go to the same place every year.

"Where you done so good that time?"

"Yeh. Got my limit in two hours. Lots of birds up there."

"Good feed in there, too. Open enough so the shooting shouldn't be *too* rough," I speculated. I'd never shot at a grouse there, and had never seen Ron shoot at one. Never even seen a track. Five years ago I'd seen one of Ron's old empties on the ground in a likely swale, but the accumulation of leaves had since buried even *that* trace of more prosperous hunts on Ester Dome.

"Yep. Good shooting. Be sure and don't overshoot your limit. We don't want to wipe 'em out just when they're making a comeback."

"Okay."

Ester Dome is a large hill, fairly steep in places, with swales and ravines creasing its sides. The best grouse cover is located on the lower reaches of its slopes, so we never climb over halfway to the top. If we ever found a grouse on it, we would probably get him; we hunt together well, covering each other in thick spots and working ravines skillfully, without having to holler or wave at each other.

The case is the same for hunting with a good dog; there is satisfaction in hunting well, even in the absence of game.

Ron was hungry before we were halfway up to the knoll where we usually eat lunch. I gave him a candy bar from the satchel and we spread out again to work another swale. He put the candy wrapper in his pocket and was chewing the bar when he stopped. I stopped. He pointed at the ground ahead of him and I climbed up to where he stood.

"We ain't the only grouse hunters out this morning," he said, with his mouth full of chocolate, and indicated the fox tracks leading around the hill in the same direction we were heading.

"He must've been out at first light, or while it was still dark. How could a red fox sneak up on a ruffed grouse in daylight with snow on the ground?"

Ron shrugged his shoulders. "You want a fox skin, if I see him?"

"Is the season open?" I asked.

"I don't know."

"Too early for the fur to be prime. You want him?"

"No." Ron looked at where the tracks disappeared around the hill. "I just thought you might."

"No," I said, "but it makes me glad we got ptarmigan sandwiches with us. If we was hunting our lunch we wouldn't be doing so good."

"Now that you mention it, dig me out one of those sandwiches."

I started down the hill to resume my position across the swale. "It'd spoil your lunch," I told him.

Sugar Snow

The haze was burned off and the sun was bright on the snow now. It was starting to melt underfoot. By noon, we'd lose it. I was glad for the rubber lowers on my boots, with the snow wet and melting. Time and again we crossed the fox's track. It was reinforcing to happen onto the single-file row of prints in willows or alders where one expected birds to be.

I hunt grouse with Ron in the capacity of a junior partner, because he knows their habits much better than I. He took a course in college once and learned their Latin name, *rufus umbellus*, which he dropped on me one day. I looked it up later and discovered he'd gotten the "*umbellus*" right, but must've forgotten the rest, so he'd made up the "*rufus*." He is my better in grouse lore, though, so I defer to his judgment on Ester Dome, letting him choose our route while I go where I think he would want me if a grouse flushed. Sometimes I work the heavy stuff, sometimes he does.

Except for an intuitive knowledge that I imagine I have about good bird cover, which I call "bird sense," the presence of the fox's tracks was the first indication in five years that Ron really knew where the grouse would have been, had there been any. It was reassuring.

The knoll on a steep place in a stand of birches where we eat lunch was originally chosen for its view of the valleys; one can not only see a good portion of the slopes one has hunted, but can see the Goldstream and Ester Creek valleys, routes of the early gold-seekers, spread out far below, and the Chena and Tanana valleys reaching east and southeast to the horizon. The patchwork of grays and blacks between the two big rivers is Fairbanks, with steam rising from the stacks of the municipal power plant, and the occasional rumble of a jet departing the international airport west of town.

Ron got to the knoll first and laughed out loud. He leaned his shotgun against a birch tree and picked something up to show me, climbing a few yards below him and swinging the satchel off my shoulder. It was a grouse wing.

The rest of the grouse's feathers were scattered around in the melting snow, amid a welter of fox tracks. "It *is* a perfect place for a fox to rest," I said. "Look how he can watch his back trail. See how far he watched us come?"

We kicked the snow aside in two places and sat down in the dry leaves underneath. The sun was warm and the air smelled of dead, wet birch leaves.

I divided the sandwiches and set the jar of pickles between us in the snow. Ron sat with his legs stretched out in front of him, crossed, his cap pushed back and the sun on his forehead. He opened a beer and reached for the cheese.

"How can we hunt a place five years and then get beat out of the only grouse on the whole dome by a fox that don't have a shotgun and don't even know a grouse's Latin name?" he mused.

"I think it's like the story of the rabbit and the hound," I said. "You know that one?"

"No."

"Well, the hound always chased the rabbit but never caught him, so someone asked this old fart how come, and he says, 'The dog, he's just runnin' for fun; the rabbit's runnin' for his life.'"

"Oh. Did you just make that up?" Ron doesn't trust me; I guess he figures if he fabricates Latin names, I probably make up fables to suit the occasion.

"I think Aesop did. Robert Frost said about the same thing."

"In what?" He speared a sweet pickle with his pocketknife, and lifted it from the jar.

"'Two Tramps in Mud Time.'

'My right might be love, but theirs was need.
And where the two exist in twain
Theirs was the better right – agreed.'"

"Hand me another egg. One thing we can say about this hunt: we've hit everything we shot at," he rationalized.

"They call that a 'sin of omission' in journalism," I said.

"Is that anything like a 'nocturnal omission'?"

"Pass the salt. I wish I had a Llewellyn setter."

"A *what*?"

"A woolen sweater. Are you going to fink out on the pheasant hunt again?"

"No way. Lookit. Where's *he* headed?" He was watching the airport in the distance. Another jet had rumbled and was lifting off. It was a 707. It climbed and banked slowly around to the southeast, out over the Tanana Flats, still climbing.

"Seattle."

"How much longer?"

"Two more weeks."

"Let's wear our shell vests on the plane this year." Ron wanted to do that so the stewardesses would ask questions. He thinks he's unique because he goes from Alaska to Kansas to hunt, when everyone else comes from everywhere in the world to Alaska, to hunt.

"Okay."

"These grouse oughtn't to treat us this way. They're just making it rougher for the pheasants next month," he said.

"What grouse?"

John Hewitt

Walking Up Lake Trout

Big Russ was from Pennsylvania, and apparently left before catch-and-release was invented. He was raised during the Depression, lived a rural subsistence lifestyle, and his familiarity with shooting moving things resulted in his occupying the tail gunner's seat of a B-24 Liberator in the Pacific Theater, of which he said, "Never be a tail gunner. They're the farthest person in the plane from a door you can get out."

Where fish were concerned, he subscribed to the whack-'em-and-stack-'em philosophy. He was the last person you'd tell about any new hotspot you'd discovered, though he was generous with directions to his own favorite spots. On the one famous occasion that he got checked after a typically successful day astream, and, amazingly, passed with flying colors, he admitted afterward to being pretty worried. Besides the legal limit of ten in his gunnysack, which he'd shown the officer, he'd had another thirty in his rucksack and ten in each hip boot. The warden was satisfied with just a "creel check," and, as they say in the city, the perpetrator walked.

He preceded me to Alaska by fifteen years and Mary by twenty, so we trusted in his knowledge of fishing spots and his judgment that "the good old days are about gone." What was left seemed pretty abundant to us.

Potato farming was one of the very few agricultural pursuits proven profitable in Alaska's interior, and Big Russ was one of the men, mostly WWII veterans, who proved it. He was always good for a couple of weeks' work in the spring during planting, and two or three more in the fall during harvest. Mary particularly liked planting, when she sorted and culled potatoes that I brought out of the big root cellars in wheelbarrows, and Russ's wife, Julie, ran them through the cutter. Little Russ drove the flatbed to the field with the seed potatoes we'd processed, loaded them in the planter, and Big Russ drove the old John Deere around the fields, dragging the planter. Except at lunch, when he regaled us with stories of days gone by.

One place he spoke of aroused my interest because it was his only lake trout story. It was also the only time I knew of that he'd flown into a fishing spot in a bush plane. Deep in the Alaska Range was a lake, he claimed, where the fish were so numerous they were stunted, and you never caught one over three pounds. Still ... if you were from Kansas and thought a sun perch the size of your hand was a nice fish and had once, in your youth, made a 1,500-mile drive to Manitoba to catch lake trout, and failed ... well, a lake full of hungry (he said) trout as long as your forearm was enough to set your imagination percolating.

At $2 an hour, Mary and I were never flush enough to consider chartering an airplane for a fishing trip, but Big Russ' accounts of this lake always concluded with the assurance that "Hell, John, a young guy like you could probably *walk* in there and get 'em – if the snow in the passes isn't too deep. You wouldn't want to go before

July Fourth."

I invested $2 in a government topographical map and mulled over various routes. Then I showed it to Mary. She furrowed her freckled brow, scratched her red head, held a No. 2 pencil beside the miles scale and then over the proposed route, humming mindlessly.

"So," she said, "this is *it?* You guys talk like this hike needs Sir Edmund Hillary, and it can't be over twenty-five miles. What's the big deal?"

Which pretty much decided it, except for the details. Footwear of choice would be L.L. Bean boots; food for five days; a one-burner stove in case there was no wood; rain gear, top and bottom; tent, pads and sleeping bags, and for tackle, a pair of ultralight spinning rods and reels with 6-lb. test Stren. And a small lure assortment. And a shotgun with slugs. The chances of seeing a grizzly were good to very good. Many newcomers to the North embrace this prospect, seeing in it the excuse to buy a large-caliber revolver and wear it everywhere like Judge Roy Bean or Wyatt Earp. Each to his own. It beats a walking stick. Shooting a bear with a shotgun has been, in my experience, much like switching off an electric light. Doubtless people have killed them with revolvers; it's just that no one I've met has.

Of more immediate and real concern was a creek on the track in to where we planned to jump off. If it was even a little high, I probably wouldn't elect to drive the Bronco through it. Many Alaskan outdoors adventures begin and end with a large piece of machinery in a creek or mudhole. One of mine had. There is nothing positive to be said about three or four days of a brief hunting season spent on the same acre, cranking on a handyman jack that tries to kill you every time you drop your guard. So we accepted that, at worst, we'd have to leave the vehicle on the near side of the creek and hike an extra ten miles in and back out.

When the time came in July, the creek crossing looked makeable, though one never knows until one tries, so I screwed up my courage and hit it at about ten miles per hour. The gamble in not creeping through is that the advantage of momentum might not outweigh the possibility of splashed water drowning out the engine. This time it worked.

The miners whose claims and cabins lay farther in on the informal trail drove front-end loaders or old military six-by-sixes, or really husky four-wheel-drive pickups, and crossed regularly with no hint of adventure. They also had even bigger equipment to fire up and tow themselves out if they stalled in the ford.

We parked the Bronco at the bend in the trail, which placed us closest to our destination, pulled it well out of the way, shouldered our packs and headed off cross-country. The going was typically Alaskan, occasionally wet and tussocky, somewhat brushy, generally quite spongy underfoot. One mile per hour was good time, and about a quart of sweat.

Recently I stopped for gas in south-central Colorado, and an old gentleman there remarked on what rugged country it was. I am too polite to disagree with someone's opinion on such matters, but only a few miles earlier I had remarked on how like a golf course this part of Colorado seemed. Scrub grass. Scattered pines. No brush of any kind. A little steep here and there, perhaps. But good country for horses, of which we'd seen quite a few. In an Alaskan's opinion, if you can ride a horse there, how rough can it be?

Luck was with us. After a very few miles we came onto a miner's two-track that went roughly in the direction we wanted to go, but didn't show on our map.

"Piece of cake now," Mary said, striding out for the first time at a normal walking pace. Yeah, boy. The trail forked off up a side valley, but we followed it anyway, reasoning that, though it might add a couple of miles to our route, it would save us half a day's time because we weren't bushwhacking.

I got a little uneasy when the trail took us right through someone's diggings, however, and told Mary we'd better detour a little and let him know who we were and what we were up to. In Kansas, few things are as sacrosanct as personal property rights, and I've never made the adjustment to the Alaskan ethic, where the average snowmachiner gets indignant to the point of physical hostility at the mere suggestion that some person might actually *own* the ground under the snow and prefer not to have him use it.

Smoke was coming out of the stovepipe of one of the shacks, so we headed in that direction. There was what appeared to be a tunnel mouth farther up the valley, with great piles of what I took to be ore piled nearby. A hard-rock operation, in country where placer mining was the rule.

The owner was inside, covered from head to toe in flour, and jumped a foot at our knock. "Figgered since I hadn't had any bread in a month, I'd better knock off and make some. Except I ain't very good at it." He hadn't observed our approach out the cabin's many windows (which branded it a summer dwelling), focused as he was on the foreign process of turning flour into bread.

His name was Lemuel Botts and, according to him, the trail he'd left walking his Cat in to the Susitna River and thence to his claim in the 1950s became one end of the Denali Highway. He had a good location and had been offered a half-million for it, but declined, taking that as further proof he was on to something good. Or, he could've been "up North" on a Cat earning the big bucks on the Pipeline then in progress (he held a card in the Operating Engineers union in Anchorage), but preferred to work his own claim.

Outside, a very Spartan garden was doing its best but seemed to be producing only rhubarb with much success, and half of that had bolted. The usual collection of abandoned and rusting machinery was scattered haphazardly about the little open valley, and gave the impression of better times gone by, but Mr. Botts was as optimistic as only miners can be ("I been into some better stuff lately. I can't wait to mill it and see what I got.").

He had, of course, been to our lake, and others we had not heard of, but had not fished them. Saw the fish, though. It just seemed a lot of work, walking all the way back there to catch a fish. He recommended which pass to ascend, once we were past his tunnel, to come out closest to our lake, and described another old trail not on our map, up the near side of the main valley, that might make our trek much easier. We took our leave and topped over his pass, and he was right on every score.

"It's a nice spot," Mary said, " but it seems to me you'd get a little lonesome in here after ten or twenty years."

"I would," I said.

We saw a grizzly track on the trail beyond the pass, which made me feel better about lugging the old pump gun all that way. Dusk came on and, if we'd wanted to press it, we could have made it all the way, but we got hungry for supper and called a halt. There were no trees, so we knew we had to use the few hours of twilight that pass for a July night at that latitude to sleep in the shade the mountains provided.

Late the next morning when we crested the last rise heading up the valley the lake appeared before us, prettier than either of us had imagined. It was turquoise in the shallows at each end, shelving off into deep blue water quite near its side shores in some places and completely free of ice, which had been a minor worry. Every bald lakeside knob, it seemed, held a ptarmigan cock, still raucously in the middle of the mating season, which we thought ended in March or April. It was a tough spot for a light sleeper.

"Wouldn't change a thing," Mary said, unrolling the tent.

The fish were there, all right. You could see them in the impossibly clear water, cruising the bottom even in the shallows.

"Who ever heard of fishing for lake trout you can *see?*" I said after we were set up. No takers. After two hours of meandering the shore in separate directions and casting, we rejoined at camp for a council of war and lunch.

"Now what?" Mary asked.

"Boy, you got me," I replied. "We may have to just fight it out along this line if it takes all summer."

"I've tried everything I brought," she said. "Sometimes they even shy away from the lure."

"So I noticed," I said. "Wish I had some pork rinds or something. If we ever catch one, I'll make pork-rind imitations out of fish-belly skin and *then* I bet they'll change their tune."

Sight-fishing for other kinds of fish in other places, I'd noticed that where a single would always refuse you, two were easier to get to strike, competing for the meal, perhaps. So I tried to target pairs, though pairs were scarce. Finally, a #2 Mepps retrieved between two cruising fish elicited a savage strike, and I shortly had the material for faux pork rinds.

They worked, at least now and then. The wariness of the fish I took to be a product of a lifetime of feeding on minuscule freshwater shrimp, with which their stomachs were invariably plugged, and which no lure we owned even remotely resembled. Striking at a minnow imitation must've come from some generations-old genetic coding and not real experience. I could only guess the belly strips added some scent to the equation, as they did more to harm the lure's action than to help it.

We caught a total of four, cleaning two and leaving two on the stringer overnight. I managed to fry the two in chunks in my small backpacking skillet over a willow-stick fire, while Mary cooked rice over the backpacker's stove. They were a lot to eat, but we finished them, cleaned the utensils somewhat haphazardly and repaired happily to the tent to listen to the ptarmigans' cacophonous serenade, which we learned to sleep through.

"How about," I suggested before we dropped off, "we fish one more day, keep four more if we can catch them, clean them the next morning, pack them in snow in a garbage bag in my pack and do the hike out in one day? It's mostly downhill, and we know the way now."

"Fine with me," Mary said. Her estimate of the place had gone up with each strike she'd had. "But you know what I think? About Big Russ and his 'good old days'? I think that was really just a time in his life. How could it have been better than this? Twenty-five years from now, I'll bet *we'll* be calling *this* trip the same thing."

"Probably. If the bears don't eat us on the way out."

Subsequently we tied the knot, after which the incidence of Mary being correct in her suppositions fell off sharply. It's been twenty-five years since that trip, however, and that time she pretty much hit the nail on the head.

The Last Drink in the Bottle

There was a road camp a few miles from Minto where Ron was making the call. It was noon, and if the call verified what he already suspected, that his and Dave's crew had gone back to work on the Pipeline, this would be his last morning on the Flats for a year.

He had gotten up earlier than usual in camp that morning, quietly, while Dave and I slept, and slipped away on foot to hunt a pond at the edge of the marsh a half mile upriver from camp. I expect he wanted to be out at first light, by himself, to savor separately each of the multitude of sensations that, combined, make up the duck hunter's sunrise hour on the marsh, just as he always holds a bottle's last shot of brandy in his mouth for so long, rolling it on his tongue and tasting it more completely than any other drink from the bottle before swallowing.

The last morning of the last day is when one takes time to notice the many things one usually overlooks, threatened finally by the prospect of a year of nothing but memories before the next chance.

Dave walked from the riverbank to meet the truck returning.

From where I sat on the bow of the canoe, I caught the words "... last night." So they had already missed a night's work. I got up and eased the canoe back in the water till it floated free, and swung it in to the shore while Ron climbed into his waders. I sat both sacks of decoys out on the bank to lighten the load, stepped in, sat down and started the motor. It muttered evenly.

"It's going to be pretty close," he said as he approached the bow where his gun was. "We can be in town in five hours if you and I make a fast trip to camp for our gear. You can break camp later." He didn't want to be late for work after missing one night already.

He sat his ammunition box out on the ground by the decoys, and unloaded his gun while Dave unloaded the other. When he handed Dave his empty gun, I lost him, like I lost my brother when I carried his duffel bag into the B.O.Q. at Ft. Benning eight years ago. As long as Ron had his shotgun, he was still a duck hunter, the way I like him best. Now he was a laborer again, like Dave, like four thousand others on the Pipeline. He put the empty spare gas can beside the ammunition box and got in.

"Are you leaving today, or staying?" he asked over his shoulder. I'd been turning it over in my mind. The weather was holding, for late September, and the leaves had all gone to yellow. Going to town meant another Pipeline job for me. Staying would cost a hundred and fifty dollars a day in missed wages, that I needed to finance a November pheasant trip to Kansas. But I'd hitch-hiked that one before. And I hadn't had a last sunrise to savor, as Ron had...hadn't squeezed a day or an hour until I had the essence of it.

"Staying." I shoved off with my paddle and brought the bow out with two strokes, before putting the idling motor in gear.

"You would," he said, with his back to me. He wanted to stay, too, but it was impossible. I knew he'd hoped that I'd stay. If I'd said

The Last Drink in the Bottle

I was leaving, he'd have argued against it. "Stay," he'd have said, "the weather's perfect. Maybe the northern birds will come down."

"Siphon him some gas out of the truck with the hose behind the seat," he told Dave, pointing at the empty can on shore.

"Separating the men from the boys around here today," I rubbed it in. "Be down to the *real* hard core tomorrow morning," and opened the throttle all the way. The long canoe, practically empty, knifed downriver as the bow rose and trimmed out at speed.

On the way to camp, occasional small bunches of mallards erupted from the rushes bordering the river, noiselessly, with the outboard sound so loud and close, each bunch climbing vertically, necks straight and tails flared wide, like mallards on calendar prints. Ron turned his head slightly to watch them.

He likes to watch ducks in the air the way I do, and on the last day each flock holds the infinite promise of plenty of birds for the next year. "We left a lot for seed," he said after I'd shut the motor off and the bow had slid through the rushes onto the mud riverbank in front of camp.

Two sleeping bags, Dave's leather boots, pipe tobacco and the ice chest were all he had in camp. The rest was mine: the tent, stove, lantern, pads, grub box, axe, saw, and extra clothes. I helped him carry the ice chest through the mud to the canoe. It held thirty-two ducks, picked, singed and gutted. The three he'd gotten that morning were in the truck. He and Dave would go home with one bird short of their limit.

And I would be left with the canoe, gear and the whole Flats to myself, no time limit and three days' bag limit, eighteen ducks, to try and get. I was pretty sure I could get the ducks in three days. Then I'd leave to get them home, wrapped, and in the freezer. Three days it would probably be…to savor the last drink in the bottle.

We walked the canoe back out along the trail it makes through the rushes into knee-deep water, climbed in and paddled out beyond the weeds before I tipped the motor down. Warm yet, it started on the first pull and I put it in gear and swung the bow out into the river, upstream, opening it up as it straightened out.

Ron was looking back over his shoulder past me at the camp as its clearing grew smaller and disappeared, then he glanced at me. I nodded my head to the right. A half mile out over the Flats, forty big Canadas were coming down, wings set. He saw them and looked back and spoke soundlessly into the outboard noise. "Northern birds," his lips said, and he grinned his duck-hunting grin.

****

I mixed oil into the five gallons of gas in the spare can and put it as far forward ahead of the bow seat as possible, with the decoys, to hold the bow down on the way back to camp. Ron and Dave were gone. Three Natives watched from the bluff above the boat ramp.

They could see the whole of the flats from up there, or all of the lakes within ten miles of the village. Separated by great expanses of rushes that waved and winnowed in the wind like a ripe wheat field, dotted with islands of yellow birches, the lakes were deserted now, with the dozens of trucks, boat trailers and once-a-year duck hunters of the opening day/Labor Day weekend crowd only an unpleasant memory in the village, like June's mosquitoes. October, and freeze-up, were close enough to feel at dusk and see at daybreak along the lake edges, where the canoe paddle bit through skim ice.

Back in the river with the nearly-empty canoe, the cluster of houses and the three watching Natives fell quickly astern, and I leaned her into the first bend. She felt light and quick, more respon-

The Last Drink in the Bottle

sive with no one else in her, and I could see better over the bow with no one sitting there. I looked back and Minto was out of sight.

It was ten years to the month since I'd stepped off the plane in Fairbanks for the first time, with an extra pair of Levis, a chamois cloth shirt from Macy's in Kansas City, a wool jacket, a pair of leather boots, and my 20 gauge. Ten years to the week that I'd stepped into a canoe for the first time, bow seat, with Butch paddling stern and the twenty in my lap, hunting the only thing Alaska offered that I'd ever hunted before, in a way I'd never tried.

Twenty years to the month since I'd first carried the 20 gauge, brand new then, to the blind on the Kansas River, helped put out the decoys, and taken my place beside my dad as a duck hunter at last. Dad and Gramps, Tiny and Tom and I, opening morning, 1955. All gone now, except Dad. And me.

More geese were sloping down over the Flats. Maybe Ron hadn't been fooling – maybe they *were* northern birds. They cupped their wings and disappeared behind the horizon line of rushes.

Five seasons on the Flats and I'd never explored even a tenth of the lake system nearest the village, which is itself less than a tenth of the Flats. There had always been others to get shooting for – Ron, Dad, and Mary – so I'd always taken them to the places that I knew, that I'd explored five years before.

Until this year. On the second day with Ron and Dave I'd persuaded them of the potential in exploring, or at least Ron had humored my whim. I'd alternately run the motor and paddled that day, paddling while the other two kept ready for flushing ducks. The dog, Garfield, couldn't keep still between Ron and Dave, and the noise of his toenails on the bottom of the canoe had spooked many of the birds out of range.

Finally, Ron had wanted to try pass shooting. Dave had gotten out with him. I would explore and try jump shooting by myself, out of the canoe. There was a bluff in the distance that I wanted to climb, to look down from and commit the lay of the lakes to memory, and to see if I could see where the geese stayed.

I had paddled about as close to the bluff as the lake I was on would take me, when the mallard had flushed. The 12 gauge was in my lap. I dropped the paddle and grabbed for it. This unaccustomed delay gave him a good start but he'd still looked good when the barrel came ahead of him. He'd folded dead, and at the shot a pintail had jumped, close also. Other ducks had jumped from other lakes and nearby potholes, mostly mallards, but none in range, so I'd gotten on the pintail and dropped him within ten feet of the mallard.

There'd been no way to get to the bluff that day. There was another, closer lake, but getting into it through the maze of channels, passages, and dead ends would have taken hours of paddling. I'd picked up another mallard, and had been paddling back towards the channel entrance to the lake I was in when I'd heard an outboard coming. I'd veered into the rushes, stopped thirty feet from the lake edge, and laid back against the gunnysack-covered motor to wait.

A stubby riverboat with two figures in it had planed into the lake, one in the bow with his gun in hand, the other running the motor. They were following the edge where I had paddled, but the weeds were too thick and they'd gurgled to an abrupt stop. The gunner almost went over the bow.

"Jesus Christ, take it easy!" he said. His voice had carried the two hundred yards over the water as though he were in the canoe with me. They hadn't known I was there.

"Aw, it's these goddamn weeds," his partner'd replied, cleaning the prop. Underway again, they'd gone slower, the outboard squalling and gurgling. They'd passed within fifty feet of me, both white

The Last Drink in the Bottle

men. I didn't move.

"Not a single goddamn duck!" the gunner said. I looked at the three on the gunnysack at my feet, remembered the several hundred I'd chased off the lake with my first shot, and grinned. I wished for Ron. He'd have enjoyed it. But he might've hollered "QUACK! QUACK!" and then we'd have had to speak to them.

With the sun nearing the horizon, I'd picked Ron and Dave up and we'd reached camp about dark. They'd gotten two. Returning to the same area again the following day, I'd let them out at their pass shooting spots, put decoys out there and left to explore in another direction. I enjoyed the exploring, and abandoned the finding of a route to the bluff in favor of locating a new campsite to move to, to eliminate the two-hour morning and evening boat ride.

I'd been finding more ducks, too. I only got a shot once, because I ran the motor quite a bit that day. I'd doubled on mallards, found the campsite I'd been hoping for, and turned back. Ron had gotten one bluebill pass shooting.

****

So, when I watched them out of sight in Ron's truck the next day at the village, I knew exactly where I was going. It took about an hour to break camp and get everything packed into the bow of the canoe, covered and secured. I heated a can of beans and franks, ate quickly, and shoved the canoe out through the rushes again.

The wind had risen a little, out on the river and lakes, but the slight chop and the occasional spray was worth it; the wind made noise in the rushes where the ducks fed and rested, so that when I decided to begin paddling with the gun in my lap, any sounds I'd make would be covered by the wind. The canoe, more difficult to handle alone in a wind, would be all right if I kept to the lee shores. Which was where the ducks would be, anyway.

I didn't mind the spray in my face and the water trickling off my rain jacket. It seemed a little more like duck weather with a drop of water hanging from the end of my nose.

Passing them, I remembered all the good spots of years gone by, and the parts of the hunts I'd lived at each of them. Mary's goose. And Ron's triple. The only triple on ducks I've ever seen him make, standing up in the middle of the canoe using my full-choked pump gun, Mary and Dad in the bow letting him have the shot, him shooting his best with my twelve at his shoulder, pumping and shooting crisp and quick and calm, mallards jumping ahead and on both sides, and the three shots and one-two-three mallards falling almost but not quite simultaneously; two empties floating beside the canoe and the gun coming down from his shoulder, the third empty jacked out absently and splashing and feathers still in the air, Mary reaching out with her paddle "Hang on, Ron!" and digging in while he squats quickly with the gun across his knees, the canoe pushing through the rushes toward the first bird and Ron not saying anything yet, and you could tell Dad was as happy as if he'd gotten them himself when he said, "All *mallards*, Ron!" leaning forward to look for the second one now.

And Ron's one-handed hen mallard shot, behind him over his right shoulder, no way to get his feet pointed the right direction in the bow seat, letting go with his left hand, big right hand white-knuckled at the pistol grip supporting the weight of the gun, butt in his shoulder, squinting, and I watched him instead of the duck to see if he'd drop the shotgun overboard at the shot. He didn't, and when I heard her splash behind me I began backing the canoe to her and laughed. "I'll be hearing about this one for awhile," I'd said.

Soon the remembered spots were behind me and there were two big lakes to cross before I'd have to ram the canoe as far as it would go back into the rushes under power, tip the motor up and get out to tow it to the next lake.

New country! Always the separate thrill of just seeing what's around the next bend, or beyond the bluff, distinct from the thrill of shooting. And now, new country with the prospect of mallards and geese around each bend, and the search for concentration points where one could observe their patterns, slip in quietly, and consummate the hunt with skill and with grace.

One of the many satisfactions in waterfowling, or in any wing shooting, is shooting well, killing consistently and cleanly. Such shooting requires both skill and patience, the skill to hit the birds shot at, and the patience to pass up marginal shots, to wait for birds one knows they can kill cleanly. I hoped for such a hunt.

Pulling the canoe across the neck of rushes, I could see the island standing out from shore three miles ahead, solid yellow with birch leaves. Out of sight behind it lay the entrance to the lake I'd camp on. I got back in and started the outboard, and was within a mile of the island when I shut it off and tipped it up. I was approaching a narrow passage into another lake, one side was in the lee, and it was time to start hunting. With luck, I could get a start on my limit before setting up camp.

I reached for the pump gun, laid it in my lap with the barrel over the thwart ahead of me, checked to be sure it had three loads of #5 shot in it, and began paddling easily and quietly. Rare as it was to see a duck on the water among the rushes before it jumped, there he was, a mallard drake, and only about a canoe length off the bow, frozen in an attitude of alarm, neck stretched high, eye on me, unblinking.

I laid the paddle gently across the oak gunwales as the momentum from the last stroke closed the distance, just got my hands on the twelve, and he exploded upwards. It was not a difficult shot, straightaway and not too high, easy enough that I didn't have to concentrate on it and could be gearing my mind and senses for the expected second shot at other birds out of sight now but probably in range, which the first shot would flush. He fell, but had been alone. Others jumped, far down the lake out of range. I thrust the canoe ahead into the rushes, got out and waded to the bow, where he lay on his back in the water, feet paddling slowly in the air.

He was in the eclipse plumage, a little maroon coming into his breast, some green to his head and light gray to his underside, but resembling a hen more than a classic, spring-plumage drake. He would have quite a few pinfeathers, his winter and spring wardrobe, just sprouting. The only mallard one sees in interior Alaska in September in proper spring plumage would be the rare redleg. In seven years I've seen one.

By the time I reached the island, I had five mallards on the gunnysack at my feet, in a row on their backs. There were lots of ducks in the area, and the slowness inherent in dropping the paddle and picking up the gun seemed compensated for by the silence gained

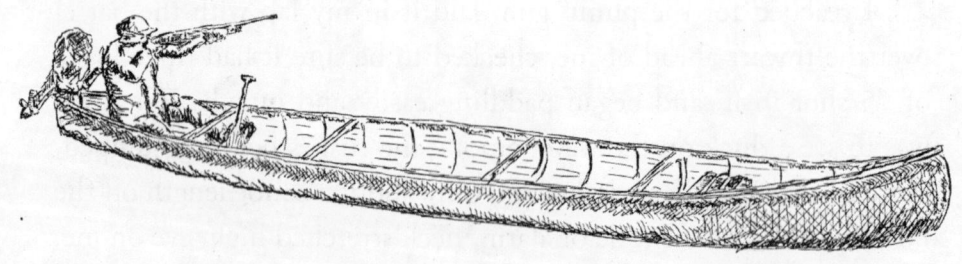

through hunting alone. I was getting the canoe much closer to the birds before the flush than I'd ever been able to get with other gunners along.

My silence practically cost me the redleg. Redlegs, as I had come to understand them in my duck hunting childhood, were a mallard subspecies, maybe indistinct, but certainly recognized, which nested further north than any of the others. They were significantly larger, more brilliant in plumage, and their legs were beautifully bright red-orange. A duck hunter's duck; the most desirable mallard of all.

I'd seen some on the Kansas River when I was nine, in December in a snowstorm on a day when the river ran ice, the year before I got my shotgun. Dad hadn't gotten a shot. They weren't decoying.

That was 1954. The next ones I saw, in a snowstorm again on the same river, were in 1968. They are the latest migrating of all mallards, and it takes snow to move them. This time, fourteen years after the first bunch, I decoyed three one morning in the blind by myself, and, shooting Dad's modified twelve, took the closest drake and hit him the first shot, stayed on him, hit him again and slanted him down the second shot, and finally folded him on the third shot. Pete bought him in alive, and I had to hit his head on the gunstock. I measured his wingspan on the shotgun, holding one tip on the end of the barrel, and notching the stock with my pocket knife behind the pistol grip where the other wingtip reached. Forty-one inches, tip to tip.

I'd taken the only other I'd ever seen or shot at, in '72 in Alaska across a lake from Ron. It was the first he'd seen. Two redlegs in twenty years.

I paddled right by the third one. Close in to the rushes, hugging the lee shore of a narrow slough, sculling with the broad-bladed canoe paddle, not lifting it from the water, perfectly quiet, I was aware of the possibility of slipping by feeding mallards and was about to lay the paddle down, pick the gun up, stand up and look back when he came up. At four o'clock from the bow's twelve o'clock, behind me and to my right, the worst quarter to shoot towards for a right-handed shooter facing forwards, he presented the most difficult flushing shot in the book from a canoe. Ron's one-handed shot.

The paddle clattered into the canoe and I had my eye on him before my hands were on the gun. He was an eyeful. Bright green head, distinct white ring around his neck, russet breast, stark contrast of white on black in his tail and blue speculums flashing on his wings, and red legs underneath, he was a bird of another time and place, an habitué of snowstorms, out of place there in September.

But the color of the country was wrong, too. The gold should have been gone that late in September, the birches bare and white. Ducks like this, flushing against the red of the lakeshore willows, up through the gold of the birches, green of the spruce and deep browns of the high country, into a bright blue sky, lived only in the minds of duck hunters, and on the canvases of wildlife artists.

It was a flush that would carry me comfortably through the airports and bus stations, cold mornings and often-empty skies of November Kansas duck hunts, miles of the Alcan at 30 below with my footprints in the blowing snow strung out behind me, hitchhiking back to Alaska with the pump gun dismantled in my pack after the money ran out in Whitehorse, and, finally, through the mind-numbing monotony of a winter in the construction camps on the Pipeline. I would keep that mallard in my mind the way others keep snapshots of their wives and children in their wallets.

He had been so close when he jumped. Now he was at speed and good range, almost in the clear, but the gun was there and on him, awkwardly, twisted so far around in the seat and not a smooth swing but a quick one, shooting for a point ahead of him jerkily and no follow-through. Spot shooting, what others would call a snap shot. First shot or not at all; there would be no time for a second.

He must have been in the center of the pattern. Back down through the browns and gold, greens and reds out of sight into the rushes with a splash, drops of water hanging in the air above the rushes and only a few of his gray breast feathers up in the blue, drifting downwind.

I picked him up carefully from where he floated belly-down, turned him over, and stroked down the tufts of breast feathers the shot had raised, going in. His legs were extravagant red-orange. He was a pound or more heavier than the other mallards, and seemed half again as big, though his size was part illusion, owing to his being the only duck in the canoe with all his down grown in. He would have no pinfeathers.

I would save him for a special occasion. Perhaps I'd cook him for Ron, in the winter, cook him in the oven in aluminum foil, breast down in his own juices, so that his skin would be brown and crisp with the delicate duck taste, and underneath his breast meat succulent and tender, falling from the bone, serve him with brown rice and cranberry sauce and expensive wine. It would have to be for Ron. No one else I know in Alaska could appreciate a duck like this one.

It was a mile to where I planned to camp. I could have been there in five minutes running the outboard, but there was some good afternoon left and the big drake on top of the others in the canoe made my limit. I paddled the lake shore, exploring sloughs and potholes back from the edges, investigating entrances to other lakes, flushing mallards and pintails with regularity, enjoying being able to watch them without having to shoot, trying to get close enough to see their small, dark eyes when they jumped. I spent two hours getting to camp.

The campsite was ideal. Pulled in against the bank, the canoe was invisible to anyone else on the lake. The thick spruce would hide the campfire smoke, yet there was an opening in the lakeshore foliage so that, sitting before the fire cooking breakfast or picking ducks, one could look down the lake southeast towards the sunrise. I could hear geese down there somewhere now.

The bow touched shore and a ruffed grouse flushed and sailed out of sight through the spruce where I planned to pitch the tent. He would have been good for breakfast. I still had bacon and eggs from town in the grub box, though. And the local grouse population was low in its cycle. A shot would disturb the quiet here at the new camp...frighten away something that I might otherwise have gotten to see: moose, or lynx, wolf or mink or marten. And I might *miss*, and lose the satisfaction and completeness of the last mallard, the big redleg. He'd be gone from my mind for the moment, then, and I'd have a missed grouse to think about, and a lesser chance of seeing a mink or marten. Besides, I like bacon and eggs for breakfast outdoors in the morning, and the bacon smells good, frying. The grouse was safe from me.

****

The three-man tent went up quickly. The mosquito netting in the rear window still sagged, with the bear's claw-holes in it showing the size of his front foot, and one of his other muddy paw-prints still visible on top of the fly. I'd straightened the aluminum poles so that, pitched, the tent looked undamaged.

We called it "Clyde's bear" because of the vendetta Dad had

with it after it stole a gunny sack from him with his coffee can full of Mary's chocolate chip cookies and two picked mallards in it, the only birds he'd gotten the morning after the night the tent had been squashed.

We'd been in the tent, Dad and Ron and I, sleeping the sleep of exhaustion after almost no sleep for two nights. We'd picked ducks until midnight by Coleman lantern light, in a humorless stupor, and hearing the splashing down the river shore that was the bear circling to get our wind, passed it off as a beaver or moose. Nothing mattered that night but finishing the ducks and sleep.

Waking the next morning, I'd wondered at the tent sagging onto my sleeping bag. It had withstood a 60-knot blow on the coast north of Nome the winter before, and with its external frame, was structurally impossible to blow down or collapse. The footprints on top told the story. Dad, the perennial light sleeper, barely had time to register his usual "I didn't sleep a wink all night" complaint, when I found the bear's claw marks in the mosquito netting six inches from his nose. He wouldn't believe the story until he'd crawled out and seen the tracks on the tent. "Must've dozed off a minute or two there," he'd said.

But I was guiding for an outfitter in the mountains that year, duck hunting on a ten-day break between clients, and we had to pull out the evening after the bear had pirated Dad's cookies and mallards, leaving me with a tracked-up tent and Dad with bear tracks all over his memories of that hunt.

Years and many hunts and camps later, he will stop picking a duck (or whatever he is doing) and look at us sternly and say, with conviction, "We could've *got* that bear if we'd stayed one more night." The bear would've made excellent sausage. Perhaps we should have stayed. It made a good story to tell, either way. Particularly for Dad, in his own duck blind in Kansas, where bears are rarely a threat, and Terry never quite believes him: "By God, Terry, it's the *truth!* John's got the tracks on top his tent to prove it."

"Yeh, Clyde. Never even woke you guys up. Want some coffee?"

****

From my seat beside the fire, in leather boots with my waders inside out nearby to dry, I could see a prime piece of shoreline, all within two hundred yards, where the falling level of the lake had exposed a long mud bar, covered now with goose tracks and droppings. It was separated from the pond inshore of it by a strip of grass on dry ground; it was on the pond that I'd killed the two mallards while exploring the day before, and discovered the goose sign and settled on the location for camp.

Without goose decoys, it was a gamble. I was just trying to insert myself unobtrusively into their pattern, at least as much as I knew of it then, by camping with a view of a favorite resting place, and a built-in, noiseless approach. I could slip back into the spruce, down into the pond, and, waist-deep, wade across it hidden from the geese on the bar by the grass, and be in good range before abandoning my cover.

It wasn't my plan to sit idly by waiting for this to come to pass, though. The geese might never use the bar again. But it seemed a sensible way to pass those daylight hours I'd doubtless be spending in camp, picking ducks as I was doing now. I was getting something worthwhile accomplished (the picking) and yet hunting, too, after a fashion. Beyond the mud bar and pond I could see to the end of the lake, a half mile, and slivers of other lakes beyond, between islands, among hundreds of acres of rushes.

Somewhere through those distant lakes the river channel wound. I would explore it later. Across the lake, beyond the nearest yellow island and other, further yellow islands, countless more lakes and thousands of acres of marsh, lay the bluff. I could see it from camp, miles away, accessible by an approach from this direction, if I could pick the lock of the lake system. There would be time for the bluff, too. Except for its bald face, the rest of the bluff's hill was gold with birch, like the islands.

The breeze lay in the evening, and the lake went calm. The stars came out, above the tall spruce, and beyond the hills north of camp, far off, I heard wolves. The hair stood up on the back of my neck, and I shivered. Wolves make me do that, or, rather, hearing them at night does. I added two sticks of wood to the fire and listened, forgetting the duck in my lap while the wolves howled.

Wolves at night touch something in me deeper than my intellect reaches, something primeval and basic that the physical safety of the shotgun leaning against the tree, and the closeness to the fire, can do nothing to allay. A fear so nameless and central to the core of the wilderness and the predator-prey relationship that it's not for me to reason away with logic, and I relish it when it happens, and am thankful it exists, that for all my technological and intellectual superiority, there is still something beyond the circle of my firelight that strips the fabric of civilization away and makes me put more wood on the fire, and look over my shoulder into the dark.

I picked four ducks, added some rice to Ron's leftover duck soup of the night before, and simmered it while coffee water heated. The wood smoke went straight up between the tall spruces and didn't get in my eyes, and resting geese down in the other lakes conversed in low tones, while now and then a wakeful mallard hen somewhere across the lake quacked in the night.

I'd brought my goose loads up from the canoe when I'd made camp, and the twelve was loaded with them, three-inch BBs...I'd take it into the tent with me after supper, in case a bear got after my groceries in the night. I could use the sausage. And I'd be ready if geese came in to the bar in the morning while I was picking the last two mallards. I'd saved the redleg, to pick last.

I was glad I had him to look at and wake up to in the morning, but sorry I had to pick him. It would be like running a lawnmower through a flower garden. Some hunters would have saved him for a taxidermist. Stuffed ducks rarely do justice to the beauty and grace that a living duck is, and the most skillfully stuffed still collect dust on their green heads and yellow beaks and brown eye, and this duck deserved better. His appearance, alive, coming up out of the rushes into the blue sky, was secure in my mind, more secure than a photograph or taxidermy could ever make it. And I could still cook him and tell Ron about him again in the winter, and share him down through the years in the duck camps and blinds of the future.

The shoveler soup, always a result of mistaken identity, a flush from a blind quarter, a snap shot, and the sinking feeling when one of us picks up the big-billed rascal we mistook for a mallard, was Ron's only culinary contribution to the autumn ritual. With rice to give it a little body, carrots and celery diced up for flavor, salt and pepper and ashes from his pipe, it was delicious and filling. I ate a slice of bread and butter with it, and made coffee in a soot-blackened three-pound coffee can with a wire bail for a handle. There was one large can of Elberta peach halves in syrup left, which I opened with my C-ration can opener, ate half of, drank some of the juice from, and put by for the next night.

I laid my waders, dry now from the campfire heat, inside the tent, and undressed, rolling up my wool shirt and pants and laying them aside. I'd use my down jacket in a nylon stuff bag, wrapped with my flannel shirt, for a pillow. I closed my eyes, stretched out in the down bag on the pad, relaxed and tried to remember the landmarks and the exact route I'd come to the new camp by, then remembered the first drake and the others and stayed awake just long enough to remember, in all its crystal detail, the last one, the big redleg.

Awaking at first light, I laid still awhile, listening to the marsh waking up beyond the open tent door. No wind. Geese talking, getting ready to move, away off down the lakes. Mallards chuckling and from time to time the whistle of wings, and a long skidding splash – diving ducks landing in the deep water out off the bar. It had frosted, and the crystals coating the grub box beside the dead fire caught the light in the east.

The mallards were out there for sure. If yesterday had been any indication, I could hunt them at leisure and take my limit in two hours. So there was no urgency to get going, to get in the canoe and get duck loads in the gun and be off. I got up and dressed in the pre-dawn darkness inside the tent only to be out by the fire so I could see where the geese went when they moved, and because being up at the sunrise hour had been such a fine part of the ritual for so many years, I was loath to abandon it just because there was no longer any necessity for being on the marsh at shooting time.

The geese moved while the fire was burning down to coals and the coffee water coming to a boil. I wished for my binoculars, but could see the flying geese well enough without, lifting above the rushes between the islands a mile away, fanning out in flocks over the flats in several directions. Most of them flew out of sight and out of hearing. I would look, when I had time, for the place they had spent the night, a mud bar along the lake or river shore probably, and decide whether or not to wait for them there.

I fried two eggs sunny side up and got them both onto the hot enamel plate beside the bacon without breaking the yolks, toasted the bread in the skillet, and salted and peppered the eggs. There was butter and strawberry jam for the toast, and sugar for the canteen cup full of coffee. The sun came up orange from behind the hills beyond the lakes where the geese had spent the night, while I ate the eggs and drank the coffee. I washed the dish and silverware, put them away, and started picking the smaller mallard, drinking my second cup of coffee.

****

The geese came while I was picking the redleg. I sat still and watched them come, low over the water, wings set, not working, straight in and not talking except among themselves a little, Canadas, about fifty of them; the lowest bird on the left end of the flock dropped his feet and backpedalled with his wings as his feet touched the mirror surface of the lake and made two long streaks in the water like two bass feeding side by side before his body planed in, and he folded his wings, floating on the water, rocking gently fore and aft on waves of his own making, head up, looking. The others were down, too, a hundred yards off shore, not spooky, but cautious.

Lesser Canadas, I could tell, now that they were close and on the water, talking a little more. I didn't move. If they swam to the mud bar, I'd have my chance. Until then, there was nothing to do but hold still and wait.

They began swimming in, satisfied that the bar held no danger, and they all made long wakes in the smooth water. The diving ducks in the deep water paid no attention.

The Last Drink in the Bottle

I heard the boat back down the lake behind me, toward the village, and began to worry. But it was a bigger motor, probably a large riverboat, hopefully going moose hunting east up the river. It would not come through my lake, but pass instead a half mile south, through a more direct chain of lakes. The out-of-the-way location was one reason I'd decided on this spot.

The first geese touched shore and walked out, more graceful on land somehow than domestic geese, alert, looking. Half the flock was out and I hadn't moved, waiting for them all to be on shore where I was sure they'd stay, before sliding off my seat and back into the spruce for the stalk. I'd have to get into my waders. There were extra goose loads in the chest pocket of them. I'd laid my plan well. The gun was within reach. Two more minutes.

Boom! Boom! Boom! The shots from the invisible riverboat on the other lakes rolled across the water. They must've run up on some divers who'd stayed under too long. The geese leapt into the air and flared with a speed belying their size, all squawking at once.

The motor's drone never changed tempo. They hadn't hit anything. Probably hadn't even been in range. It reminded me of how reluctant I often am to identify myself, socially, as a hunter, fearing being lumped together in many peoples' minds with hunters like these, who may be the only kind of hunters many people ever see. It made me thankful again to have had Ron for seven years, Tom in Kansas for fifteen, Dad for twenty, and Gramps, for one.

I was momentarily angry trying to accept the idea of having missed out entirely on the geese, but the anger had subsided before I finished picking the redleg. They hadn't killed anything, their lack of concern for the law notwithstanding. They'd deprived me of a good chance for a once-a-year shot, but I'd shot geese before. I would shoot geese again. And the geese were all well, somewhere else on the

Flats by now, and all would make the migration. Maybe next year. They always come back.

It's not the fact of success or failure, I remembered trying to explain to a potential father-in-law once, but how a man handles the success or failure that's the measure of the man. He thought I was making excuses for having quit a good job to go hunting.

And I knew they *would* come to my mud bar, now. Perhaps another flock that same day. This knowledge, having seen them do it once, was more valuable than two or three lesser Canadas, dead, would have been. Now I had confidence in my choice of campsites, could look forward to bringing Dad and Ron here, getting them a shot at a goose right in front of camp. To have gotten one by myself would have been nice. But not necessary. I threw some twigs on the fire and singed the redleg.

****

By midmorning, I had paddled downshore east into a narrow lake and a *cul de sac*, a strip of land separating the narrow slough I was in from a half-mile-long lake with ducks scattered across and around it. There were good weeds for cover on the neck of land but no ducks were within range, so I dropped back, left the canoe and circled ahead through the woods to try a sneak. The woods were dry, and noisy. When I got to the shore in shooting position, the ducks had moved down the shore both directions, warily.

I waited. Teal came back first, six greenwings, and fed within twenty feet of me. Fourteen widgeon were next; they moved on to feed back towards the canoe.

I tensed at a rush of wings overhead and froze. Several great wingbeats in one place above me, and silence. Raven? The teal were

The Last Drink in the Bottle

nervous now. The widgeon had swum together in a tight group and stopped feeding. I turned my head slowly. Eagle. He sat in the top of a dead spruce nearby, close enough to hit with a rock. He turned his white head, scanning the shoreline for dead ducks caught in the weeds or washed ashore.

His yellow beak was curved sharply. His stare was piercing when he fixed it on me. Great hooked talons held him upright on the branch. I had never been closer to an eagle. He *must* have seen me. But when he left his perch to drop low out over the water and then swoop up to another perch a quarter mile further downshore, he didn't seem alarmed. His flight chased up a lot of ducks that settled in across the lake. He must have been trying to sort a cripple out of the random bunches on the lake. My teal and widgeon resumed feeding.

I withdrew into the woods and moved halfway back to the canoe, hoping to better my position. The widgeon fed down within range again. Two mallards, straight offshore out of range, watched the widgeon feeding in front of me and swam in to join them. A drake and a hen. I thought of Dad and Gramps and their stories of the duck hunting in the Midwest when live decoys were still legal, and they kept a half-dozen apiece, and wondered if it had ever happened like this in those pre-Roosevelt Prohibition days when Dad was the age that I am now.

The mallards passed the point of no return, swimming steadily. Now I would get a shot, whatever happened. I should get at least one of them. Fifteen yards out they stopped and went to tipping up, feeding among the widgeon. The longer I let them feed, the more tense I became, so I waited for the hen to get her head under, stood up, and yelled, relying on the adrenalin catharsis of the flush to release the tension. It did. It always does.

The drake, as I'd planned, was up first, followed by the widgeon and the hen. Too close, I had to wait him out. Waiting a bird out is bad for my shooting, generally – better for me to shoot the moment I'm on the bird well, but when they're too close and the shot charge would ruin them for the table, they have to be waited out.

I took him at about thirty-five yards. He tumbled at the shot, I was on another again quickly, pumped, and – the hen was still going! The third shot brought her down. I'd known the instant I'd seen her larger silhouette among the widgeon what I'd done; shot a widgeon with the second shot, by mistake.

Ducks had jumped all over the lake and for a minute or two the sky was full of them, so I squatted down in the grass and reloaded. A minute later, with things settling down, a single mallard came back down the lake, craning her neck, quacking. She spotted the three floating offshore, and set her wings. Just as though to decoys, she settled in, and I dropped her beside the widgeon.

Four shots, four ducks. My shooting always improves when I'm alone, and except for having to finish off a cripple the day before, I'd taken a bird with each shot, and now had run ten straight.

I waited before going for the canoe to retrieve, and caught a movement out of the corner of my eye. On the neck of land, where I'd left the canoe, a Native was dragging a short, shallow one-man canoe, and was looking at my birds in the water. He hadn't seen me, and he looked puzzled. He was only seventy yards away.

He'd been just coming up the slough to hunt this spot as I had, when I shot. Without intending to, I'd spoiled his stalk. He was doubtless from Minto, and had probably hunted this spot all his life, thirty or forty seasons. Although people from his village had no more legal right to hunt the lakes than I did, I regretted my position. His many years there, compared with my five, gave him grandfather rights as I saw it, and I was the newcomer, the trespasser. The hunters who'd spooked the geese earlier had probably been from his village, but they had nothing to do with him or me. I would find which way he planned to hunt, and hunt elsewhere.

He still hadn't seen me. I blacken my face and hands every morning with charcoal from the campfire ashes, wear a camouflage flannel shirt and a camouflage cap, and chest waders. I waved at him. He laughed then, and waved back. I walked the lakeshore around to talk with him.

"Got two, huh?" he asked. I shook my head no, and held up four fingers.

"Four," I said. He looked back at the ducks on the water.

"Oh yeh. Two in by shore."

"Uh-huh." He was friendly enough. Still feeling each other out, but not guardedly. "You have a rifle," I pointed at the bolt-action tied to a thwart in his tiny canoe, beside his shotgun. "Hunting moose?" He looked at the rifle and shrugged.

"Moose…duck…whatever I see. Got nothing so far. You hear airplane land?"

"About an hour ago?"

"Uh-huh."

"Yeh. Who was it?"

"Fish and Game. Want to see my license."

"Checking everybody?"

"Guess so. You want me to get your ducks?"

"Well…okay. I'd appreciate it. If you're headed down the lake east here, I'll go back the way I came and hunt south."

"Hunt anywhere you want. Hunt this lake too, if you want."

"No. You go ahead."

"Okay. I get your ducks," and he slid the little boat into the water, knelt in the center of it and paddled with his long, thin homemade paddle to where the ducks floated. When he returned, they were all in a pile in front of him in the bottom of the canoe.

"You want a mallard?" I asked. He hesitated and looked at me.

"Sure. You betcha." So I left him the nicest one, the drake. "Thank you. Have something to take home now."

"You live in the village?"

"Yes. You from Fairbanks?"

"Yeh. John Hewitt's my name," and I extended my hand.

"Alfred Frank, me," he replied, shaking my hand. I wondered where he'd learned to say "Alfred Frank, me." It was the way Cree Indians I'd met on the Quebec shore of James Bay introduced themselves, a French construction: "Johnny Minocquagan, me," or "Harry Hughboy, me."

"Good luck, Alfred. If I see a moose I'll come find you."

"Okay," he smiled, "good luck to you, too."

"Say, are you paddling all the way back to the village tonight?"

"Uh-huh. Not too far. Do it all the time. You got camp?"

"About a mile back down the shore." He furrowed his brow, remembering.

"Didn't see it."

"No. You can't see it from the water unless you see the fire at night."

"Oh. Okay. See you later."

"Okay Alfred. Good luck, now."

"You betcha."

We had learned a lot about each other. He knew that I'd hidden my camp so that it wouldn't attract strangers from the Flats. He knew I'd killed four ducks with four shots. He didn't know whether I'd shot them on the water or not. It didn't matter to him.

I knew he'd shoot ducks on the water. It didn't matter to me. He was a lifelong subsistence hunter. His code made more sense for him than mine would have.

There were many riverboats in the village. He must own or have access to one. But he'd chosen to hunt the way I did, rather than the way the unseen crew in the riverboat that morning had. I respected him for that. He'd come several miles, paddling, since daylight, and I respected him for that. I always respect a hunter that takes his hunting seriously, and is willing to work for his game.

He looked to be forty or fifty, it was hard to tell. Thirty seasons, at least, in this duck hunter's paradise, that it had taken me most of my life to find, and the rest of my life to learn about. It was the reason I lived in Alaska. I was happy about meeting Alfred.

With the Pipeline and its minority hiring policies, he must be able to earn enough in a few weeks to buy his family's groceries for a year; white man's food, canned vegetables, fruit, butter and milk, and meat. Perhaps our reasons for being on the Flats were more similar than I'd at first thought.

There were two more mallards in my canoe two hours later. I lacked one of having my limit. If Alfred had seen anything, he hadn't shot. I paddled out of a slough behind a birch island which had been mostly reduced to birch stumps by beavers, and saw his canoe pulled up on the shore. Wood smoke drifted up from the other side of the island. I paddled around to look.

He was drinking tea with his back to the shore, looking down at his little fire. I paddled on down to him and eased the bow of the canoe to a stop six feet from where he stood. He hadn't heard me. He started to turn around and saw the bow and exclaimed, "Ha! You sneaked up on Alfred!" He was amused at not having heard me. "You want some tea?"

"Sure," I said, and shoved my canoe ashore. I fished under my seat for the canteen cup, which I both drank from and bailed with, stood up and walked the length of the canoe.

"Say, how long your canoe, anyway?"

"Twenty-three and a half feet," I said. He whistled.

"Biggest canoe I ever seen. You make it yourself?"

"Uh-huh. Five years ago. It's fiberglass over spruce planking. I made it to hunt ducks with. They make them this big in Canada, but they're too high and wide for sneaking ducks. They look like riverboats. You make yours?"

"Yes. Some of us in the village make our own. Too small to haul moose in, though. Good for muskrats. You haul moose in yours?"

"Sure. It'll carry a lot of weight. Yours is a better duck boat for one man."

"You doing all right with yours." He pointed to my ducks. "You killed another duck back there. I found him floating in the middle of the lake, dead. I give him back, but," he nodded at some bones beside the fire, "I ate him already. Good, too. Get you some tea there." I poured tea in my cup and put in sugar from his cloth bag, and stirred it with a plastic C-ration spoon from my shirt picket.

"I must have hit one I didn't mean to. I killed all four that I aimed at."

"He was way down the lake. You crippled him and he flew down there and died."

"I'm glad you found him then."

"Eagle would have found him. You see the eagle looking for cripples?"

"Yeh. Before you came. Did he find any?"

"Eagle always find something to eat." The tea was black and strong, but sweet. I drank slowly, and we talked of the Pipeline (he worked out of the same local union I did), our shotguns (they were identical), and the hunting.

"Last day for me. Got to go to the Pipeline," Alfred said as he put his tea and sugar, spoon and tin can billy in a canvas bag and rolled it up. "How about you?"

"One more day. I'll leave tomorrow afternoon. Lucky to have this good weather this time of year."

"Uh-huh." He squinted to the north. "Going to change soon." He walked across the island to his canoe, stowed his bag and paddled around to where I was sitting in mine. "Well, I see you. Maybe you get you a goose tomorrow."

"Hope so, Alfred. Good luck. Thanks for the tea. See you next year maybe."

"You betcha," he said, and we both dipped our paddles into the water and the two canoes glided apart. I last saw him far away, slipping through a narrow channel into another lake, working his way back to the village. I never heard him shoot.

So he was doing the same thing I was. Holding the last drink in the bottle in his mouth as long as he could.

****

I had enough of the afternoon left to shoot another mallard and paddle to the bluff, and climb it. On top were the ashes from many fires, probably people from the village come there on snow machines across the ice during the November moose season, climbing the hill to look out over the Flats for moose. You could see for miles from up there, clear back to the village, and south to the Nenana Spur, the ridgeline that was the southern tip of the Flats, forty miles away, blue and hazy in the distance.

I stayed for an hour. There were geese on a lake to the south, inaccessible except by walking. I made a mental note of how to get there next year. Geese were coming in to another lake, northwest, between me and camp and accessible by canoe. They were half a mile away but I saw a few leave to go to another lake, marked their path and saw where I could hide myself and the canoe within two hundred yards of the raft of geese on the lake, behind some screening brush. I'd get a good shot if more left by the same route.

On the way down the hill, I jammed an eight-inch willow stump through the ankle of my waders. The Natives had cut off the small willows and poplars with an axe when the snow was deep, so they could bring snow machines to the top of the bluff, and the stumps now stuck up eight inches and were sharp on top. The two times in other years that the same thing happened to me, it had been beaver cuttings in tall grass.

I had to wade waist-deep water to get to the canoe, and I hurried, lest the rising water level in my right leg reach my crotch and spill over into the left leg, filling it also. Once in the canoe, I hung my wet leg over the side and let the water drain out through the hole. It had filled almost to the crotch.

I was still warm from the walk. The chill would set in, I knew, once I was in position for the geese, with nothing to do but sit. My circulation would slow down, and cold creep in. I'd remember that I'd been forgetting to be thankful for dry feet. So much one takes for granted. I'd try to patch the waders later, by the campfire. But now, the geese were waiting.

Mallards and pintails traded over me, once I was in position, offering fine pass shooting, but I had my ducks. At least I was in the right place. They all passed right overhead, low.

Three hours passed, slowly and coldly. Foot wet and cold, I listened to the geese, saw others arrive to join them and swell their numbers, and watched the ducks. A few geese would fly, and I'd grip the gun, hearing their wingbeats beyond the brush, but they'd settle down again with the big bunch. They couldn't see me, nor I them, but I could hear them, and they sounded closer than I knew they really were.

The sun was going down, and the air was cooling noticeably. The slight breeze, instead of laying as usual, came around to the north and was picking up. Maybe Alfred was right. Weather change coming.

With a sound like thunder rolling, they were in the air, and coming. I could see them through the brush, strung out for three hundred yards, rank upon rank of them, all coming straight towards me, all talking. At last! The cold foot no longer existed.

A hundred and fifty yards out, twenty feet off the water, coming straight on like a great wave, they started to split. I didn't move, chin tucked in to my chest, peeking out from under the bill of my cap, gun in my hands. Did they see me? The flock cleaved in two, half to my right, half to my left, talking excitedly, the universal pandemonium of flushing geese.

At the only possible time I came up on the closest bird on my left. Three loads of three-inch BBs in the pump gun and a good long lead; I swung with him, followed through, and lifted my cheek off the stock.

Marginal. Too chancy. Good chance of a cripple. I'd lost a crippled big Canada six seasons before, trying too long a shot. Seventy yards at the closest, they'd been. And I'd let them go. I waited to see if I'd be glad, or wish later that I'd shot.

In the end, I was glad. It had been the right thing to do. I've never been a sky-buster. Letting them go was good. Killing one would have been good. Missing or crippling would *not* have been good.

The wet foot, the three hours of enduring the discomfort, were good. I'd done everything that I could do. It had almost worked. I'd had my adrenalin and my existentialist moment; I'd chosen not to shoot. What I stood to lose, if I'd shot and missed, wasn't balanced by the goose that I might've had in the canoe if I'd connected.

I had the spot to come back to another year, too. And I'd been to the top of the bluff. I'd explored all the lakes and sloughs that I wanted to this year, and had the lay of the marsh in my mind. I'd met another hunter worth knowing. I had the wet-foot willow-stump story to tell Ron: "Goddamn," he'd say, shaking his head, "you just go around *lookin'* for stumps to poke through your boot, don't you?"

I had one more campfire, one more supper, one more night in my warm sleeping bag with the smell of spruce needles in the night air, and one more morning's hunting. The gold was still on all the hills. It was fixed in my memory, behind the rising redleg.

Picking ducks that night, I noted the wind rising yet. By the time I turned in, it was a roar high in the spruces. A tent among spruces is my favorite place to be during a blow. I went to sleep thinking that tomorrow, the gold would be gone.

It was after midnight when I woke. Something. Something woke me. I raised my head off my pillow to listen with both ears. Just the wind, nothing more. Then it came again, faint and faraway and high up, over the wind in the spruces. Geese! Six days of hearing geese almost constantly, and I was wide awake instantly, another kind of shiver tingling down my spine. Not resting geese, or feeding or flushing geese. The voices were high and north, over the hills, beyond the Flats.

Travelling geese! Northern birds! Down from the Flats of the Yukon, high up and coming on the north wind in the teeth of the season's first good blow, big Canadas, old birds with many migrations, and youngsters on their first, navigating in the dark by some instinct or tradition I couldn't comprehend, completing another cycle, verifying again the existence of the great mystery, and making me a part of it.

I lay awake and listened to them passing, impossibly high over the tent in the spruces, faintening finally and gone to the south. Another flock followed, and another, before I slept again. Many times I awoke before first light, each time to the sound of travelling geese. The passing of the northern birds! And I had gotten to witness it. The night in the tent would be with me as long as the memory of the redleg against the yellow hills.

Sunrise, breakfast, and my last morning for a year on the marsh. The gun was in my lap, paddle in my hands, as I worked the lake edges silently, awaiting the flushes. The gold *was* gone: the yellow leaves were all on the ground among the rose hips, and the hills were that much closer to winter. Autumn was over in one night.

If the last day's ducks were anticlimactic, it wasn't because the old keenness wasn't there. I was still as eager for the shot as I had been two days or twenty years before. I ran four more birds without missing, and found them all easily, because none were cripples.

Just after noon, I keyed on another flush behind me and to my right, the redleg shot again. I'd been too quiet and had sculled by another duck; gun in my hands now and coming around and ahead of him, spot-shooting as before without follow-through, gun recoiling and mallard tumbling out at good range, dead bird, I lowered the gun to my lap and watched the rushes move with the waves he'd made falling, not believing what my eyes had told me I'd find out there floating in the rushes.

Another redleg.

Four redlegs in twenty years, and two of them on the same trip, both drakes. Now I had one to take home in all its brilliance to show Ron. I lacked one duck of having my possession limit, but I wanted the second redleg for my last duck, to remember.

I unloaded the gun and laid it forward of the thwart, out of reach, choked the outboard, and started it. I'd held the last drink in the bottle in my mouth long enough now; it had been rich and sweet, and I could swallow.

Cornered

Hiram was normal once. The way I know is, I spent two hours discussing the issue while trying to get to sleep in a tiny travel trailer in southeast Washington a couple of years ago, with a fellow who had gone to junior high school with him. We were both suffering the onset of what felt like rigor mortis, brought on by trying (without success) to keep up with a German shorthair in chukar country. Our efforts, at sleep anyway, were thwarted by a third party who had only had to keep up with a size extra-small Brittany bitch, and was consequently not only snoring loudly, but loudly digesting his contribution to the trip cuisine, which he called "Shepherd's pie," and which had smelled a great deal better warming up in the propane oven than it did now after two hours in his alimentary system.

Zillich, who owned the shorthair, had been present at the exact moment Hiram ran off the track, figuratively speaking, at a party celebrating the end of the tourist season at the hotel where they both worked for the summer at McKinley Park in Alaska in about 1963.

Rebellion against what he perceived to be "middle-class values" was at the root of Hiram's departure from the straight and narrow, which one feels safe in saying, thirty-six years later, is permanent. Thereafter, the most scathing and damning pronouncement Hiram could make about an idea or activity or dwelling or automobile or shotgun or fishing rod was that it was "too middle class."

Take putting up firewood: He preferred scavenging his from any available source (buying it would've been even worse than gathering it ahead of time) even though it might be dark out and the temperature 40 below zero. This fundamental of his personal philosophy was one of the most visible items that his first marriage stubbed its toe on. To be fair, my own first marriage was on a fairly similar trajectory, though not for want of an annual five or so cords of split and dried firewood in my yard by each duck season.

Now, if you're like everyone in my family since I can remember, including Terry, whom my mother unofficially adopted late in high school and referred to as her "triplet," the preseason part of duck hunting was an enjoyable interlude in and of itself. The scouting part and the building duck blinds part, that is. We were generally so wound up after getting our feet wet in the hunting season with dove openers that whacking a path through bull nettles and dragging drift logs across sandbars was a worthwhile outlet. And once the blind or blinds were finished, you could sit in them through the sundown hour and imagine how it would be once the mallards were in, appearing like faint wisps of smoke above the horizon. In your mind's eye you'd see them, where their final circle would carry them if the wind lay from the northwest, before cupping their wings, dumping altitude and dropping their feet.

In Alaska, though, Hiram vetoed out of hand my suggestion that we visit our opening-day spot for a little preseason scouting, maybe throw together a blind or two. "Nope," he said, "too middle class." And that was that. The spot was only five miles from my cabin the way the crow flies, but our road system was not too sophisticated and I had to drive forty miles to get there. This took two hours on opening morning, as the route passed the Drop Inn Café in town, where my rig automatically wheeled in and parked in the black dark, in spite of Hiram's protests. He didn't do breakfast. Too middle class. I had a personal philosophy of my own by then, and ham and eggs was one of its major precepts. I wasn't born in Kansas for nothing.

One of the advantages of taking *your* car or *your* boat is that, at crunch time, you get to make the important calls, such as this one. The next place I stopped was on the road a few feet short of the turn-in to the old gravel pit where we customarily parked. Hiram ran a short patrol to ascertain whether the short, innocuous little lane was safe to drive.

The only thing duck hunters hate worse than anti-hunters is each other, we'd discovered two years previous. Two late-rising young gentlemen of the teenage persuasion had been heard to swear impressively two years before when they'd stumbled out onto the bank of the slough and were greeted by a six-shot fusillade from our two pump guns, a hail of falling waterfowl, and an enthusiastic cripple chase by Hiram in chest waders, punctuated by several mostly ineffective single blasts that only spurred the errant widgeon to greater efforts. The duck had the current behind him and I could barely keep abreast of him while thrashing through willows on the bank, while Hiram was slowed by an increasingly large fleet of decoys he was towing, like an early-day Bristol Bay salmon tender under power, towing the little gillnetters, their sails down, to the fishing grounds.

The boys weren't impressed but had apparently stolen a page from my own playbook ("Don't get mad – get even") because, the following year, though we again had the place to ourselves, our two vehicles had a total of five flats when we got back to them at mid-morning, secondary to having driven unknowingly over a nail-studded plank buried across the access lane at its narrowest point, which, after we'd passed over it, had been dug up and tossed into the woods. And I thought I'd seen my last punji stick once I exited the Republic of Vietnam.

Hiram shuffled his leather-booted feet up one side of the lane in my headlights, and back down the other. "Hmmmph," he said, climbing back in, "kids these days give up pretty easy."

My perennially dim view of human nature being what it is, I insisted that he precede me on foot down the path, once we'd parked and debarked, carrying a double bag of decoys apiece. When we arrived at the water's edge without incident, I was thoroughly puzzled. I had not only been a kid fairly recently myself, I'd been a fairly scheming and vindictive one, and the mounting evidence that our tormentors from the nearby trailer park had abandoned their project of driving us from hunting grounds they considered theirs alone only further aroused my suspicions.

"There is something here, Hiram," I said, " that we seem to be missing."

"Like what, Bobby Lee?"

"You think they've given up on us, obviously. *I* think that that's exactly what they *want* us to think. I think we've walked into a trap. Only, I don't know what."

"You think too much."

"I'm thinking either a coil of barbed wire underwater, or they're back yonder putting sugar in my gas tank, or there's a big-ass crocodile out there in the dark. Lead on. I'm right behind you."

Hiram's hiding place was mainly east of me across the slough. This meant that, as light came on by degrees, I could see birds coming from his direction and warn him.

Neither he nor I could see ducks coming from my direction until they were essentially already in range.

When the noise started a minute or two before shooting time, in the woods behind Hiram, my suspicions rekindled. It was a strange noise, a kind of high-pitched whine. It grew progressively louder.

"Bobby Lee!" Hiram called, sounding a little alarmed, "What's that noise?"

"Don't ask me, Hiram," I replied, "but you're about to find out. It's getting a lot closer."

Now there was a faint glow, far through the spruce and birch behind him. The louder the whine became, the brighter the glow. My response, rooted in a practical life spent avoiding science fiction movies, was, "Now, how're them silly sonsabitches putting *this* scenario on?"

Hiram, on the other hand, had not missed many movies and was becoming more agitated at the prospect of starring in a real-life one: *Glommed by Aliens on Opening Day*. My imagination has never been able to conjure up a life form that could walk through three loads of lead #4s at close range, even 2 ¾ " 1¼ oz. loads. Hiram was seventy-five yards distant, however, and peeling a pack of extraterrestrials off him without some ancillary casualties might be problematic, even with my trusty full choke. Just, as Kesey's protagonist's uncle hollered when the hogs got him down in *Sometimes a Great Notion*, shoot into the wad, one supposed.

The glow became an actual light, then two, then four, then six, moving horizontally in pairs at what appeared to be an enormous speed only a couple hundred yards behind Hiram, ten or fifteen feet above the ground, through trees I *knew* were not two feet apart.

"*Run*, Bobby Lee!" he finally hollered. "*Run!*"

To hell with *that*, I figured. For one thing, *he* wasn't running yet. For another, if indeed it was a squadron of extraterrestrial bogeymen, he was a lot closer to them than I was. And, finally, it had just turned shooting time, it was opening day, the decoys were out, and the territorial teenagers were nowhere to be seen. Running *anywhere* was out of the question, at least for a half hour or so. The first ten minutes can be the day's best shooting.

When the lights merged into three and crossed the slough upstream, you could make out red lights following them.

"Hey," Hiram hollered again, "I think those things are *cars*!"

"Hiram," I said, "they were twenty feet off the *ground*!"

I saw the ducks then, a dozen or so out of the pinkening southeast, low and silhouetted just above the spruce tops which constituted our horizon. "Watch 'em! Watch 'em now, upstream and low, almost on you!"

Fire streaked six feet out of Hiram's muzzle and the widgeon exploded upward, one arcing silently to the water. He fired again before the closest was in range of me, and I shot three times at two birds, dropping both. I could see rings on the water from at least two that Hiram must've got. Reloading, I waded out to gather up my last one and wait for the current to bring the others to me.

The sound came again, but it wasn't the least bit scary once you knew it was cars. Two more passed. Guys about like us, probably, albeit with steady jobs, on their way to work.

"Hiram," I said, raking in the first duck with my gun muzzle, "someone built a road through our duck spot."

"I see that," he said, and indeed, from where I was, the guard rail and three culverts to let the slough underneath were becoming faintly visible.

"Would've known if we had done a little scouting," I said.

"What does it *mean*, though?" he asked, echoing a literature professor in whose class we'd met, who always asked that about some passage or other in a novel.

"It's what my high school English teacher warned us about in 1962, Hiram, urban sprawl. When it's finally solid houses from Topeka to Denver. I thought we'd be safe from it in Alaska in our lifetimes, but it's caught up to our asses already."

"Now what do we do?"

"Get *down*! There's a single coming, big duck."

It was a mallard hen, from the sound of it once it spotted our decoys and set its wings. Hiram made a nice shot on it and I was already in the middle of the slough to make the retrieve.

"I think that's a good spot for you for the next few minutes, Bobby Lee," Hiram said. "So, what do we do next?"

"Move downstream out of sight around the bend. I've always thought it might be better down there, anyhow. We can get five, maybe ten more years outa this place. Then, move again. Unless you want to buy a lot on the bank here and build a house and shoot ducks off your back porch until your neighbors vote you into the city limits and call the police on you every opening day."

"Nope," he said with some finality. "Way too middle class."

Staying in Touch

I was setting up the nylon mountain tent in the clearing beside my cabin when I heard the truck engine slow down and stop at the end of the lane. The tent was damp yet, but an hour or two in the warm June sun would have it and the sleeping bag bone dry and ready to put away.

The engine rapped up again, and slowly got louder. It had to be Julie. Julie is my trapping partner's mother, and the only person in Alaska who'd lock their hubs and go to low range four-wheel-drive to get to my cabin two months after the lane has dried out following breakup.

Julie and Big Russ live three miles away and farm potatoes and have a telephone, two sons, a daughter, a riverboat and no canoe paddles. Hopefully she would just want to borrow some paddles. It was the time of year when all of us with boats can't seem to keep them out of the water.

But they have the phone…something Outside could have happened. Or young Russ's chainsaw could've kicked back on him again, up on the Yukon. He'd need another pint of blood; our blood types match.

I had meant to cut the brome grass in the yard with the scythe after I got the tent up, but I sat down on a five-gallon can of mixed outboard gas instead. I couldn't let Julie catch me working.

She crawled into sight at five miles per hour, transfer case whining, skirted the two long canoes on sawhorses, pulled tight up against the garden fence, shut her engine off, and climbed down. Nothing serious this time: she was grinning, noting the weeds where the garden should have been, and more weeds in the vacant flower beds.

"Garden looks real nice, John-Boy," she said. The Woods have a T.V. also.

"Uh-huh."

"Yard, too. Real nice. You going to bale it this year?" I've never hayed the yard or the clearing. They're not mine, and I've been watching the willows and birch reclaim them for nine years.

"What's up?" I asked.

I knew what she was going to say. "You had a phone call," I said to myself.

"You had a phone call," she said. She was really grinning now. Mary. "Who?" I said, as though anyone else would be trying to reach me by the Woods.

"Mary. She wants you to call her, right away, in Whitehorse." Julie likes Mary. The two of them used to gang up on me cutting seed potatoes during planting in the spring, and during harvest.

"What about?"

"She didn't say."

"What *did* she say?"

"She wrecked her truck."

"Is she all right?"

"She *said* she was."
"Let's go."

The sound of her voice on the phone did the same thing for me that seeing her handwriting on an envelope in my mailbox does: made me instantly sad, as two gravestones two hundred miles apart make me sad when I see them. They all remind me of things I had once. Good times, mostly.

"John?"

"Mary?"

"Are you all right?"

"*Me? You*'re the one that wrecked the truck."

"Oh, that was nothing. You just sounded funny, was all. Are you sure you're all right?"

"Except for my broken heart. But it's on the mend. Or it *was*. What's cookin'?"

She laughed. "Well, uh, Ruby's having her face lifted." Ruby was her truck. "Mary's out of a job and wants to go float a river somewhere, but no one she knows in Whitehorse has a canoe or the time or inclination, so what's John doing the next two or three weeks?"

John had to think that one over. It had been a nice clean break early in September the year before, no loose ends left untied when she left after the first duck hunt. With duck season underway and other seasons just opening, John had had enough to occupy himself with that the finality of her leaving hadn't sunk in until Christmastime back at the cabin, alone. She was missed on the hunts, but others were missing, too. She and others were the frosting on the cake; the ducks, pheasants, weather, sunrises, campfires and autumn easing into winter were the meat and potatoes, just like always.

It took five seconds to think over. "Same thing he's been doing the past three weeks."

"Oh? What's that?"

"Watching the riverbank slip by. Where we going?"

"You really want to go?"

"Of course not. My heart's ninety-five percent scar tissue already. It's got so it breaks instinctively whenever I get near a redhead. Broke it last week passing an Irish setter on the street."

"Don't be silly. You *really* want to go?"

"Just tell me where and when and which canoe...the phone bill's gonna break me." I was glad she couldn't see me when she spoke the river's name into the receiver. I shivered and probably paled a little.

We'd run across the Macmillan twice in our reading, once in a Jack London short story set in 1887, and once in a book by Charles Sheldon, hunting sheep in the Yukon in 1905. Neither author had known anyone who had travelled the South Fork that Mary wanted to run, from its source on the continental divide, high in the Canadian Rockies.

It was not the danger, such as it might be, that the river held that made me shiver. It was the not knowing. For me, the river was a complete void - absolutely unknown, a complete mystery. Someone had surely been its length. Unrun rivers were few and far between in 1976. But Mary didn't know of it. Nor did I.

I'm not a whitewater canoeist. Canoes have always been a tool that I use to get me to better hunting and fishing. Handling a canoe well in difficult situations is a satisfaction of a certain kind, but I don't seek out such situations to try myself against.

Whitewater canoeing, like wing shooting or fly casting, is no more and no less than a set of skills which one can acquire if one wants to. No mystery; mystique, perhaps, but no mystery. Anyone with the time and the desire can do it. I've never bothered.

It's dangerous, first. People get killed at it. Once you're dead, as far as I know, you miss a lot of duck seasons. Like rock climbing and some other things which I choose not to do, it's a good clean, healthy way to find out how one will handle oneself in the crunch.

I found that out in the war, which was neither a good nor clean nor healthy place to find out anything, and enough crises have arisen spontaneously since then to keep my memory fresh, and to spare any necessity at all for going looking for them.

I saw a whitewater canoe once, though. It looked like a two-holer kayak, decked completely and with more tumblehome built into it than Grumman, Kennebec or I built into any of mine. Mine are all open, lacking even so much as a spray cover to make them seaworthy in white water.

There are a whole raft of paddle strokes that whitewater aficionados use to, for instance, hold their positions in the river, move crosscurrent or even upcurrent. My own skills are not that sophisticated. I belong to the pick-your-route, cross-your-fingers and paddle-like-hell school of river running. It works for me, but like I said, I avoid man-eating rivers.

Charles Sheldon had been up the Macmillan to the Forks, about two-thirds of our float, in a small steam launch. Then he'd ascended the North Fork partway, lining a Peterborough canoe, and had returned downstream after the hunt with his trophies, when the river ran slush ice.

But the North Fork was inaccessible, except by air. A little-known and less-used WWII vintage one-lane, travel-at-your-own-risk road provided access to the South Fork. The South Fork was the big blank spot on the map we didn't have.

There were other rivers in the Yukon Territory. Wild river surveys had been done by the government, and the mimeographed results were available for a nominal handling fee, complete with difficulty ratings on a I to VI scale, suggested campsites, portages, and fishing holes. Some of the floats, like Whitehorse-Dawson on the Yukon, had become quite popular. For twenty-five cents, a person could find out what he or she was getting into. I didn't waste my breath making the suggestion.

"Why did she pick the only accessible river in the Territory that she knew absolutely nothing about?" Anne asked afterward.

"Because she's Mary," was all I could offer.

"What do you think?" Mary asked, after she'd named the river she had in mind.

"Lucky it's you asking," I said.

"Why?"

"I wouldn't run it with anyone else." That was a fact. Mary's one of the people (all of whom I can count on the fingers of one hand) that I've *always* been able to count on when the chips are down. One of the others can't swim. One is married to someone else. One is dead. One teaches school in Michigan. Having this most critical requirement out of the way, the rest would be simple: just a matter of logistics, weather, luck, and the Big Question Mark. What *was* in that valley the first hundred and fifty miles, above the Forks?

"Do you think we can make it?" Good old Mary. She always left me a way out, just as she always kept a way out open for herself.

"We'll know by the Fourth of July," I said.

"Worried?"

"I think we'll have to use the Kennebec, and waterproof everything. One fishing rod, freeze-dried food, nothing that can't be fitted into two packs. We'll need every inch of freeboard that we can squeeze out of her."

"We can decide that when we get together," she said. "How soon can you be down?"

"Sunday at the latest."

"That's *four* days."

"Best I can do. I just came in off a three-week trip and I got some loose ends to tie up." I had a date that night.

"What river?"

"Chena, Tanana, Fish Creek, the Yukon, up the Tozitna to Russ and Ann's and Helen and Stanley's, cut some cabin logs for Russ and came back with the outboard." I'd been in my long square-stern canoe.

"Well, then, don't leave without me. I'll come up to Fairbanks and ride back with you. Be there in a day or two."

"Your truck's broke."

"My thumb's not."

"Somebody in Whitehorse you're trying to avoid?"

"Just got the itchy foot. Will you be home tomorrow?"

"Be to dinner at Will and Anne's from two till midnight."

"What's for dinner?"

"Mallards."

"You cooking them?"

"Yep."

"I'll be there. Thaw one out for me."

"I got one shoveller left that'll be just the ticket."

Click.

She was one hour late for dinner. Six hundred miles of dirt and pavement, four rides, up all night. Late because her last ride drove slow, trying to talk her into partnering up with him on his trapline, the next winter. He was sheepish when I said hello in Anne's yard.

I'd worked with him at Prudhoe Bay and on the Yukon River Bridge two winters before. The North's a small place.

She cried for a moment, later, when she walked into the cabin again. It'd been home for a good part of four years. Then we went out to the root cellar, swung wide the big door to let the moonlight in, and she ran her hand down the side of the upside-down Kennebec.

The Kennebec. Spotted in a Traverse City, Michigan backyard by my old partner, Butch, on the lookout for an ailing Old Town for me, spring of '69. "Been there at least three winters," he'd said. "Pretty tough shape." We'd gone to look at it. He was right. Fourteen years outdoors upside-down on sawhorses under Michigan snowfalls had rotted the stems and gunwales clear off. The canvas was rotten and cracked, peeling off over the long gouge that had broken seven ribs.

"Hit a stump and dumped her on the Two-Heart in 1955," the owner said. "You can have her for fifteen dollars."

"Lot of work there," Butch warned. "I don't know if it's worth it." Not the money. The time. It'd take a month or two. But Butch, Butch, look at her lines! Yeh, her ribs are broke, yeh, the canvas is falling off and she needs gunwales and stems, but *look* at her! A lady's a lady, whatever you dress her in.

Kennebec. Folded during WWII, the owner said. He'd bought her secondhand. She had to be thirty years old. Maybe fifty. Someday I could check. I grinned at Butch, and reached for my wallet. We went to the truck to dig out his tie-down ropes. She was my first canoe.

It took Mary and I two full days of driving to get within a hundred miles of our put-in point. There was no bridge over the last river to cross, and the ferry was closed for the night.

There was a settlement, a cluster of cabins, airstrip, and a bush hotel of sorts. We backtracked fifteen miles and camped beside a lake. The tent was no sooner up than Mary wouldn't have it but we put the Kennebec in the lake and try for pike.

Three weeks in my longer, beamier canoe had dulled my sense of balance. The Kennebec, at eighteen feet, took a little getting used to, but soon I was as comfortable in it as I've always been.

Butch had taught me about lowering the seats: "It's the difference between sitting *in* a canoe and sitting *on* it. Originally bolted fast to the underneath side of the inwales, they were now eight inches lower, so that in the stern I could push back until the converging sides gripped my hips and be as sensitive to tipping as good carpentry and my own responses would allow.

Later we gathered wood and built a fire and cooked supper. Afterwards, Mary slept easily and deeply. I was wakeful. Yes, it had been her idea. Yes, I was breaking some of my own rules: use maps, if you can get them. If you have doubts, don't. But it was my canoe. My car. My skill, or lack of it – I'd paddle stern. Finally, and in spite of everything else, like in the war running an infantry platoon, I was responsible. If everything went to hell, as it might, there would be no one else to blame.

If we lost the boat…well, I'm used to losing things. She taught me that, herself. I could get another boat. If we lost me, she'd be all right – she could and would walk out alone. The same willfulness that had carried her away from me in the past when things got too close and routine would be her ticket back to civilization without me to show the way. For once, I was glad for it.

If we lost her, though…she was the only thing on the trip that couldn't be replaced.

I had ham and eggs at the hotel the next morning. Mary had eaten her breakfast while I rolled up the tent; yogurt and fresh fruit. The man at the cash register came out to pump gas for us and noticed the canoe. He asked where we were heading, and shook his head when we told him.

"Don't do it without asking Jack the foreman at the maintenance camp seventy-five miles up about it first. He knows more about it than anyone. There were two men from Minnesota through here two weeks ago, went up with a canoe and came back without. I don't know the details, but stop and ask Jack."

Okay. You bet. I looked at Mary. She shrugged her shoulders and grinned. Back in the car, she voiced her opinion. "*Any*body can lose a canoe. Don't mean a thing." Jesus. Because she's Mary. God-*damn* redheads anyhow, sometimes...

Jack wasn't at the camp, but we met him a few miles further, and flagged him down. The epitome of an equipment operator. Fifties, built like a bulldozer.

"Hello. Are you Jack?"

"Yep. Going canoeing?"

"We planned to."

"In the South Fork?"

"Yes."

"You'll *never* make it." I glanced at Mary. Her eyes narrowed a little, her mouth pursed, and I was glad she had the grace not to say what she was thinking. Lots of people tell me what to do. No one tells Mary what to do, or what she can't do. Jack's manner wasn't exactly conciliatory – he didn't want us to run the river, period. He was trying to intimidate us. We needed facts.

Mary was thinking, "We don't tell you about road grading – don't tell us about running rivers." What she said was, "Have you ever been down it?"

"No, and don't ever care to. I just know there's canyons down there somewhere and two fellows a week ago never even made it to the canyons; lost their canoe and all their gear the first day."

"How far did they get?" I asked.

"Less than a mile. They were lucky – still close to the road. If they'd made it on down a ways..." he let the sentence hang for emphasis, and shook his head, "that's some of the roughest country in Canada. Maybe they'd have made it out, maybe they wouldn't."

This was the best news yet. Less than a mile. Ninety percent of the swampings and dumpings I hear about happen in the first mile. The fact that our predecessors had dumped and lost everything could either say everything about the river, or nothing.

The fact that they dumped – well, there might have been lots of reasons. Jack later remarked that one of them had dropped his paddle overboard and they broadsided a rock and dumped with only one paddle in hand. And lost everything. Fact one: they either didn't carry a spare paddle, or carried it in such a location that it wasn't readily accessible, or lost their cool at the critical moment and didn't grab it.

Fact two: they lost everything; must not have had it all lashed in. Their mistakes, or what we knew of them, were inexcusable. What the Marines call piss-poor prior planning. Any reservations we had upon first hearing of the mishap disappeared.

"Person living here could get a lot of good mileage out of a riverboat, if he had one..." I remarked, on a hunch. Jack brightened.

"Sure can. *That's* what *I* like. I've got me a..." and went on to describe his rig, an equipment operator's dream: twin outboards with more combined horsepower than my automobile, all three of my own outboards, my chain saw, and Mary's food grinder with

Mary on the crank. Hydraulic lift. Remote throttle. Electric start.

Riverboats are a way of life in the North. Canoes are an anachronism. So the truth was out: Jack wasn't against running the river – he was against the *idea* of a canoe. An understandable bias. Canoes are obsolete. The road Jack pushed dirt around on for a living had been obsolete since the day in 1945 that Douglas MacArthur had accepted the surrender on the deck of the Missouri.

I talked riverboats with Jack awhile, amiably, and he suggested a launching spot back down the road. We'd already noticed it, but he took us back and pointed it out.

We untied the Kennebec and tied bow and stern ropes on her. We'd tie them together if we needed to line it. Loading the canoe did not take long; there wasn't that much to put in.

There are roads in the North (more well-travelled ones) where to leave a car or truck overnight unattended is to invite stripping – tires, battery, tools, jack, anything not welded on. It is one of many pitfalls that experienced travellers take into consideration.

Here, I left the car unlocked and the keys in the ignition, as in genuinely remote areas, Northerners still leave their cabins unlocked, firewood cut and matches at hand. Anyone afoot here would need the car worse than I did, use it, and, hopefully, return it afterwards.

The river was flat as far as we could see in both directions. The short stretch of white water that had claimed the previous canoe was behind us already, upstream, in sight of the bridge. If what was below was no worse, it would be a pleasant trip.

The current, though, was swift, and the water deep. We climbed in, Mary first and then myself, holding on to a piece of caved-in bank as the current tugged at the canoe and I got settled. I looked at Mary's back, her long red hair down over her checked flannel shirt. It wasn't too late to call it off. Float an easier river. My paddle was in my right hand.

Her head turned. She saw the look on my face, and laughed. "Lost your jam already?"

I tried to smile. "Did we leave the water running in the tub or anything?" Neither of us has a tub, or running water.

"Lead on, McDuff," she said. I turned loose, dug in two strokes to set us right with the current, and shivered again.

"I think I'll get my camera out," Mary said. She had brought her new Nikkormat and telephoto. "We'll have time to put it away if the water gets bad, won't we?"

"I think so. As long as the river's no worse than this it'll be all right. Tie the strap to the carrying thwart in front of you, and leave the long lens on. If we see anything to take pictures of we'll want to be quiet." There isn't any compromise that I know of; either the camera gear is close at hand for quick use, exposed to splashing and vulnerable to quick dumping, or it's put away somewhere waterproof and not there when you need it.

The valley was wide and park-like; fine big stands of spruce, cabin-log size, fronted much of the riverbank, and spread up the slopes to timberline. Smaller stands of birch, aspen and cottonwood stood on the inside of the bends, with the ever-present margin of willows separating them from the gravel bars the river was building. As the current undercut the banks on the outside of the bends, the tall spruce leaned out and out and finally toppled, then swung downstream held fast by their root system to the crumbling bank, and formed their own spruce-trunk riprap. The swift water eddied and churned behind them, but the current's momentum was broken and the erosion of the rest of the spruce woods retarded. An admirable rear-guard action.

Beaver sign was everywhere, but it was too early in the afternoon yet to expect to see them at work. The only sound was the current working against the sweepers, cutbanks and gravel bars, and the rhythm of the paddles dipping.

I watched the smooth sandbars at the lower ends of the gravel bars for bear tracks, and was a little relieved to see only moose; pairs, cows and calves, and sometimes singles. Bulls, perhaps. They'd be showing antlers, not large yet, and of course still very much in the velvet.

Relieved because I had chosen not to bring a gun. We were unarmed in grizzly country, a condition my best friends in the bush would find foolhardy.

An hour onto the river, paddling in silence, I froze Mary with a low "Shhh!" and went to a sculling stroke myself. She saw the cow and calf a hundred yards ahead, near the right bank, and untied her camera.

The calf, small and red as moose calves always are when newborn, slept on a tiny sandbar thirty feet from shore. Its mother cropped green willows overhanging the bank, ignoring the river as an avenue of predatory approach. The upstream wind was in our favor.

I held the bow downriver and let the current deliver us past them. The slight burble of the water against the odd hanging limb or sweeper covered the click of the shutter, and the rasp of the film advancing. A photographic moment of truth was approaching: there would only be a few seconds when the pair would be lined up and in the picture together, due to the narrow field of the telephoto. The river hushed, waiting for it.

Five more seconds. Three, two – the big head swung around, jaw chewing, willows out either side of her mouth behind her Roman nose. An ear flicked a fraction of a second before she saw us, and as quick as the ear flicked, she swapped ends to face us.

She gave no audible signal, but the quickness of her move snatched the calf to its feet and toward her. Dappled light falling in shafts on the pair through the leaves backlit the spray. The shutter clicked.

There was no danger. The river between was too deep. But the cow's ears were laid back, her head low and spine hair standing up stiffly like a dog's, nothing in her bearing suggesting flight or fear. If we wanted her calf, it would have to be over her dead body, no quarter asked and none given.

Tom Walker watched a cow moose in a like situation give a grizzly the same option. Hungry, he took the chance. He lost, both his meal and ultimately, his life. Russ Wood, when he was a kid, saw a stray dog play the game in deep snow, for fun, and lose. "Hey," he'll tell you, "she kept comin' down on him after he was *long* dead. I make hotcakes thicker than that dog when she was through. I always figure if a grizzly gets ahold of you, even a sow with cubs, its ten to one you'll live through it. Moose with a calf gets you, it's a hundred to one you won't."

We drifted another hundred feet. She caught our wind and bolted.

"I think I got them just right," Mary said. "It was too fast to bracket the action so I just took one."

Before she got her lens cap back on we were playing leap-frog down the river with a kingfisher, and for forty-five minutes he'd fly, alight, we'd paddle, drift, stalk him, and glide by his perch, framing him with spruce and mountains, composing his portrait with a canoe paddle, wilderness, and lots of time.

When he lost interest in us, finally, and disappeared back the way we'd come,

Mary put the camera away and surveyed the river ahead and

behind.

"What would be nice," she posited, "would be a little rough water, for variety. Just to keep it from getting monotonous."

"Mary Mary Mary."

"If there's a canyon down here, let's get on with it."

"There ain't going to be any avoiding it, like we did the cow." The valley was narrowing perceptibly.

The noise did not start faintly, as surf heard from a great distance; rather, we passed around a sharp bend, from three hours where it wasn't, into a straight smooth stretch where it was, into two days and nights where there was no escaping it.

The river ahead seemed to run point-blank and full-tilt into a rising wall of rock. The only clue to its fate was a haze of mist drifting back upriver, emanating from what, at that distance, appeared to be a narrow cleft in the rock, on the left.

"Holy Jesus," I said.

We paddled gingerly, and I put us in against the right bank, the better to see what lay beyond the cleft. In lieu of all the books I'd never read on whitewater canoeing, I was writing my own as I went. It had one chapter, entitled "Be Cautious," which was one sentence long: "Don't commit yourself to anything you haven't looked at first, or can't see the end of…go slow."

As we drew nearer, the defile widened into a respectable canyon. The river narrowed, and narrowed, and narrowed, gaining speed, and, unrippled by rocks or standing waves, vanished smoothly through a slot twenty feet wide. Falls. White mist rose below the slot, and the river was no longer visible at all. We put ashore, tied up, and walked down to look.

"Portage," I said.

"Here?" We were backed in against a cliff.

"On the other bank."

"Then what?"

"Walk below and see what's around that next bend."

We lined back upstream, and dug across on an angle, paddling for all we were worth, not losing ground to the falls, but not gaining, either. I walked down to look.

The soft, delicate sphagnum moss underfoot bore no sign of anyone ever having used this, the obvious and only portage. The twenty-foot falls were impassable, by my judgment, in any boat at any river stage, although perhaps I underestimate the capabilities of whitewater purists and their equipment. Suffice to say it was impassable for canoeists of my caliber, in any boat.

The rapids below them were not bad, however, climaxing with a swift, narrow downhill sprint and an unavoidable four-foot falls over a large boulder flanked by larger boulders. But the pool below was flat calm, deep and green, where the current stalled before a right turn and a quarter mile of slow water. Without this pool to collect ourselves if something went wrong, I wouldn't have tried it.

At that, there was a small question mark in this first fragment of the Big Question Mark: What did the boiling white water where the little fall spilled into the deep green conceal? Nothing, hopefully. Nothing, probably. Nothing, at any rate, that would kill us.

I explained the plan to Mary, we made the portage, loaded the canoe, lashed things in, and gave the boat to the river. Hit it right where I wanted to. Except that it was faster than I'd anticipated, things went off as planned, and twenty seconds found us squirting between the flanking boulders right on target, adrenalin on schedule, three and a half feet of daylight under Mary in the bow, tipping down, knifing into the froth, shipping over both gunwales forward an amount of water which, but for the calm pool below us and gravel bar to pull out on, would have been disastrous.

Then the stern cleared the falls, daylight below me, down down into the boil and "Crrrunch!" right under my seat. I felt the jolt to the roots of my teeth. So there *was* something under there, after all. One-third full of water, we paddled heavily across the pool, got out, dumped the water out and I inspected the damage. Two ribs broken. Planking holed. Needing a patch, but nothing serious, that couldn't wait until we camped.

Mary was exhilarated. I was wishing the same thing I'd been wishing since she'd suggested the river on the telephone, that I knew how long the bad water would last.

"What d'you think?" she asked.

"I think you ought to have on your leather boots."

"They'd get wet."

"No wetter than mine. We ought to wearing everything we need to walk out of here with, in case we lose the boat."

"Tennis shoes are fine for me."

The falls and first rapids set the pattern for the next two days: walk ahead, survey the danger, choose a route around or through it, and back to the canoe to follow through. I was worried most of the time, as the Kennebec took the river's best shots in her ribs, and the quart of fiberglass resin in my patching kit diminished with each repair: we were down to just a half pint. In the war of attrition that we seemed to have entered with the river, the river was winning.

We camped the third night above a spot we'd have to portage before we could get back on the water. Mary ate heartily, and predicted a great day ahead. She hadn't walked the water below the portage. I had no appetite, even for tea, and finally lay bone-tired in my sleeping bag, and couldn't sleep. The river beyond the mosquito netting churned and roared. Sleepless, I dressed and climbed the bluff behind camp to escape, if only for a moment, the tumultuous river noise.

It was quiet up there in the first dew-laden moments of the new day, the river below muttering, almost silent at that distance, the tent and canoe on the narrow beach looking like highwater flotsam. I walked downstream again, for another look at the run ahead of us. It looked so harmless from so far away.

It didn't look any better than it had looked the night before, once I was down and gauging each stretch of water against our boat and our skills. It would be the worst yet.

There was nothing there that much worse than some places we'd already run. But there were five bad spots in rapid succession, with no sanctuary between to rest, to empty water out of the canoe, or to repair it. The fourth and fifth spots *were* the worst we'd tried yet, made doubly dangerous by the water above them: each we could probably run safely, providing we entered them at just the right spot, bone dry. If we picked up too much water on the haystacks and standing waves preceding them – if the canoe were heavy with several inches of water sloshing back and forth under the gear – if I'd misjudged any of the difficulties – if a frog had wings he wouldn't bump his ass every time he jumps.

"What's the verdict?" Mary asked, poking her breakfast fire when I returned.

"Run it," I said.

From where we loaded up below the portage, the first two rough spots were visible, then the river disappeared around a bend. In the bend, I knew, a quarter mile below us, was the third bad one. It would straighten out, then, a half mile of steep, fast water preceding the final pair of obstacles. Below that, we could probably beach if we had to.

Mary climbed in, picked up her paddle, and addressed the river. I did the same. Untying was always my worst moment, because the possibility of changing one's mind still existed. If I was scared walking the river and sizing it up, I was terrified untying. Perhaps the only reason that I persisted with the simple knot that suddenly became so difficult was the knowledge that getting it untied and shoving off was my only salvation.

It never failed. As soon as the bank was beyond reach, the canoe floating free and committed, for the moment, to a piece of river, any trace of residual fear or doubt vanished. The real danger, such as it was, was not half so bad as imagined danger yet unknown and unfaced. There are no moments for a soldier so difficult as the moments preceding an assault. The case must be the same for prizefighters and sky divers.

For now, Mary's usual bravado failed. "You really think we can do this one?" I shoved off, paddled out and relished the new calm and absence of doubt.

"What you see," I said, "ain't one-half so bad as what's around that bend. We can do it if we stay dry the first half mile. Just paddle like hell."

We took five or ten gallons of water each from a half-dozen inconsequential standing waves in quick succession, shot into the bend pretty much on course but a little heavy, hit the unavoidable haystack there and in the blink of an eye were no longer afloat. I have no memory of the water being cold.

I had been so concerned about dumping, and assumed that that would accompany swamping, that I hadn't considered just swamping.

"We're okay!" I hollered to Mary. Gunwales under, bow and stern out, heads and shoulders and arms out, we were sweeping downriver towards the two dangerous spots not out of control, but at the entire mercy of the current. Well, not quite entire; with effort, I could keep her bow downstream. Mary carried her paddle at high port, poking this way or that to keep us clear of rocks.

She flashed me her I-think-we-did-it-again smile, concerned but not frightened, and laughed: Cap'n Hewitt, Old Never-Say-Die, up to his T-shirt pocket in the river, going down with his ship in the best stiff-upper-lip nautical tradition, did not seem to arouse any sympathy in her.

Ahead, the current raced over a wide, round boulder and boiled into a broad, unavoidable haystack. We didn't hit it quite right. She slipped sideways off it, down into the haystack bow-foremost, tipping, and rolled lazily.

Butch, who'd sat me in the front seat of his Old Town and started the whole thing so many years back, in Michigan, bailed us out. In addition to his instruction and his advice, he'd literally put the paddle in my hand that I now held. Of his own design, whittled, shaped and laminated by his own hand, broad-bladed for racing, it made the difference. The stroke was instinctive, straight down with all my strength. The canoe tipped ninety degrees before I got the roll stopped and the keel back underneath us where it belonged.

The final danger, a small falls with a great boulder hulking midstream just below, neared as the canoe sank even lower in the water. The packs and stuff bags, tied shut over clothes and sleeping bags, were losing their buoyancy as water soaked in, and only our torsos were yet above the water when we spilled over the slight falls.

Again, there were rocks in the foam below; had we been empty, we'd never have touched them. Weighted as we were, with a ton of water inside, we sat down heavily on them and the hull gave like an eggshell. The noise was terrific, the three holes were gaping, but the damage, for the moment, was of no consequence: already full of water, our situation couldn't have been worsened short of the hull breaking in half or overturning.

The boulder waited ahead with the current breaking against it, but a light nudge from Mary's paddle tip was all it took to steer our bow around it, and the current did the rest.

We pulled for the left bank, racing by fifty feet away, as the boulder fell astern. The next bend, with its unexplored mysteries, loomed closer.

"Okay, jump!" I said, when we were within five feet of the bank, and we both did, out into the waist-deep water. We set our feet into the rocky bottom and tried to hold the boat. The current threatened to tear it out of our hands, but I held it long enough for Mary to secure the stern line to a tree, and we were, if not sound, at least safe.

Once we'd heaved it sternfirst an inch at a time, out of the water, Mary untied the lashing ropes and rigged a clothesline further up the bank to dry our gear, while I unloaded. I turned her over....the Two-Heart, on her worst day, had never treated the Kennebec like this. I broke out the patching resin, and the cloth. It would be like patching a caesarean section with bandaids.

"Is it bad?" Mary called down from the smoky fire she'd built in the center of her clotheslines.

"Busted fifteen or twenty more ribs. She won't stand another beating like that."

"We've lost the bread." Mary was inventorying the grub. "It's soaked. And the rice. And lentils. Bulgur, too." All the old-fashioned, newly fashionable food she insisted on bringing. The freeze-dried meals, vacuum-packed in foil, were dry. Our food supply was cut in half. But there were fish in the river.

"How's your camera and binoculars?" I knew what the answer

must be.

"Full of water." Film ruined.

When I finished the patches, speeded up by the bright sun warming the resin and the hull, I walked below to see what lay ahead. Compared to what we'd come through, it wasn't bad. I wasn't as intimidated by the river now – we'd plumbed one dark corner of the unknown, and discovered that swamping isn't tantamount to catastrophe. We could run a river swamped just as we could run it dry, if we had to. It was one less thing to be afraid of.

So we loaded up and ran a mile, put in to the other shore, climbed the bluff and walked ahead over a point that hid the downriver valley. As we topped the little ridge and emerged through the aspen, the river below straightened into a long, smooth run and wound out of sight far to the west, between gravel bars. Willow stands, spruce forests, slow and flat and safe.

"I don't believe it," I said.

"We made it," Mary said, "home free..."

"Lot of river left..."

"The worst is behind us."

"We'll see." I was slow to relax.

Back on the river, we rounded the last point with a flourish of paddles and coasted down the last half mile of diminishing whitewater into an opulent green valley as verdant and lush as any we'd ever seen.

This would be the finest that the river had to offer. We paddled through the heat of the day, smelling only our own sweat, and splashed water onto our faces to cool off. The Kennebec glided silently into the cool evening.

Streamside scents, burnt from the air by the midday sun, became more plain. The willows, warm yet, had a smell all their own, as did the wild roses. Spruces, when the river passed between towering stands of them, cast long shadows and smelled pungent, pitchy.

There were hillsides rising steeply when the river approached one or the other sides of the valley in against the mountains. The hillsides were sometimes solid lupine, acres and acres of steep, fragrant lavender. As the air cooled, it moved down the mountainsides, as campfire smoke would show, and the sweet scent on the cooling air flowed out over the water like mist in the early mornings.

A large backwater, an old river channel dammed by beavers, opened in the left bank, offering a harbor, so I pulled in, looking for a campsite. We were alone, away from even the now-soft sound of the river passing, with only beavers for company, in absolute wilderness. And the canyons behind us.

"This is what I've been looking for, I said. "I could eat a horse." I pitched the tent among spruces while Mary built a fire and watched the beavers investigate the canoe. They idled by at a safe distance, pushing their wakes across the mirror surface with their noses, and, not finding us a threat, went off to cut willows down shore.

"Where's John Muir when you need him?" Mary said, at supper. It's not many places we get to that we fancy he'd appreciate. This was one.

There would be another canyon, downstream, not threatening. We would run it intact and dry. There would be camps like this one for another week, and Canada geese with their broods around every bend. A nighthawk nesting on a gravel bar, defending her eggs. A bull moose in a backwater, looking the wrong way, that we approached close enough to touch, who never knew we'd passed. A wolf caught flat-footed one evening, yards from cover when we rounded a bend.

Fish, when we wanted to catch them, to eat, to stretch our dwindling supply of edibles. Sunshine each morning to dry the dew on the tent. Trapping cabins, abandoned. A long-deserted trading post and outbuildings, with a nineteen-year-old spruce growing up through the collapsed floorboards and caved-in sod roof. But not a single footprint, anywhere.

Finally, two trappers, the Wilkinson brothers, living, gardening, fishing and trapping beside that river since 1927, the year their father brought them into that country at the ages of eight and ten.

We spent our last afternoon and night with them, warming up to their tied sled dogs, their home-canned moosemeat, their understated stories of winters gone by, quietly envying them the times they'd seen, their simple, independent lifestyles and their wealth of experiences. We had taken our chances on the river for eight days, in the most forgiving season of the year; they had taken their chances for fifty years, in all seasons, in situations sometimes so much more hopeless than ours had been at worst that our trip's dangers paled by comparison.

They were outdoorsmen of the first order, had learned of necessity and incorporated into their daily routine skills that a whole generation would later seek out, not as the means to an end that the skills were for these two, but as an end in themselves.

Ed and Jared accompanied us to the settlement, loaded our canoe and gear and us in one of their riverboats, in fact, and made arrangements for our things to be looked after there, before disappearing back upstream.

The tourist season was starting, and quite a few passed us on the road shoulder with our thumbs out before a leadfooted mining engineer in a rented pickup stopped. He set us afoot again in Whitehorse in record time, where we overnighted and picked up Mary's truck at the garage.

The Bronco was as I'd left it, keys in the ignition. We drove south and west for the Dawson road, and overnighted one last time.

Next day, we stopped for supper and to say goodbye at Carmacks, a settlement bearing the name of the man that panned the first ounce of gold out of a tributary of the Klondike. The food was not very good, and while I paid for it, Mary went out and gassed up her truck. She was leaning against it, hand on the gas pump handle, staring absently at the Yukon rolling by, whistling.

The tune was "Four Strong Winds," Ian Tyson:

"…But our good times are all gone,
And I'm bound for movin' on…"

I pulled up across the pump from her and when her truck was full she filled mine.

"Peter bid a job at Mayo. If he gets it, it'll be a month's work," she said.

"Well, hope it works out." I went and paid for the gas. She was in her truck, engine idling, whistling again,

"…Still I wish you'd change your mind,
If I asked you one more time…"

"Stay in touch," she said. I climbed in and started my engine. "And if you can figure a way, would you send my shotgun down?"

"Sure. Good luck."

"You, too." She put it in gear and pulled out onto the dirt highway, heading south. I pulled out and turned north.

Her red Chevy grew tinier and tinier in my rearview mirror, trailing its dust cloud, and disappeared altogether.

I leaned forward and looked up through the windshield at the inside of the Kennebec, at the place where Mary's feet had been for eight days. All the ribs I could see there were broken.

Hiram's Theme Song

Hiram was pretty much a failure at hibernation. Like an alcoholic who refuses to admit that drinking has become a problem, he was slow to get the message when our wives left, and then later our girlfriends. Quicker to see the writing on the wall and take action than Hiram, I was up to fifteen hours of sleep per night by the middle of December and down to two meals per day. I was even getting to like it, except the wood stove in the cabin held a fire for only about seven hours if you set it just right, and by the time it was light out and I got up, the water would be skimmed over with ice in the little coffee percolator I'd bought to replace the one the wife took.

The more optimistic outlook Hiram adopted was that as long as there was a bar still open you technically weren't without a girlfriend. He didn't share my view that in Fairbanks, Alaska, where the guy-to-girl ratio then was probably three or four to one, any girl still occupying a barstool by herself at closing time was damaged goods.

Besides experimenting with hibernation, we were doing a little writing. I had placed a piece with a hardcore hook-and-bullet magazine, and Hiram had cracked the market at *Sports Illustrated,* which paid the most, so we were pretty much concentrating our efforts there. It being a New York publication, they had an endless supply of rejection slips with which they were exceedingly generous. Conventional wisdom had it that if Stalin and Khrushchev's successors finally lost patience with the Cold War and pushed the button, New York would be the first place on the continent to get vaporized. Which might be an improvement, I figured. At least it would get rid of all the rejection slips in one swoop. I wasn't making much of a dent in them, burning them in my wood stove one at a time.

Hiram's small success had gone to his head, and he had eschewed renting and gone out and bought the cheapest item any local real-estate agent listed. It cost about one-seventh as much as a new pickup does now, was less than a shotgun's range from the northwest to the southeast property corner if you stood on one and fired at the other (which, from the look of the siding, someone had tried several times) and was located at the end of a street later officially (and aptly) named Runamuck Drive. The not-so-aptly termed "improvements" consisted of a worn-out travel trailer with a wanigan tacked to one side. And an outhouse even an Okie would've torn down.

Hemingway's heirs had only recently published *Islands in the Stream,* which I had bought and we both read, so the first spring of Hiram's brief and only tenure as landed gentry, when the dead slough curving across his property filled with water and ran a one-mile-per-hour current that made his home accessible only to those with hip boots, his friends began referring to his estate as "The Island in the Slough." It kept him amused until the water receded, though, ferrying company to his doorstep, hip-booted, by towing them in his first wife's galvanized doublewide bathtub. The doorstep was three old pallets stacked up, and when someone tipped the concrete block off them they floated away.

Technically, the place had plumbing, but that froze up permanently while we were off on our final duck hunt of the season, and he went back to hauling water from a local spring, as I did, and using the outhouse. My outhouse was bigger than his but not as deep, and I stored my duck decoys in it, stacked up against the wall like cordwood. One of the girlfriends Hiram dragged over for my approval and a duck dinner objected to being watched by forty-eight fake mallards while she did her business. Didn't much care for my roast duck, either. Her approval rating was very low. Seriously damaged goods.

I had a freezer in my shed, bought for five dollars from an old bachelor in Lemeta named Bill, who bought broken appliances surplused in truckload lots from the local Army base and repaired them. The freezers were actually refrigerators with the control turned as cold as it would go. A freezer had to last only until October, at which time you unplugged it until April. There were both ducks and pheasants in it, which I mainly saved for company.

My daily two meals never varied, and this drove Hiram nuts. Two eggs, bacon, toast and jam with coffee for breakfast/lunch, and two Oscar Meyer hot dogs sliced lengthwise and fried for lunch/supper, served open-faced on two slices of whole-wheat toast with ketchup and zucchini relish. And coffee. Milk had always been my favorite drink, but keeping some around, fresh and unfrozen, had gotten to be too much trouble. I had given it up and was probably contracting a fatal case of osteoporosis, which I had not heard of yet. Writers needed, Hiram insisted, to live on the edge, and two hot dogs a day with no milk was the edge I chose.

For exercise, I'd suit up in wool pants and the Eddie Bauer down parka my wife must've figured she wouldn't need in her new life and hiked the three-quarters of a mile to my mailbox. There might be a letter from Mary in Canada. Or an acceptance letter from *S.I.* Yeah, right. My mother wrote once a week, rain or shine, with the results of Terry and Old Clyde's most recent speculation in snow goose and mallard futures.

It was getting on toward Christmas, as I had Hiram's present (a square bottle of Amaretto di Saronno) bought, when the envelope showed up in the snow-covered mailbox. Brookline, Massachusetts, postmark. I turned around and headed home, pondering my as-yet-unrefuted theory that Darwin had been wrong and the most advanced life form was really black-capped and boreal chickadees. They didn't fight wars or pay bills or get sent rejection slips or get left by girlfriends or even need an Eddie Bauer parka with a wolf/wolverine ruff to stay outdoors all year.

Once back at the cabin I poured half a coffee can full of sunflower seeds into the birdfeeder, carried in three armfuls of firewood to top off the wood box, looked around the clearing to see if the fox was about and went inside, rediscovering the letter when I hung up the parka behind the door. There were two five-dollar Army surplus over-stuffed chairs in the cabin in front of the east and west windows. I sat down in the west one, next to the wood stove, and read my mail. It set off Midwestern radar. In Kansas, deals one gets offered in the mail that sound too good to be true usually are.

Well. One of two things: If this sonofabitch is a scam artist, he's the best-writing one who ever tried to beat me out of thirty bucks. Or, if he's on the up-and-up, my prayers are answered. And Hiram's, too – if they accept unsolicited submissions.

Before I got out of the chair I'd written a check for two years of the as-yet-only-proposed *Gray's Sporting Journal*, and a two-page query letter outlining the kind of writing Hiram and I did and generally making us out to be a lot more refined and dependable and cosmopolitan than we were, assuming this was the sort of writer Ed Gray, whom I guessed to be about fifty, would like to have in his new magazine.

Then I plugged in the no-longer-new Bronco so it would start in a while, and whipped up a sumptuous repast of hot dogs on brown bread. And coffee. Hiram had invested in a telephone as befitted his faster-paced life, a gilded baroque nostalgia piece that looked as though it belonged in a New Orleans bordello. More committed to the simple life, I had no phone, and sharing the latest journalistic gossip with him would entail a one-hour one-way expedition. Before leaving I wrapped the Amaretto in Christmas paper from the salvaged-paper sack in the closet, the bottom of which was frozen to the wall.

The situation at Hiram's was not good. Typical, but not good. He was crouched behind his portable typewriter trying to rewrite something, his least-favorite task. A piece of kindling the size of a chopstick protruded from the hangar deck of his typewriter, and fell out every five minutes. Without it, he had no capital letters, which worked for e.e. cummings and *archy* and *mehitabel*, but had never caught on in mainstream outdoors writing.

There was a small, sad spruce tree propped up in a large peach can with no water in it, decorated haphazardly with a variety of pitiful homemade ornaments and no lights. Both ears of the rabbit-ear antenna atop the small black-and-white television were snapped off, apparent victims of a domestic disagreement over who was going to watch what.

The current girlfriend was not in evidence, her real Teamster boyfriend having returned unexpectedly from the Slope and reclaimed her.

"Well, Bobby Lee," he said, brightening at an excuse to quit rewriting. "We, uh, celebrating Christmas early this year, are we?"

"Whatever," I said. "Today, next week, makes no difference to me." He took the wrapped Amaretto from me, felt it thoroughly through the paper, shook it vigorously and listened to it gurgle.

"Today it is," he said, and reached into a sack on the floor and handed me, unwrapped, a new copy of Richard Brautigan's *A Confederate General from Big Sur,* in paperback. "Merry Christmas, Bobby Lee."

"Aw, Hiram," I said. "You shouldn't have."

"Wait'll you see what what's-her-name gave me before she left." He rooted through a junk drawer and withdrew a box containing a somewhat expensive lock-back hunting knife that had only recently come into vogue. "How about *that?*"

"Geez, Hiram, you just open everything when it suits you?"

"After you open something they're less likely to change their mind and take it back. Ah," he said, tearing paper from the bottle, "time for a little duck-camp cheer," and he unscrewed the lid and tipped the bottle back before extending it to me, smacking his lips. "What did we do before this stuff?"

"Peppermint schnapps," I said, taking a drink. "But Hiram, I saved the best for last. There's a new huntin' and fishin' magazine out of Boston that sounds like someone invented it precisely for us to write for. I got a blurb here I just got today, and a letter I wrote 'em on our behalf, and money for a two-year subscription just so's they know we're not *total* deadbeats. It all sounds a little higher class than we're used to."

"Don't know, Bobby Lee," he said, scanning the brochure. "*Sports Illustrated* been pretty good to old Hiram. But it might be a place where we could send our *Sports Illustrated* rejections. Sort of recycle them."

"Suit yourself, Hiram," I declared, " but from today on I believe *Sports Illustrated* can just kiss my ass. Ain't a single hunter or fisherman there, and Ed Gray, whoever he is, is obviously both. Or a hell of a bullshitter. Don't you ever get tired of the same old rejection slips all the time?"

"I get personal letters, Bobby Lee. But what have you got up your sleeve if this Ed Gray don't like our stuff, either?"

"Well," I said, "I been thinking about than on the way over here, Hiram. It's my belief that life has been preparing us uniquely well to write country and western songs."

"Not us," Hiram said, taking a really long pull on the bottle and swishing it noisily through the gaps inside his mouth where two teeth were missing. "Someone already wrote 'Born to Lose'."

John Hewitt

Maneaters of Moose Creek

When Dr. Carper started snoring again just before daylight, I gave up and rolled out. Frost coated the inside of the tent, and between the snores and the condensed breath erupting regularly from the tiny breathing opening in his sleeping bag, he might easily have been mistaken for a steam locomotive, stuck in neutral.

My leather boots were frozen and I had to thaw them out under my arms before I could wedge my feet inside. It was Arctic-pac weather, but my pacs were in Fairbanks. Brake had extended the hunt four days in a last-ditch, end-of-the-season attempt to see that the clients had *something* to take home. And to see that the guides didn't start another winter with empty freezers.

The boots were as cold inside as they'd been every other morning. "Jesus," I said, and crawled out into the snow.

Another two inches had fallen during the night, and covered my pack. I shook it and put it on, heading for the knoll that we did much of our spotting from. A lantern was on in Brake's tent; Doc Shoemaker was probably up early, inoculating Brake and himself for swine flu or Russian measles. Doctor Carper had complained earlier of being constipated, and in addition to pills of a dozen varieties, two injections, a quart of reconstituted prunes and a handful of suppositories, Doc Shoemaker had recommended surgery.

There were fresh footprints in the snow on the trail, and Brake was at the knoll when I got there, sitting on his own pack, hunched over his spotting scope, dribbling tobacco juice out of the corner of his mouth into his beard.

"Spit once in a while, for Christ's sake," I said. Seeing the outfitter before breakfast always spoils my appetite. He jumped and looked up. "Jesus, don't sneak up on me like that. Ah thought you was a b'ar."

"You *wish* Ah was a b'ar," I said. "Be the *first* shootable thing you seen this season within five miles of here."

"Ah *tol'* yuh an' Ah *tol'* yuh, we allus git our moose rat thar by thet lake. Ah don't know *what* went wrong this year."

"In 1946, when I was still crappin' my pants, you got a moose there."

"Thet's jist exackly whut Ah keep tellin' yuh…we *allus* got our moose *rat thar*…"

"You seen 'em yet?"

"Hail, yes. Rat whar they was yestiddy mornin'."

"And the morning before that. And the one before that." I leaned down and squinted into his scope. Between the tobacco juice on the eyepiece and the lint and part of a chocolate bar stuck to the objective lens, I couldn't even make out the draw where the bull and his cows had been feeding.

"Christ," I said, and dug in my pack for my own scope and tripod. He leaned forward and squinted into his.

"Well, hail, yuh knocked it off. Now whar'd thet big sumbitch go to?"

"I got him," I breathed, focusing mine and increasing the power. It was still not quite light enough to tell much, or anything at all, unless you knew what you were looking at, but the white-palmed antlers in the red willow were familiar to us by now. "Can't see the cows yet, though."

"Nope, but they're thar, all right," Brake said fiddling with his focus, "rat whar Ah wanted 'em. 'Cause now, b'Gawd, we *got* 'em."

I set back on my pack and looked at him. He was glued to the scope, dead serious, and as optimistic as only a skunked outfitter on the fourteenth day of a ten-day hunt can be. "Now I have by God heard it all. You're not gonna let one of those knee-jerks *shoot* that sorry sonofabitch way over there, are you?"

"Hail no. I got an idee."

"It better have somebody in it besides *me* to pack that big peckerhead down off that mountain. You're talkin' about *eight* round trips, and the damn *plane* be here this time tomorrow. Jesus. It'll be *dark* by the time we get one of those old farts *over* there, even. Leave me twelve hours of goddamn *night* to get him back here, eight trips, five miles one way, um, eighty divided by twelve, oh hell yes, fine, all I got to do is walk seven miles an hour for twelve hours, carrying a hundred and fifty pounds at a whack across a five-mile niggerhead flat in the dark. Hell yes. When do we start?"

"Ah *tol'* yuh, Ah got an idee. Won't have to pack thet big devil but a quarter mile. Ah'm goan send *you*," he jabbed the stump of his trigger finger at me, "over yonder to thet little knob on the skyline thar…"

"You mean that *mountain* clear out there on the goddamn *horizon?*"

"Thet's what Ah said. Lemme finish – whar yuh hook around

an' sorta, you know, sweep back through thet piece o' country thar," sweeping his hand over the willow thicket where the moose were, most of Moose Creek valley, and a spruce stand the size of the state of Delaware, "an', uh…kind of try an' *ease* 'im back this way. Ah'll put the doctors by the lake an' they'll shoot 'im when he breaks cover down thar."

"What's Doc doing in the tent with the lantern on?"

"Don't change the subjeck. Now, it oughta take yuh three hours t'get over thar, be thar by ten o'clock if yuh leave now without breakfast…"

"I said, 'What's Doc doing with the lantern on?'"

"Hail, Ah don't know. Trimmin' his damn toenails. Puttin' in a repository. How in hail should *Ah* know?"

"He's reading, isn't he?"

"Uh…"

"Goddamn, I'll *ask* him and find out. What's he reading?"

"Uh…"

"Oh no. No no no no. *Maneaters of Kwala Lampoor*, isn't it?"

"Uh…"

"Well *that* goddamn does it. That's it. That is by God *all!* I told you, goddamn you, either that goddamn book stays in town this year or by God *I* do."

"Hail, *Ah* didn't put it in. Didn't even know it was along. The ol' lady musta stuck it in with mah stuff. Tol' me she wanted me to press her some tunder flowers for her, guess she figgered Ah'd need a book tuh press 'em in. Doc found it last night."

"Has he been up all night?"

"Well, uh…"

"This moose drive was his idea, wasn't it?"

"Well…"

"A drive. A drive? A goddamn *moose* drive? No no no no..."

"*Ah* know it won't work, but goddamnit it's prob'ly the *last* hunt the pore ol' fart'll ever make. Nothin' *else* worked. Now he says he allus wanted to go to India an' sit in a whatchacallit in a tree an' shoot a tagger, but never made it an'...hail, Ah jist didn't have the heart to tell 'im no."

"I bet you told him it was a good idea, too. Couldn't miss and you didn't know why you didn't think of it yourself. Didn't you?"

"Well, uh..."

"No no no no."

"Hail, *Ah*'m the one got to climb a way up thar in thet spruce stob in the cold an' build the whatchacallit."

"Machan."

"That's it."

"Ah ha. Ha ha ha. Hahahahahahaha!"

"Le's go git yuh some breakfast. Ah guess we can spare a hour."

There had been no shots. The sun was long down but my binoculars gathered just enough light to see the new platform in the big lone spruce at the end of the lake. I broke cover a mile away and headed down the lakeshore. There was a fire beyond, in camp, and a lantern in one of the tents.

The three sets of tracks I'd been on since noon were over an hour old now. I hadn't seen the bull or the cows for two hours, but they'd seemed to have travelling on their minds the last time I'd moved them.

The tracks passed within two hundred yards of the tree, and headed straight towards camp. Three sets of footprints joined them and covered them up. Brake sat beside the fire, alone, on a stool I'd chainsawed out of a dead spruce, looking into the flames. He looked ten years older than I knew he was. One side of the cook tent sagged, where the moose had tripped over the ropes and pulled up the pegs. Brake didn't look up.

"Were they both in their blinds when the moose passed?"

"Yup."

"Shoemaker in the tree?"

"Yup."

"And the bull walked right by?"

"Cow, too."

"Too long a shot for Carper?"

"We was clear acrost the lake. Hit was Doc Shoemaker's bull. He was bigger'n we thought."

"I know. I seen him too. But how did he…I mean, there wasn't no brush or nothing. How could he set there in that tree and not see? Was he…?"

"Reading thet book."

In the tent, a page turned.

Maneaters of Moose Creek

The author and Tom Walker with clients, 1971 – photo by Tom Walker

John Hewitt

Ted Zercher's Sandwiches

Clyde carried a metal lunch pail every day of his working life. The day he retired, he carried it, accompanied by Pete, the hundred-pound Lab, who was seven that year, to the alley and ceremoniously dropped it in the trash can. Mom told me about it in a letter. His attitude towards the ubiquitous sandwiches the lunch pail had always contained was scornful, at best. In fact, he would rather have called lunch "dinner", as Kansas farmers did, and eaten a sit-down meal at noon, as Ted Zercher did on wheat harvest crews before Clyde was born, and as all of us did when pheasant hunting. Clyde was not against sandwiches per se, he was against the *idea* of a sandwich. One of the only two or three times we ever saw him angry was in a restaurant for supper when all they had was hamburgers. He had just finished driving thirty-six hours nonstop, from Dryden, Ontario to Topeka, with Tom and I wrestling in the back seat, though.

So Mary was on thin ice the morning she, in charge of lunch for a day of duck hunting, made sandwiches. The usual thing, since before I could remember, was to take something requiring cooking, and to build a fire. The something was always wieners. Clyde's scorn for sandwiches somehow did not extend to hot dogs.

Mary had been around a couple of years and, due to my first wife's previous defection, was pretty much one of the family. Her shiny new 12 gauge, a Model 1100, looked quite glamorous in the blind between Clyde's ancient and Terry's middle-aged Model 12s. Shooting that morning had been good; that is, we'd had chances at a couple of decent bunches of mallards and had nine or so greenheads between the four of us. Not bad for before Thanksgiving. It was above freezing, so no one was suffering and needed a fire. Mary and Pete had gone on one excursion down the sandbar to below the island earlier, seeing if the beavers had been working and the deer out on the bar at night. They had.

Toward noon, or at least eleven, after a two-hour lull, Terry inquired after lunch and Mary got out the satchel and passed out sandwiches and black coffee. Five years younger than Terry and I, she was as much a product of the Sixties as we were of the white-bread Fifties. The two most worthwhile aspects of the Sixties, discounting the Winchester AA shotgun shell, were distilled in her character: a willingness, even an insistence to try new things, and a penchant for baking esoteric whole-grain breads.

Clyde accepted his oversized, brown-bread sandwich stoically, peeked under the top slice of bread, and recoiled.

"Mary…" he asked, "what *is* this stuff?"

"Sprouts. Alfalfa sprouts."

"Really?" He extracted a few between his thumb and forefinger, and sampled them. "Hey, those are pretty good. Seventy years old and never heard of a sprout. You have to go out and dig these up somewhere?"

Ted Zercher's Sandwiches

Terry, halfway through his sandwich already and scanning the sky nervously, laughed with his mouth full and broadcast sprouts and chunks of tomato, pickle, and unidentified ingredients onto the logs the blind was built from, where Pete scavenged them.

"No, Clyde, you put the seeds in a quart jar with water and a special lid. Kay's got one. In a couple days it's full of these deals. You rinse them every now and then," Terry said.

Clyde tried a bite. "Say," he said, "Frances never made a sandwich like *this*. What all's in here, Mary?"

She rattled off the half-dozen principle components, half of which were cheeses none of us had heard of or could've spelled. He chewed and swallowed and had a swig of coffee.

"Man. Those Ball Park franks will never seem the same," he said.

"You got that right," said Terry, licking his fingers. He claimed to hate hot dogs and to only eat them to humor Clyde and I.

"Bunch up in the bend," Terry said.

"Yeh," Clyde said after swallowing again, "but they're going the other way. I think they were on the water up there."

Mary looked at me with her eyebrows knit. I handed her my binoculars. When you played who-can-spot-the-ducks-first with Clyde and Terry, you'd best start with at least 7x35s.

"Hey," Clyde said, "did I ever tell you about Ted Zercher's sandwiches?"

"Nope."

"Nope."

I'd heard about them a time or two but Mary and Terry hadn't.

"Back when he and I first started hunting together, in '29, and came up here the first time, in '34, there was quite the gang of us that took two weeks off for quail and hunted every day. Joe Becker was the cook and kind of took care of the food. But it'd dwindle off

The author with Jessie

to just Ted and I by the end of duck season, so one of us had to do it.

"One Saturday, he said he'd take care of it – I should've known better – and I said okay. Well, it was a morning to remember, a real red-letter day, and since even then Ted was over fifty and we had no dog, I'd been halfway to the bridge two or three times after swimming cripples, in over my hip boots. Lord. I'd only get halfway back, still downstream a quarter mile, and he'd have another bunch working. Shot that little twenty just like a rifle, Lloyd Stansbury used to say. It was one of the earliest Model 12s, way older than mine, and only took special shells, shorter than modern ones. Two-and-a-half inches, I think. That was before he got snow in it and blew the end of the barrel up and the girls at his shop got him the new one for Christmas, that he shot the last twenty years and shot the cat with the day before he died.

"So, before I even would get back he'd have three more down. And he could knock 'em down a *lot* further than he could kill them, so I'd just wade out and try to keep the swimmers from getting past me in the current. Usually he'd manage to kill them on the water and I just had to head 'em off.

"When it finally calmed down enough that I got back to the blind and got me some coffee – we had the old glass thermoses in those days, would break if you looked at 'em with your eyes crossed – he asked me, did I want a sandwich? 'Sure,' I told him.

"Well you should've seen this damn sandwich he hauled out. It was bigger than Mary's, and he had *two* of them for me. And *stink*? Oh Christ, you should've smelled the thing. 'What in hell is *this* thing, Ted?' I says, and he says, 'Limburger and Bermuda onion… try it, it's really good.'

"I was hungry enough to eat a horse, but I was afraid if I tried to eat this damn thing, it'd give me dry heaves. I just sat there and looked at it. If we'd had a dog, he'd have had him a nice snack.

"'Oh, for Christ's sake, Clyde,' Ted said, 'go on and eat the damn thing. Here, I'll hold your nose so you can't smell it – that's what I did the first time,' and he reached over and I grabbed my nose myself and told him I could hold my own nose. So I took a bite."

"Well?" Mary asked. I had finished my sandwich and poured more coffee all around.

"You know what? That was the best damn sandwich I ever ate. It had big slabs of Bermuda onion in there, and slices of dill pickles Ted made every year in the basement – I *knew* those were good, beforehand – and mustard and enough horseradish to cure a bull moose of a common cold. Ted made the sandwiches every time we went for the next ten years. Until his first coronary."

"Doctor make him give them up, then?" Terry asked.

"No, he just kind of lost interest in 'em. If it hadn't been for those damn sandwiches of his, we could've had him to the hospital six hours sooner."

A flock of mergansers appeared upriver. Terry and Clyde waited to see if Mary or I would bite on them.

"Ducks!" Mary finally said.

"Mergansers," I corrected.

"Oh, yeh," she said. "What did cheese and onion sandwiches have to do with a heart attack?"

"Aw… Ted lost his only boy, Teddy, in… what was it, '25? Then his youngest brother, John, the one John here's named after, died of mustard gas in '34, right in the same bedroom, the one the twins shared later. Was gassed in '18 but it took him sixteen years to die. Ted's wife, Katharine, died of breast cancer in the same room, in '38. So he had a lot to be sad about, even forgetting the brother he shot trying to clean the family shotgun when he was nine.

"He'd get into the Glenmore, and by midnight us and his Mary Liz'd all be in bed and he'd be down there feeling sorry for himself and hungry on top of it, so he'd make these damn sandwiches that – it was one of those nights he was drunk when he ruined the whole year's dill pickles by adding kerosene to the crocks instead of vinegar – these sandwiches, well, God only knows what all he'd put in them. All the stuff he liked. Raw radishes and turnips, cold chicken livers and sardines, you name it. Then, he'd wash them down with a pint or a quart of straight cream, whatever he could find. Milk in those days wasn't homogenized, and we got ours from a farmer and Frances skimmed off the cream and made butter with it. Unless Ted got to it first.

"Sometimes, between the whiskey, these godawful sandwiches, and the cream, he'd get a gut-ache. Then he'd lay around and moan like a cow in trouble trying to have a calf.

"Frances, she sleeps like a rock, you know, always has, she wakes up about 5:30, probably to nurse the twins. They were right there in the crib…it was February…not quite ten months old I guess, and she listens a minute, and says, 'Clyde! Wake up! There's something wrong with Ted!' Little Tom was named after Ted, you know, Mary. Ted was "Theodore Thomas' and Tom was 'Thomas Theodore'. He wouldn't let Frances name him 'Ted' after losing his own to typhoid."

"So what'd you do?" Mary asked.

"Well, you could hear him down in that same bedroom, 'Cly-y-y-y-yde…Fra-a-a-ances…he-e-e-elp. He-e-e-elp.' Real weak, almost couldn't tell what he was saying.

"'Aw, Frances,' I told her, 'he's been doing that since half past twelve. He just got looped up and made another one of those damn sandwiches of his, and now he's got the stomach ache.' It wasn't like I hadn't heard all this a few times before."

"But you know your Mom. Always worrying. So she jumps up out of bed like one of *you kids* was sick," he said, just a trace of wonder in his voice, "and she *ran* down the hall. His pulse was just about gone. In the end, the doctor said only 10 percent of the people in his shape lived as long as ten more years. He was 58. He lacked two months of making eleven, in the end. But that was the end of those damn sandwiches."

"Ducks!" Terry whispered, and started the hail call on his big Lohman. We all hunched over and froze, and watched them approaching, impossibly high, through a crack between the logs.

"Never decoy those," Clyde said. Terry kept calling, anyway.

"Mary," Clyde continued, grinning very faintly, "did you ever try any limburger cheese?"

The Year the Swan Decoyed

"Bobby Lee, you're gonna have to *do* something about this log." Hiram, never an enthusiastic duck plucker, reached for his bottle. He was covered with down from head to toe - beard, eyebrows, wool shirt, unlaced shoe pacs, and lap. Blowing more down from the lip of his bottle, he studied it, tipped it up, and gagged.

"What's the matter with the log?"

"God-damn *down* in my *brandy*!"

"That's what they put lids on bottles for, Hiram. What's wrong with the log?"

Hiram hacked and spit, and swirled the brandy in the bottle, holding it near the Coleman lantern and examining it for more down. Finding none, he tried another swig, swallowed, and smacked his lips.

"Aah," he said, and readjusted his rump, wincing. "The trouble with this log is, it hurts my ass."

He was right, for once. "Hiram, we been sitting on this log just like it is for ten years now. Why change it?"

"I guess you got to know sooner or later, Bobby Lee…"

"Know what?"

"Next week, maybe they's gonna be a new ass on the log."

"Next week I got to be back to work. Whose new ass?"

"Well, uh…"

"You getting married? *Again*?"

"Not exactly. This trip may *look* like a duck hunt, but… Well, it's really more of a *scouting* trip." Hiram had not been to Minto for three years. I should have suspected an angle.

"Scouting for what? And for whom?"

"You remember that girl I went to New York last winter to see?"

"You said it only lasted a week."

"Four and a half days. But at this party…"

"What party?"

"There's lots of parties in New York, Bobby Lee. Every night. At this party, there was two book publishers. One little one and one great big one. They both had too much to drink, and was having words. The little one, whether he knowed it or not, was about to get his head tore off."

"One less New Yorker."

"But you know how I been trying to get somebody interested in publishing my stories in a book?"

"Let me guess: you stepped in and blind-sided the big one, cold-cocked him, and out of gratitude the little one's going to bring your book out."

"Close…except the big one got back up and tried to stuff me down the toilet."

"I told you publishing a book wasn't going to be easy."

"It may have been worth it, Bobby Lee."

"Were these two publishers boys, or girls?"

"Boys. The little one drove me back to my hotel and…"

"This may be going to be worse than I thought."

"No, no, no. He was straight. But he likes to hunt. Sort of."

"Oh-oh. The new ass on the log?"

"Precisely. You'll like him."

"That's what you *always* say. Does he have his own shotgun? I sold my other one, you know."

"Of course. It's a double-barrel. He says."

"Pass the bottle."

I spotted the double headed my way on the baggage conveyor and nabbed it. Hiram had met the plane while I parked the truck. They'd stopped at the cocktail lounge for a quick one, Hiram being Hiram and New Yorkers being New Yorkers. Oly beer and a dry martini, probably.

The case was a Browning product, imitation leather, brand new, about what one would expect out of a New York book publisher who liked to hunt, sort of. The second case brought the hair up on the back of my neck. I glanced around to see if I had the wrong one already, but no one was approaching me irately. Twice the second case circled on the conveyor, like a wary drake mallard making his mind up. It was all leather, and at least as old as I am. Hiram hadn't said anything about two guns. On the third circle, I grabbed it.

Twenty minutes later, the baggage claim area was deserted, save for me, the two gun cases, and four Abercrombie and Fitch-looking duffel bags milling around on the conveyor. They had leather handles and straps and name tag windows, big zippers, and were also new. It took three trips to get it all in the truck. I shook the old leather case violently and listened, and locked it in the truck's cab.

Back in the lounge, a spirited one-sided conversation was in progress, which I could hear easily from outside the door. I listened while Hiram lied to the publisher about the number of birds we'd taken on the scouting trip, the number of shells it had taken, the size of my tent, the nature of the food we'd bought for the trip (mostly wieners and pork & beans), and the weather. It occurred to me then that Hiram had probably missed his true calling – big game outfitting. I'd heard old timers forty years in the business not half so smooth. Maybe he'd learned something in New York after all, besides how big of book publishers not to pick fights with.

Despairing of hearing anything more incriminating than the usual small-time exaggerations, I stepped on in. She was the only one of the three at the table who faced the door, and no stranger to eye contact. I instinctively glanced back over my shoulder, but no one else was there. The lounge of Fairbanks International was no place for *this* woman: she belonged in the centerfold of any one of three magazines I could think of, none of which was *Field & Stream*. I had a premonition that I might be walking into an ambush, one of Hiram's elaborate practical jokes. "Come on, ambush," I said to myself, and did a creditable imitation of Sean Connery's James Bond, given the handicap of a six-day beard, errant flecks of down on my corduroys, dirt under my fingernails, and dried marsh mud on my Jones-style cap.

"Bobby Lee! Sit down! I want you to meet some friends of mine. This is Hal Van Zant of Dingham, Smith and Brown, the publishing company. And this is Roxanne Brennan."

"Pleased to meet you, John," he said, half rising and extending his hand. "We've been hearing all about you." He had a fair handshake, for a New Yorker.

"Hi," she said, smiling. She had a mouthful of teeth as white as a flock of lesser snows on a sandbar.

I nodded at them both, failing to think of anything appropriate to say. She was drinking margaritas. Her empties looked elegant on the table beside Ron's Oly bottles. She was also one ahead of him.

"The stuff's all in the back of the truck. Maybe we ought to be easing out that way."

The cab of the truck was a little crowded. It was an aging International, found unfit for duty by the U.S. Government the same year I was, and surplused. Most people in Alaska with character drive such rigs. Mine had been a front line combat troop on the garbage run at McKinley Park, as witnessed by the grizzly claw marks on the driver's door and the chew-marks on the front fenders. If they gave trucks Purple Hearts, it'd have had a sackful. On the dashboard were sixteen orderly notches, filed there by whoever drove the truck and neutralized bears: he apparently had been a triple ace in the grizzly wars.

Four adults made for a tight fit in the cockpit, however, which problem Hiram solved by hoisting Roxanne onto his lap. "Take the long way home, Bobby Lee," he said. So much for the polish I'd hoped he might have acquired in the East.

Roxanne's entry into the sporting goods store occasioned a rare lull in the interminable cross-counter firearms discussions between clerks and non-buying customers. There was a lot of maneuvering and jockeying for position to see who was going to get to sell her a nonresident hunting license. Hiram loved it. Mr. Van Zant picked up a battered 16 gauge Mossberg bolt action off the used gun rack and appraised it attentively. I repaired to the ammunition shelf and checked a box of .22 long rifles to be sure it still said "Range One Mile – Be Careful" on the flap. It did.

Hiram's inane one-liners were coming fast and furious now. Most he repeated twice when Roxanne didn't smile the first time.

I was making sure twelve gauge Winchester #6 Magnums were still red when she joined me with her license.

"What's the limit on ducks?" she asked.

"Ten per day, any species, any sex."

"And in possession?"

"Thirty. Three days' bag limit. It's a generous flyway."

"Yes," she said, and selected two boxes of low-base sixes.

"Um, ma'am, I've got plenty of shells at home for us. Those aren't duck loads, anyhow. We shoot magnums, generally."

She smiled her snow-goose smile and tossed her head to move an out-of-place lock off her brow. "I don't," she said.

"Oh."

"Will there be geese?"

"Well, uh, yes ma'am, sometimes. We get geese almost every trip, but not more than a couple. They're...pretty chancy."

"Have you goose loads?"

"Oh, yes ma'am. Lots. Are number twos all right? Magnums?"

She smiled again, which put me one ahead of Hiram. "Two-and-three-quarter inch?" she asked.

"Yes, ma'am. They're what Hiram shoots. I use three-inch loads for geese."

"Does he get a lot of geese?"

"One in his lifetime, that I know of." She laughed and covered her mouth, glancing mischievously around. Everyone was looking at us.

On the way back to the truck, Hiram lagged behind. "What was so funny back there?" he wanted to know.

"Beats me. All I said was that you got a goose once."

"Shit!" he said, and kicked a dent in a Cadillac's hubcap.

They unpacked at the cabin, and I provided them with plastic bags to line their duffel bags, in case the canoe ride to camp was wet. I also suggested soft gun cases, and dug out a pair of extras. Hal opened his hard case and took out the halves of his Browning side-by-side, which appeared so new as to be unfired.

"A double barrel," Hiram said, alertly. "What kind is it?"

"Browning, I think," Hal replied, experiencing some difficulty assembling the thing. Hiram assisted him.

"Hmm," Hiram puzzled, examining the locking end of the barrel-half like an ape with a flashlight. "I thought Brownings had one barrel on top of the other," then, brightening, "...missionary style," and watched Roxanne. She ignored him, absorbed in the wool socks she was stuffing into the garbage bag inside her duffel.

"Maybe, Hal, if you hold your end on the table there, upside-down, and I can get enough leverage out of this," Hiram was using the barrels like a bumper-jack handle. The two of them were grunting and succeeding in puncturing the plastic tablecloth and making an impression of the receiver in the wood tabletop when they were diverted by a quiet metallic click behind them.

Roxanne had put her own gun together.

"Goddamn, I'm glad we didn't try *that* one," Hiram said, "it's got *three* halves instead of two." Still in place in the red velvet-lined case was a second set of barrels.

"You didn't tell me you shot a double, too," Hal said, abandoning his half of his own to inspect hers. "It looks like an old one."

"Not old enough to be a collector's item," Hiram speculated. "It don't even have hammers on it."

The two of them shouldered it and swung it onto the calendar pintail.

"Doesn't seem to fit me," Hal said.

"Me, either," Hiram agreed. "The stocks on it are too small." He looked at the splinter forend and the checkered surface of the butt. "Look here – they never put a kick pad on it. Or even a plastic thing."

"I'll be darned," Hal said.

"What can I say?" Roxanne said.

I took my turn with the gun and the pintail. There was more drop in the stock than our pumps, that was certain. I opened it and it was tight yet smooth, not too stiff, but not too loose, either. And, right where the book says it's supposed to be, was its whole story: "J. Purdey Sons, Ltd." I've always said there were two things left in life for me – shooting my first canvasback, and seeing my first Purdey. Now just the canvasback.

She was watching me, bemused. There was a slight hint of suppressed laughter around the corners of her eyes and mouth, and where she stood near me in the sunlight from the west window, I noticed the little wrinkles there, too. From a distance or in poor light, you'd miss them every time.

"See a lot of those in Alaska, Mr. Hewitt?"

"No ma'am. Not until now. But I read the book. Where did you, uh…?"

"Acquire it? From an English gentleman I was…formerly associated with."

"Ow! Ow! Ow!" hollered Hiram, shaking his left hand and sucking his index finger. "Get me a band-aid, Bobby Lee. God-*damn* double-barrels, anyway."

Hal was holding his own gun, minus the forend, closed and locked, with a piece of my tablecloth and, presumably, Hiram's skin sticking out from between the barrels and breech.

I handed the Purdey back. "Full and full?" I asked.

"Yes," she said. "Will I need the open barrels?"

"There are grouse behind camp sometimes – the dog knows where. Pretty thick back there, though. No guarantees."

"I'll take them, then," she said, and slipped the shorter barrels in among her wool socks.

We had stashed the decoys and spare outboard and gas on the scouting trip, so while the Bronco might barely have held the four of us and our gear, we'd need the truck for the trip home. Hiram drove the bear-chewed flatbed and I, the four-wheel drive. To his disgruntlement, Hal chose to ride with him, which left Roxanne on the good half of the Bronco's seat, Jessie's chin on her shoulder.

"This is a luxury I envy you," she said, scratching the golden behind the ears.

"You mean the dog? Anybody with a gun like yours ought to be able to afford a dozen like that one."

"No. The money's the least of it. It…helps to know where you're going to be the next while."

"Oh. You travel, then?"

"When the opportunity arises."

"And like it?"

"Oh, yes. But it rules out other things. Dogs. Children."

"I guess it would."

A squirrel darted across the road. Jessie dived off her pile of duffel into Roxanne's lap, and mashed her nose against the windshield, whacking our passenger in the face with her tail.

"Jessie! No!" I ordered, and she hunkered on the seat between us. Roxanne was laughing.

"You have a keen dog."

"It's usually just her and me, so I haven't taught her car manners. She gets a lot of mileage out of squirrels."

"Don't break her of it on my account. I like to see a dog keen for something. People, too. What are you keen for?"

"Ducks."

"Just ducks?"

"You saw the pictures on the wall back at the cabin. I fool around at a lot of things; build canoes now and then, fish at the right time of year. Carpenter some. Write a little, like Hiram. Travel a little. Mainly hunt ducks, though."

"Where do you travel?"

"To better places to hunt ducks."

"What about Jessie?"

"She goes, too."

"That's nice. And Hiram?"

"Hiram goes sometimes. But he's kind of afraid life might be passing him by. He likes to get into the fast lane occasionally." She laughed at that.

"But what's he keen for?"

"Women, probably."

"You're not?"

"I'm in a tight corner now, aren't I? Well, I was married once."

"Oh. And…"

"Now I'm not."

"Now you've got Hiram."

"No. Now I've got Jessie, and two good places to hunt ducks, and some memories I wouldn't trade. I don't really know what Hiram's got. Himself, maybe."

"Is he really as… ubiquitous as he seems?"

"Well… there's really *two* Hirams: one is keen for the hunt, like Jessie. Patient, observant, next to impervious to physical discomfort, generous – if he's got any money, he'll buy *all* the groceries and gas and whiskey and shells; if he's had the good shooting today, he'll see that someone else gets it tomorrow."

"And the other?"

"The other Hiram comes out when you throw a woman into the equation. It makes him into a clown. He performs and shows off and there's no help for him, short of subtracting the woman."

"Oh. Do his affairs last long?"

"No. I think he wears thin pretty fast. Bear in mind that what you're hearing is the pot calling the kettle black."

"Your affairs are short, also?"

"Up to now. There's something about me – I don't know what it is – that arouses an unfortunate impulse in most of the women I've known."

"What impulse is that?"

"The impulse to change me…clean me up, make me over into something more socially acceptable. Something with a career. All I've got to show for it is a half-dozen neckties, a graduate degree I'll never use for anything, and an aversion to most things newly fashionable. You know what a non-slip retriever is?"

"Yes."

"Well, that's what the…ladies I've known seem to want out of me, but I was born breaking at the shot. And Hiram, he breaks at the flush, if he's even within sight."

"You still haven't answered my question."

"Which one?"

"About whether you're keen for women, your marriage notwithstanding."

"Oh, yeh. Let me put it this way: I'm not single by choice. I'd *like* to be married well, but one bad marriage was plenty. It made me cautious. Jessie's pretty spooked on electric fences since she got jolted a couple times, but it doesn't make her stay home during duck season." Cresting a ridge, we raised a small mountain range over the horizon.

"What mountains are those?" Roxanne asked.

"The Sawtooths. We'll be right in under them in two hours. When we pass them five days from now, on the way home, that snow that's on the peaks will be clear down to the road at their feet."

"What do you do for a living?"

"Mainly carpenter work. Laborer up north in the oil fields. Yourself?"

"Lots of things. Most recently I was a cocktail waitress at a country club."

"Pay all right?"

"Three dollars an hour, plus tips. But you meet people. You get asked to go places."

"Like to Alaska with Mr. Van Zant?"

"Yes, like that."

"I can see you doing that. You look a little like the woman in the Black Velvet ad."

She grinned and looked out the side window. "No – another agency got that one."

"You model then?"

"Past tense. A wrinkle puts you back on the streets in that business."

"Oh. Must have been something for a while, though."

"For every million-dollar face, there are hundreds in the trenches, barely making the rent. Did Hiram say you'd guided for big game?"

"Probably."

"Well, of the thousand or so dollars a day a hunt costs, how much did you get?"

"Thirty, usually. Fifty, once."

"Were you exploited, then?"

"I'd rather call it finding things out. I usually go into things with both eyes open, except with Hiram."

"This trip has all the raw material for a Hemingway short story: failed model going off with disillusioned guide for who-knows-what."

"When we get to the part where you have to shoot somebody in the back of the head, shoot Hiram; he's the oldest. And don't use your gun – it's too good for him. Use mine."

In the village, children played in the perennial derelict automobiles, which sank lower into the earth with each passing year. An old Indian, afoot, grinned and waved near the village store, and, to balance him out, a younger one came out on his porch to give us the finger.

"Not too happy to see us," Roxanne commented.

"No. Some think the game here is exclusively for them. And when they get to town and get a few drinks in them, they get a whole lot more out of some whites than just the finger. It's a two-way street."

We were loading the two canoes when the two old timers walked down the long hill and surveyed our outfit.

"Two canoes this year," Alfred said.

"Who's she?" Peter wanted to know.

"She's from back East," I said. "Come a long way to hunt ducks here. Roxanne, this is Peter and Alfred." The two of them ducked their heads at her.

"You should get man to get ducks for you. Hard work hunting out there."

"I'd starve to death," Roxanne said. "Hiram here has hunted all his life, shot one goose."

Alfred and Peter looked at Hiram and laughed. "Maybe you can teach him to make baskets or something. He's a good boy." Everyone laughed, even Hiram.

I found the center of a ten-foot piece of rope, tied a knot in it to leave a loop there, and fastened the ends to either end of the thwart behind the bow seat of the Kennebec, with the loop underneath, centered on the keel.

"Bobby Lee, why don't you just…"

"It's called a 'towing bridle,' Hiram. Trust me."

"But it'd be easier to…"

"When was the last time I took your advice, rigging canoes? Haul the rest of that stuff down here and we'll load her up," I said, knotting the heavy nylon towing rope into the loop and slipping the Kennebec into the water.

Roxanne was done charming Alfred and Peter, who stood beside the Bronco, smiling beatifically. She walked to the water's edge, knelt, and touched the gunwale of the Kennebec, rocking it gently.

"Somebody put a lot of work into this one," she said.

"Half a summer."

"And the long one?"

"A whole summer. It's been worth it, though."

Hiram dropped two duffel bags at my feet. "What did Alfred and Peter have to say?" he asked.

"Well, I had an offer of a half interest in a trapline and a third in a fishwheel. Kind of them, but I have other commitments."

"Those two haven't seen the near side of seventy since before they moved the village," Hiram said, somewhat derisively.

"You obviously have had no experience with older men," Roxanne said. "You would be more generous."

Peter looked at Alfred and raised both eyebrows dramatically. Alfred opened and shut his toothless mouth three times, but no words came out. They turned, with their hands still in their pockets, and started for the village, grinning and discussing something excitedly, in Athabascan.

Most of the gear went into the towed canoe, and the hunters, guns and dog into the long one.

"Should we load up here?" Mr. Van Zant asked.

"No. We leave the guns cased when we're travelling. After we get some kind of camp set up to come back to, we load up and see what's flying."

"Oh, okay. When in Rome…"

"Had we better get into our rain gear?" Roxanne asked.

"That's always a good idea," I said, "in case there's some slop."

At camp, with all the new hands, Hiram had a week's firewood dragged in and sawed up before I was done with the tents.

"Well, well," he said, tripping over one of the parachute cord fly ropes of the big tent, "what have we here?"

"This," I said, unrolling my two-man mountain tent, "is the Annex. I thought we'd need somewhere to throw the extra stuff, so I brought the two-man along. It'll make a good warehouse."

"Uh-huh. We all sleeping in the big one?"

"Always did before. Unless someone's got some other plan."

Roxanne and Jessie came up the path, followed by Mr. Van Zant. The woman and dog stopped in front of a small copse of spruce, where a narrow shaft of late September sun fell, backlighting the dog's luxuriant auburn feathering and the woman's blond hair.

"Have you two never seen a woman and a dog before?" she asked. I had to reply quickly, to head off Hiram's one-liner.

"Not like you two. The only time I ever seen anything around here in your class was the year the swan decoyed."

"Bobby Lee, how come I don't remember that?"

"You wasn't here. I told you about it three years ago."

"Oh."

Mr. Van Zant was peeking in the big tent. He went inside and looked around. "It smells funny in here," he said. Roxanne followed him in.

"Woodsmoke," she said. "And bacon. You cook in here?"

"Well, not usually. But we did one moose season six years ago when it was new and it rained for two weeks. I'd forgot about that."

Hiram took advantage of my being occupied with the little tent to usurp another of my accustomed chores, unrolling the pads and sleeping bags. I knew without looking he'd have me on the spruce root where I always put him, and the rest arranged so that no one was closer to Roxanne than he himself. When I checked, I was surprised to find her bag in between his and Mr. Van Zant's.

"You're more serious about getting this book out than I thought," I said to him when we were alone, pulling waders out of a gunnysack.

"Bobby Lee, if I can get a book out, I'm home free. Just lay back and let the money roll in."

"That's what you said you was going to do with the interest off the fortune you was going to make during the Pipeline."

"This is different."

"We'll see."

After a leisurely lunch of hot dogs with cold pork and beans and hobo coffee, we considered the matter of shooting ducks.

"What's the plan, Bobby Lee?" Hiram asked. He knew exactly what he wanted to do, and would do, but he was making it seem like it was my idea, in case it didn't work.

"You in a walking mood, or you feel like sitting?"

"Been sitting all morning."

"It takes two to jump the potholes right, over toward Mystery. Whyn't you and Mr. Van Zant do that, while I slip around through Fish-hook and the Widgeon Hole and maybe see if those geese away over on Marilyn Joseph are sneakable?"

"You ain't going to take Roxanne, are you? Make her crawl through all that mud?"

"Hiram, this is an equal opportunity duck hunt. But there ain't much point in me shagging around all over Hell's half acre if *some*one ain't in the Cookie Jar at Clyde's Island with some decoys out, in case something I or you move should relocate into there."

"Ahhh, Bobby Lee, you should've been in the military."

"It seems like I was, once."

"As I was saying, it's a masterpiece. Anything gets away from Hal and I ought to funnel right through there and see the decoys."

"How does that sound to you two?" I said to the others. "We'll leave the little canoe just across from camp in case someone comes home early or late, and Jessie can stay with Roxanne, and if there's no ducks they can both take naps."

"Let's do it," said Mr. Van Zant, picking up his double and heading for the canoe, with Jessie bounding ahead and Hiram close behind. Roxanne was still wrestling with her waders.

"Why me?" she said, when they were out of earshot. I was stuffing candy bars into most of my pockets.

"Why you what?"

"Why *me* in the 'Cookie Jar'?"

"Because you're...because we...well, Hiram and I both shot our limits off that spot once this week already. You may...this may be your only trip here ever. You see?"

"And Hal?"

"He's probably all right, but he hasn't paid his dues yet."

"And I have?"

"If you know enough to shoot a Purdey and miss getting to own a dog, you've had your ticket punched in the right places somewhere along the line."

"You have things pretty well figured out, don't you?"

"I thought I did when I was a lot younger. Want some Hershey bars?"

"Sure."

Jessie wanted to get out with Hiram and Mr. Van Zant, of course, and gave me her "But life is passing me by…" look when I told her to stay in the canoe. The river was still high enough that I could pole the channel back to Clyde's Island, and she leapt lightly ashore there, familiar with every inch of the marsh within gun range. The decoys were where I'd left them, under a blown-down willow clump, in their two tied-together gunnysacks. We used the canoe to put them out.

"What commands does Jessie know?" Roxanne asked, leaning her graceful old double against a dead birch stump and opening her shell bag. It was a nice functional item that reminded me of Hiram's, except hers had never been Hiram's first wife's purse.

"'Come' means come. 'Stay' means stay. 'Down' means down. 'Fetch' means fetch, though she'll never wait to be told, if you knock something down. She'll sit and heel if you need her to."

"It sounds like she pretty much takes care of things by herself."

"That's the idea. Oh, don't waste your breath trying to call her off a retrieve; that's one time she doesn't hear you."

"Okay."

"Be back around five for the evening shoot. I'll hide over yonder then. Keep your goose loads handy."

"You, too. Write if you find work."

The geese were where I expected them to be, a long muddy crawl from cover. I was trying to decide whether the candle was worth the wax when a lone pintail helped me out by boring over, in nice range. He tumbled at the shot, splashing in in fairly open water, and the geese headed elsewhere.

I watched them as the several hundred birds separated into half a dozen flocks, and each flock followed its leaders to quieter locations. There was not enough wind or weather to keep ducks or geese moving, nor to cover any boat or paddle noise, so I was getting almost no shooting. It was probably little better for Hiram, but I was hearing an occasional "Whump!" or "Whump! Whump!" far off. I couldn't tell if it was him or Roxanne, though.

So I went back the way I had come, hid the canoe, and made myself comfortable in one of the secondary spots on the periphery of the Clyde's Island Cookie Jar. I chose one with a view of the island and, beyond, the marsh toward Mystery Lake. From there, I could observe the fortunes of the entire hunt, unless Hiram had walked his publisher off the end of the earth. Roxanne was about a quarter mile away. It would take a duck to determine whether she and the dog had succumbed to the sunshine and the marsh-hay chaise lounge Hiram had gathered together one previous afternoon.

Far away, two shots, then a third, echoed over the marsh. Low down on the horizon, several wisps of movement became individual flights of ducks, some circling and going back down, others breaking away and disappearing in the distance, and yet others getting more distinct, as they neared. I put the binoculars on them. Mallards. Then on the island. Roxanne was not visible, but Jessie was, watching the mallards. Six of them committed themselves a couple hundred yards out, centered on the flight lane that would carry them right across in front of her. They would be a shot, whether they decoyed or not.

I saw her then, rising from a crouch to shoot with both legs under her. I'd get more ducks if I always had sense enough to do that myself. She took the first bird in range, coming in. Her gun belched a faint blue cloud of powdersmoke the instant the butt touched her shoulder, and the duck had folded before the sound reached me. The second shot had the same result, and I was watching Jesse gallop out through the hock-deep water when a third shot folded a third mallard. I examined the brush for sign of Hiram or Mr. Van Zant, but found none.

Somewhat later, I could make out the two walkers, three-quarters of a mile away, taking the short route back to the second canoe, and camp. Neither seemed to be staggering under the weight of their bag. Roxanne, on the other hand, was not letting much shootable get by. I missed two chances for shots myself, concentrating on birds in the distance that I thought might pass her within range.

Toward sundown, a pair of widgeon made the fatal choice, and her second shot failed to drop the trailing bird cleanly. He faltered, caught himself, and veered in my direction. It was the kind of shot Hiram likes, a little too far to suit me, but I put an extra-long lead on it and got lucky. Faintly but unmistakably, from the island, I could hear applause, hands clapping. I stood up and bowed.

When I slipped the canoe ashore on the island, Roxanne added eight ducks to the two behind the front seat – all good ducks, too – and climbed in.

"Might as well leave the decoys for the morning shoot," I said. "You showed them no mercy tonight."

"This is a most perfect spot. I'll bet there's not another spot like this on the whole marsh."

"Actually there's two, but neither have a dry spot for a shooter or dog to sit down. And there's only bulrushes for cover. So I guess you're right; this *is* the number one spot. But you should be here during a northwest wind. Even Hiram and I get our limits then."

"Did you see him in your travels?"

"Once. They finished the day across from camp. I expect they're back there already."

"We'd better hurry then, and rescue the whiskey. Did you bring whiskey?"

"That's Hiram's department. He's forgot his socks before, and his shotgun shells, but we've never been without something to warm his insides. Even Hiram has priorities."

Something in the chemistry of the evening kept me from tipping the outboard down when we cleared the weed beds and were back in the river proper, and we paddled to camp over water as flat calm as the silence was complete. Little by little, the deepening moonless darkness swallowed the woman in the bow, until only the steady dip and pull of her paddle remained, as I steered by the faint western horizon. When we rounded the last bend before the half-mile straightaway, a new call drifted down from high overhead, up toward the stars.

"What's that?" she whispered.

"Swans," I said. "They don't stop here much."

"Oh, look! They've got a fire going at camp already."

"So they do. Maybe Hiram's good for something after all."

"That's nice. I don't usually have a fire to come home to."

"Me, either," I said.

Hiram was pacing the riverbank, silhouetted by the fire and lantern behind him, chipped enamel coffee cup in hand.

"Bobby Lee!" he called. "Is that you?"

"Yes, Hiram."

"I been worried about you."

"Been worried we'd get back before you finished the whiskey?"

"Where you been? Is the motor broke?"

"No. We just paddling. Saving gas. How'd you do?"

"We got some. Three. I *heard* some shooting at the island, though."

"We killed ten," Roxanne said, shipping her paddle as the bow slid onto the bank.

"Okay," I said to Jessie, and she jumped out. Hiram picked the coiled bow line out of the canoe with his free hand and made it fast to a driftwood root. Hal came down, cup also in hand, but stayed back from the water's edge in his low-quarter moccasins while we off-loaded the ducks and guns.

"Say," he said, "maybe Hiram and I should try that spot in the morning. Somebody did all right over there."

"Mostly Roxanne," I said. "You guys got supper all cooked?"

"Supper?" Hiram asked.

"You know. The meal you eat before bedtime."

"I've been too worried to cook. Thought we was going to have to send out a rescue party."

Roxanne had gotten free of her waders and had her camp boots on. "Here," she said, sitting down on the two-by-six we'd nailed on the log to make it more comfortable. She had a mallard in her lap, and an old fashioned fishing knife in her hand, with one long thin blade. She slit the breast skin, peeled it back, and deftly rolled the meat off one side of the breastbone with one stroke. She looked up. It must have been the looks on our faces that made her laugh.

"I bet you usually pick them," she said.

"Well, yeh," I said.

"That's fine for the ones to be eaten next week," she explained. "I'm a little hungry right now, though."

"I'll get you a – do you need a skillet, or anything?" I asked.

"Just a skillet. Some butter and a little wine." She had the other side of the breast off now, and was dicing them into chunks about the size of sugar cubes.

She kicked Hiram's fire apart and drug what coals there were off to one side. "We'll forego the marinating," she said. Soon the butter was sizzling in the skillet, and the cubed mallard went in. She shook the skillet from side to side, rolling the meat about in the butter.

"What's that?" she asked, holding the skillet off the coals to stop the sizzling.

"Sandhill cranes," I said. "When does the wine go in?"

"Any time now," she said, and added about a cup of wine to the skillet, which really went wild, foaming and boiling. Momentarily, it settled down and the wine quickly cooked away, leaving the still-rare duck awash in a browned sauce that smelled delicious. She sat the skillet on one of the wooden boxes we'd had provisions in, and lifted a piece of duck breast out on the tip of her knife blade.

"Try that," she said, extending the blade toward me. I took the meat and popped it in my mouth, and sucked on it.

"Well?" she grinned. I made a face.

"Gad, Hiram, it's the awfullest thing I ever ate. Why don't you get the wieners out while I clean up the mess in the skillet?"

"We'll see about *that*," he said, addressing the skillet with a large fork.

"Don't be bashful, Hal. Devil gets the hindmost around here," I said.

"Bobby Lee, don't talk with your mouth full."

Four ducks and most of the half gallon of wine later, Hiram caught himself nodding off and felt constrained to make conversation. "Duck hunters make the best lovers," he said.

"*Au contraire*," Roxanne replied.

"What?"

"That's French for 'no,' Hiram," I said.

"You know me, Bobby Lee. Never take no for an answer. Why 'no'?"

"Duck hunters tend to go to sleep at the wrong times," she said, without looking up.

"Sleep," Hal said, and yawned. "That may be just what the doctor ordered."

"Beds are all made," I said, "and I think the weather calls for an early start tomorrow."

"See you in the morning, then," Hal said, and headed up the path, playing a flashlight beam ahead of him.

"Bobby Lee?"

"I think I'll try and get a couple of ducks picked before it catches up to me."

"I was afraid that was going to be the other option. Roxanne?"

"I'll be along in a minute. The skillet needs cleaning. Maybe I'll work on a duck, too."

"Save me a couple," Hiram said, draining his cup and heading for the tent himself.

"Shhh. Listen now," I said to Roxanne. "He's about to the root on the path he always stumbles over in the dark." There was a moment of silence, a small commotion from up the path, and a mumbled, "Goddamnit!"

"Does Hiram ever do anything that surprises you?" Roxanne asked, pouring the water she'd heated into Jessie's bowl, and scraping the skillet with a spatula.

"Not anymore," I said. "Nor me him." I had a pintail in my lap, and the first few tufts of down I pulled from its breast revealed a happy absence of pinfeathers. Roxanne poured two fingers of Hiram's peach brandy into each of two coffee cups and sat one beside me on the log.

"Thank you," I said, handed her the pintail, and selected a mallard from the pile to pick myself.

"Thank *you*," she replied, and started picking. The new wood she'd put on the fire crackled and popped. Wings swished out over the river. She turned her head to look into the dark.

"Bufflehead or bluebills, coming in late," I said.

"This must be the nicest thing there is," she said.

"Oh, I don't know. It suits me, but maybe if I had more money, I'd..."

"You'd what?"

" Well, I guess I don't know what else I'd do. Other people seem to like other things pretty well, though. Must be a thrill to raise a colt and have him win the Kentucky Derby."

"You can't do that every year."

"That's right, too."

She finished her pintail in silence, and took a mallard. She had it half picked before she spoke.

"Somehow, it doesn't add up," she said.

"What's that?" I asked.

"You. Single."

"Oh. I, uh, might have been thinking as much about you."

"No. I just can't imagine you never having children."

"Hmmm. I...haven't thought of that for a long time."

"Perhaps I'm wrong, but it would seem a great waste, to me."

"If I were never a father?"

"Yes. I don't know that I've ever met anyone more well suited to it."

"No. I don't have... I don't even own the cabin. Just rent. Kids need a decent place to grow up. You know... a house with bedrooms and a basement, a yard to play ball in. A mom."

"I think most of the things you mention are superfluous. I don't mean to be critical. But if the chance comes along, don't pass it up." She was finished with the mallard. "Me for a sleeping bag," she said.

"Take the flashlight out of my daypack," I offered.

"That's all right." Jessie got up and followed her.

"Watch out for that root of Hiram's," I warned. She laughed.

I finished my duck, covered the food and the inside-out waders with a tarp, tucked some birchbark and dead spruce twigs under the seat log against a quick morning fire, and turned off the lantern. It dimmed and went out, and the moon, finally up, illuminated the familiar shoreline across the river. I picked up my shotgun, and followed the moonlit path to the tents.

Things there had been rearranged. Hiram and Hal were snoring lustily, harmonizing occasionally, and the duffel bags and gun cases were piled over under the thickest spruce. There were two sleeping bags in the mountain tent, one occupied, the other mine.

"Bedtime, Wilson," I said, undressing. She laughed. "That was your line, by the way," I added.

It was close quarters in the tent, it being the size it was, and her face was no more than a foot from mine once we'd both wriggled and scooted our bodies and sleeping bags into agreement with the willow roots and dead twigs I hadn't cleared before I pitched the tent.

Calm as it was, I left the door and mosquito netting unzipped, and the light from the low moon fell across her half of the tent. Her face was turned to it, eyes open, looking out over the flats, and she had her arm over the dog. Somewhere in the night sky, a flock of geese were asking questions.

"God, what a country," she said, and smiled her lovely smile.

" Your smile really takes me back," I said, smiling.

"To someone you know that smiled a lot?"

"No. To the river where I grew up. Snow geese stopped on sandbars every fall, there, for grit. Your smile reminds me of a flock of snows."

She laughed, so hard it was a moment before she could speak. Jessie woke up, raised her head, and looked quizzically from Roxanne to me.

"Well, I wasn't going to mention it, but your smile reminds me of something I saw once, too," she said.

"Where?"

"At the zoo."

"What?"

"Polar bears in love."

"Is that...are you implying that I'm...buck toothed?"

"Don't forget," she said, settling into her down-jacket pillow and closing her eyes, "you started this."

I looked at her, at her face relaxing toward sleep. There was a new tranquility there that didn't grace it waking, in its world of men and airplanes, cocktails and nylon stockings. I saw the little girl she must have been once, placid and full of wonder. She was right, of course; what I should be was a father with little girls of my own. Jessie would like that, policing up the floor around a high chair, after meals.

Sleep, the duck hunter's mistress, was winning again.

"Polar bears?" I said. Her lips parted, though her eyelids did not, and the snow geese were back, closer than before. Someone from years ago, Terry or Tom or Clyde, it was hard to tell who, called them for me: "Take 'em!" and, true to every hunter's dream I've ever had, I pulled on the nearest bird, and pulled and pulled and the gun wouldn't fire.

Is It Alberta Yet?

(Formerly appeared in *Gray's Sporting Journal* with the title "Hunting The Here-After" with it's companion piece, "Here, After The Hunting" by Ron Rau.)

Now, I don't mean to belittle Ron's credentials as a duck hunter – far from it. He takes it serious enough; the morning hasn't dawned that he wouldn't forsake a warm bed (and bedfellow) for cold hip boots and a horizontal rainstorm. What I'm sayin' is, he just didn't *know* prairie mallards.

Twenty-four hours south of Whitehorse, bowling along in Ron's old pickup, Hank Williams on the portable recorder and Ron keeping time bouncing his head off the passenger window, I spotted the first bunch.

"Whatsa matter? Why're we stoppin'?" he inquired.

"Mallards."

"Yeh? Where?"

I pointed. Two hundred circled a nearby barley field.

"Big bunch," he said. For a Michigan beaver pond, it would've been.

"Nope," I said.

"Too early for arguin'. What time *is* it?"

"Noon."

"Oh. Is it Alberta yet?"

"Yep."

"Time to buy an Alberta duck huntin' license."

"Seein' 'em and gettin' shootin' at 'em is two different things."

"Hell, it's only money. How much is a license here?"

"Fifty bucks."

"Oh. Shut up a minute, Hank," he mashed the STOP button on his recorder. "Like I was sayin'…"

"It's only money."

"Drive on."

We procured licenses from a government office so rarely asked for nonresident alien game bird licenses that they first claimed no such thing existed, and then couldn't find them, after they remembered.

"Most people here are interested in moose, you know…" the girl explained, while she filled one out for Ron. He disemboweled his billfold.

"There is ab-solutely *nothin'* you could tell me that I'd be gladder to hear than that," he said. Her pen stopped and she raised her eyes.

"Oh?" she said. She was quite attractive.

"They told me that same thing ten years ago in Alaska, an' it was the best news I ever heard."

She completed the license, and did mine. We walked out onto the street, reading our new licenses and scowling.

"Bobby Lee…" Ron started, and paused. A long time ago we encountered two low-rent hillbilly outlaws in a Flannery O'Connor short story, named Hiram and Bobby Lee; later, after reading *Deliverance*, we decided that the two nameless, perverted derelicts featured there must be Bobby Lee and Hiram, and still later, it occurred to us that if we had counterparts in Literature, it was this pair. We've been Hiram and Bobby Lee ever since, when the situation warrants. "Bobby Lee, do you got this feelin' that…that…"

"That we been took for suckers again?"

"That's it!"

"Hiram, I was just goin' to ask you the same thing. Don't they usually give you a chance to throw a baseball at some milk bottles and win a Teddy bear or somethin', though…?"

"They changed the rules."

"We allowed sixteen mallards apiece, it says."

"We spent $57.50 apiece already, not countin' gas and grub."

"That's…um…about $3.75 per duck, *if* we get our limits," I figured.

"It don't say nothin' on here about *not* gettin' our limits," Hiram looked at the back side of his license.

"If it did, nobody'd buy 'em. If all we get is one duck, he's gonna be worth a hundred an' fifteen dollars, that's fifty dollars a pound live weight, seventy-five a pound dressed."

Hiram stopped in front of the truck. "Gawd. Let's pick out a fat one."

" I believe I'd ground-sluice one for that."

"That'd be the most expensive bird we ever ate, wouldn't it?" Hiram speculated.

"Nope."

"Oh yeh, that year you came back from Kansas with just two pheasants. What'd you figure on them?"

"Five hundred apiece."

"They was worth it." It hadn't been Hiram's thousand dollars, and it was the first year I baked them for him in sour cream. He smacked his lips. "Worth every penny, as I recall."

"I can think of two pheasants worth more than *that*..." I allowed.

"Which ones?"

"The two that was your limit openin' day of the Michigan season that year you had the girl friend an' ketchup factory job in California, before I knowed you, the year Hemingway died in Idaho and you didn't even know it."

Hiram thought a minute. "Oh, yeh. But you can't say that 'cause you didn't see the girl, and besides, I spent openin' day down on the beach with her and never went back there for the hunt. I never got them two pheasants."

"That's right. But you *could*'ve had them then for a plane ticket, fifty dollars apiece. All the money in the world can't get 'em for you now."

"You're right." He brightened. "Hell, a hundred an' fifteen for a mallard is a rock-bottom *low* price then, ain't it?"

"That's how I see it. If there's a sucker around here," I said, jamming my license in my billfold, "it's the Province of Alberta for lettin' somethin' like a mallard go so cheap..."

Hiram got a road map from a service station and decided the river it showed as south of us was the place to go. I looked at it and figured the lakes north were the spot. "*Believe* me, Hiram, I was *born* and *raised* out here. They'll be stayin' on the lakes, if the lakes ain't froze."

It was Hiram's truck, so we went south, me driving, disgruntled, and him very quiet, rehearsing in his mind his "I told you so" speech for when we found The Big Thousand greenheads holed up along his river.

We found one merganser diving in the river. Finally, near sundown, he agreed to head north. The first lake was shallow, and frozen.

Is It Alberta Yet?

I drove down to the edge of the second, at a provincial park; three mallards jumped within range, and others scattered downshore.

"I *knew* we'd find 'em if we kept lookin'," he exclaimed. "Those was *in range.*"

"The lake's a sanctuary. And we *ain't* found 'em yet, Hiram. *Maybe* we found where they live. We'll get us up on a hill; if they're feedin' out in the barley, we'll see 'em or hear 'em comin' back."

We saw the first bunch, about a thousand, swarming a barley field before we got to the hill.

"*Now* we found 'em!" Hiram said. I shut off the engine and rolled my window down.

"Nope. Just one bunch, and someone else is after 'em by the light of the moon…" A station wagon was parked a quarter mile down the road, and a caller was working in a strip of brush in the center of the field. It was long after sundown, too dark to tell if there were decoys out in the stubble. "There!" I said, pointing at the muzzle flashes.

The ducks flared and the six reports only dropped one. "Too goddamn high," I judged. "Assholes."

"Little late, too," Hiram said. "What do we do now?"

"Get up on our hill," I said, starting the truck and flicking the headlights on.

On the hill, I pulled over beside another parked pickup and we got out. It was still pretty light to the west. Just over the horizon I spotted what I'd been looking for, the long thin lines getting closer. We were between them and their lake. "There's some," I said.

String after string after string swished over as the sky darkened, three ranges high and hurrying, more coming out of the west until finally, when the light faded completely, we could only hear them passing. Thousands upon thousands of mallards, staging here at the northernmost open water on the continent, gleaning the barley fields and waiting for the cold snap that would freeze their lakes and drive them south.

"*Now* we've found them," I said. It was Hiram's first look at prairie mallards.

"Jesus H. Christ," he said.

Two figures separated from a bundle of barley straw downwards the lake and climbed the hill. Both wore blue jeans. One had a blue nylon windbreaker, the other a denim jacket. Their caps were fuzzy, plaid farmer's going-to-town caps. The two shotguns were brand-new, unblemished; one expected to see a price tag flopping from the trigger guards.

"Locals," I said to Hiram, quietly.

"No ducks," he murmured. "Evening!" he hailed them. "Any luck?"

"No. We should've, but we didn't hit any," one of them replied. His accent was a pleasant cross between Montana Cowboy and Australian British.

"You own this?" I asked, indicating the harvested barley.

"Oh, no. Chap on the combine there," they pointed towards two sets of headlights creeping across another field a half mile below us. "Nice enough sort."

"Oh. You don't farm around here, then?"

They grinned. "No, not us. We're from town." He waved in the direction of the town where we'd purchased licenses. "Yourselves?"

"Yanks," I answered, "on our way from Alaska to Kansas for a pheasant hunt and saw your mallards. Couldn't pass them up."

"Bit of a drive for you, then?"

"Four or five days," Hiram said, and I thought to myself, 'Not counting eating, sleeping, hunting and breakdowns.' We'd just closed the season down in the Yukon Territory with Mary, and I'd left Fairbanks two weeks earlier, after Minto Flats had frozen tight. Hiram had followed me by a week. "Plan to be here at daylight?"

"Can't, you know. Jobs. Maybe in the evening."

"Then we wouldn't be bothering your hunting to try it here ourselves?"

"Not at all. Good luck to you. Suppertime now, got to get on home. He says the ducks cost him a lot earlier in crop damage."

"Oh. We'll speak to him later. Thank you."

"Righto. 'Night."

"'Night."

They'd cost him ten thousand dollars, he said; come in at night when it was too wet to combine, and harvested his barley for him. The geese he didn't mind – they fed only during the day and could be kept from his fields conventionally, with a shotgun. Malllards were another matter. They fed at night, too, and thwarted him. He considered them pests.

It had been a bad, wet harvest. Usually the birds would've been gone a month earlier, frozen off the lakes. No one could remember it ever having been that warm, that late, just as it had been in Alaska and the Yukon. It was the gentle beginning of the mildest winter much of the North had ever experienced.

We drove to town for chicken-fried steaks, returned, and parked in Bob's yard, a landowner we'd met earlier, en route from Beaverlodge to Grande Prairie. He wasn't home. Hiram unrolled his sleeping bag on the front seat and put the soundtrack from "The Good, the Bad, and the Ugly" on his tape player.

I excavated a trench down to the mattress, in the boar's nest in the back end, by Coleman lantern light. Waders, duffel bags, decoys, stove, grub box, shotguns, shovel, jack, tools, pots and pans and boots, brown under their layer of Alcan dust, were stacked and propped precariously on each side before I unrolled my own bag and crawled in. Not sleepy, I read the regulations.

"Oh my God! Hiram! Hiram!" I pounded on the camper shell.

"What? What?" I must've woke him up. He shut off the cassette.

"It says here that *after November 1ˢᵗ*, all restrictions is lifted an' you can hunt the sanctuaries!"

"Bullshit." Hiram is forever putting me on, and figures I try to bait him. Always when I'm telling the truth.

"No, *really*! Says right in the regulations."

"Now I gotta piss." He climbed out and I could hear him relieving himself, barefooted on the frozen ground, listening to the resting mallards a half mile away. I folded the regulations and propped my pocket watch up and shut off the lantern. The stove was jabbing me so I moved it and snuggled up to a sack of canvasback decoys. "You in charge of gettin' us up?" Hiram asked.

"Yep."

He got back in and slammed the door. A wooden canvasback toppled out of the sack and hit me between the eyes.

"Ow," I said.

"Now what?"

"Goddamn decoy jumped me."

"Need any help?" This, sarcastically.

"No." I wedged the decoy behind the stove and rubbed my forehead.

"Bobby Lee. When was Pearl Harbor?"

"Seven December, 1941."

"Know what it feels like to me up here?"

"God knows."

"Six December 1941."

When I fired up the stove in the morning, there was skim ice in the coffeepot. Hiram shifted from foot to foot beside the tailgate in the dark, sucked on his pipe, and shivered.

"Thank God for instant coffee," he said.

"An' hot chocolate," I added.

"Wearin' waders or Sorels?" he asked.

"Can't decide. Pretty cold out. Sorels, I guess."

"What if we knock one down in the water?"

"Let's carry our waders, just in case."

"What in?" He wasn't awake yet.

"The gunnysack. We'll dump the decoys out."

"You're a wonder."

"Goddamn, lookit the dust in your coffee cup." I held his cup under the lantern and wiped my thumb through it.

"Make someone a good wife, someday."

"It's *your* cup." I dumped some instant coffee on top of the dust, poured hot water on it, and handed it to him. He stirred it with his pipe stem.

"Gritty down there."

"Save you brushin' your teeth."

"You think of everything."

"Somebody's got to."

Shooting time sneaked up on us while I was emptying the canvasbacks out of their sack and wadding the waders into it.

"Hey, there they go! Get your shells, c'mon!" Hiram urged, hopping around outside the truck, looking towards the lake. I crawled out. "We're missin' the flight!" About a thousand were passing a quarter mile down the hill, low enough to the barley to be in range had we been under them. I slung the sack over my shoulder and picked up my pump gun.

"Oh Lord," Hiram said, as we walked past Bob's house and down across the barley stubble in the almost-dark, "Listen to 'em." The hen mallard uproar on the lake was tremendous; if anyone was out of bed and outdoors in Saskatchewan or British Columbia, they probably heard them.

"Don't sound safe down there to me," I whispered, "I only brought one box of shells."

"Watch 'em!" he crouched.

"Too high," I warned. Hiram's 12 gauge came to his shoulder anyway, and belched a foot or two of flame. One of the string of two hundred folded, got larger and larger, and thumped down behind us. "I'll be damned," I said. He dropped a second from another flock.

"They're closer'n they look," he whispered, running for his first in a crouch, watching. "Take these."

I led one and fired. They flared, sort of. I picked another and missed him, too. "Too high," I repeated.

"You're just missin'," Hiram said, looking for his second. "Take this bunch." I was still reloading, but I came up on them anyway, did everything the same, and fired, angry at myself for not leading them more. My mallard folded and made the long fall, hitting and bouncing above the stubble. "I'll be damned," I said again, and ran for him.

The flight lasted about fifteen minutes, and we never got more than four hundred yards from the truck.

"How many we got, Bobby Lee?" Hiram called from the fencerow he'd finally taken cover in.

"Eleven, I think. How you fixed for shells?"

"Half a box."

"Me, too." Neither of us was shooting fifty percent. He came down to my hide and laid his birds with mine. We both watched.

"Too dark at first to tell drakes from hens. How many did we get?" He meant hens.

"Four. No point system here. Eight of anything, apiece."

"Yeh, but I'd sooner shoot drakes if we can."

"Me, too."

"Is it always like this?"

"These birds ain't been hunted. They're not spooky yet; fly low and don't flare at the shot, really. They'll learn."

"But is there always this many?"

"On the prairie, you mean?"

"Yeh."

"Since before we was born. Since before the old man was born."

"I'm thirty-three this year. I've wasted half my life."

"Nice to finally hear *you* say it, Hiram."

We filled our limits down near the lake, sitting in clumps of willows and mountains of down. Hiram finished first, and concentrated on picking. I kept an eye out, reached my gun and dropped a crossing drake pintail at forty yards. Barring a stray goose, we were done for the day.

"Nice," Hiram said, with his beard full of down.

"I believe we've had a terrible accident," I theorized.

"What this time?"

"I think one of us went to sleep at the wheel and totaled the truck back on the Alcan somewhere, and we was both killed an' went to heaven."

He gouged at his beard with his dirty thumbnail. "They got duck lice in heaven?"

"Heaven for a louse has *got* to be a layout like that," I said, nodding at his beard.

"This must be it, then," he said, looking around at heaven and listening to the diminished raft of mallards out on the lake beyond the shore ice. "Looks about like I expected." He picked awhile. "When do we get a crack at the geese?"

"They're for the guys that went ta church reg'lar."

"Goddamn it."

" Ssshhh. You'll get us throwed outa here."

"I forgot."

Later, while I finished picking, he drove to town and bought an insulated ice chest to keep the dressed ducks in. He selected the most shot-up bird, diced it in his saucepan, and made soup out of it, standing behind the truck's tailgate, poking at the saucepan with a short-handled spoon while the stove generated noisily.

"Made soup" means he chopped up an onion and threw it in with the diced duck and boiled it like a pot of tea, salted and peppered it, tasted it strictly in the interests of showmanship, and summoned the multitude. I held out my bowl.

"De-lightful," he pronounced.

"Jesus, I like eatin' standin' up out here in the dark fightin' mosquitoes," I said. There probably hadn't been a mosquito there for two months, but I'd voted for a café supper in town. Since it was Hiram's truck, however...

"Bobby Lee, you'd bitch if I hanged ya with a new rope. *Now* we can shoot a extry duck for this one we're eatin'."

"Just *exactly* what I wanted to do tonight."

"I think if we work it right and get up early enough, we can get our limits the first half hour in the mornin'."

"Oh, Jesus," I shook my head, "I *knowed* you'd say that. You'll never learn, will ya?"

He bristled. "You're sayin' we can't get our limits on the morning flight?"

"I'm sayin' ya can't *count* on it like that, Hiram. Maybe the wind or weather'll change it. All we know for sure is that *once* the mallards flew low enough over that barley field so's you could shoot your limit. Tomorrow's a new day. It may be roothog or die."

"I've heard it all now."

It was even colder the next morning. A lot of the ducks left to feed earlier. The sun peeked over the hills across the lake without warmth. Hiram stroked our one duck and shook his head. "I don't believe it," he said.

"I do." I was grinning.

Back at the truck, he looked like someone had stuck his head inside a bell and rang it. "I still don't believe it. Now what do you do?"

"This is the root-hog part. We'll go lookin'."

"For what?"

"A concentration of birds feeding out. Try to get a spot where we can shoot incomers and outgoers." Hiram had coined a metaphor the day before: the mallards on the lake were like a bank account... ducks leaving were "withdrawals," ducks returning were "deposits" and as usual, he'd been so pleased with it he'd worn it out and I was refusing to traffic in it anymore.

I didn't really expect to find such a spot. The morning previous, I knew, had been largely luck; I'd seen the big bunches before, but I'd never got in on them as we had. Hiram, on the other hand, did not seem a bit incredulous when we hunted our way into a second such spot.

"Here come some more, Bobby Lee. You take 'em. I only got six shells left."

"I got about ten," I lied. "You better get some more from the truck before you run out."

"Yeh. Somebody's gotta, an' I need 'em the worst," he said, and left at a crouching trot. The truck was a half mile away, beyond a hill. He was soon out of sight. I missed an easy shot and slipped my last shell into my gun. I'd had four. I knew he'd bring *me* a box, too.

It was an even better spot than the day before. There were more ducks, flying lower. Just what I wanted. The new variable, however, was a steady west wind that we guessed at 30 miles per hour. The mallards were coming off a small lake just upwind of us a quarter mile. Our shooting seemed to bother neither the raft on the lake, nor the birds we shot at.

We couldn't hit them. Now and then we'd scratch a green head down, but mostly we missed. In just a few minutes I'd shot up my four shells and had one more drake. I put the gun aside and began picking, while the mallards passed regularly, unbelievably fast with the wind behind them. No chance for a double today. Of the four hours we were there, I'd estimate that we averaged one flock of from twenty to two hundred passing within thirty yards of our hide every four minutes.

Hiram returned, still running in his crouch. We never got used to the plenitude of game; in our crouching we were still *hunting* when there was really no need for it. We ran, crouched, and squatted all afternoon, like there would never be another flock after the one we could always see approaching.

"Why, if it ain't Gunga Din," I said. "Did ya bring me a Coke?"

"Didn't say you wanted one," he answered, handing me two full boxes of shells.

"I always want a Coke. What's *two* boxes for? I'm only allowed five more birds today."

He grinned and missed about seventy-five extra-low mallards. Then he got his notebook out. "What's...two...boxes...for?" he mimicked, laboring over the letters like a first grader. "I'm...only...allowed...five...more...birds...how do ya spell 'today'?"

"Just like it sounds."

"What's two boxes for?" he read happily. "I'm only allowed five more birds today. Terrific. I don't believe you really said that."

"I don't either."

"Where you goin'?"

"Down the line a ways," I said, picking up one of the boxes of shells. "All I hear around here is that 'withdrawal' and 'deposit' crap."

"Good luck, Hawkeye," he said. "Watch this deposit." I squatted and missed. He did not shoot. There were enough birds that we no longer had to shoot at the same flock. We'd been taking turns.

I was back in an hour with two drakes, no shells, and a sore cheek.

"Showin' 'em no mercy, I see," he observed. He had three or four more, himself.

I sat down, silent as a stone, and loaded up out of my last box. Here they came. Crouch, gun up, swing fast, fire, stare. "Sonofabitch."

"You're gonna get the Medal of Honor from the Audubon Society," he speculated.

"Hey, you know what I think?" I'd figured it out, finally.

"What?"

"I was right yesterday."

"About what?"

"Totalling your truck an' killin' ourselves." I missed again, and reloaded. "We're dead, sure as hell, but this ain't heaven. I think we wound up in The Other Place."

"May be," he agreed, and rubbed his chin with his knuckles. "They got duck lice here, too."

I shot my last box of shells down to two lonesome # 5's, one in my barrel and one in my magazine. I needed two ducks. Hiram had his limit. He had shells I could borrow. He couldn't wait.

I let ten flocks pass, watching them. Finally, I brushed the feathers off my sleeves, picked the gun up, shouldered it a couple of times, winced as I cheeked the stock, set back, and waited. Hiram could hardly stand it. I expected him to wet his pants when I missed.

The flock broke over the lakeshore trees and skimmed towards us, using the wind and flying like all the rest, faster than any mallards I'd ever tried to shoot before in my life. I picked my drake and fired coming in, before he was abreast of us, at about thirty-five yards. He tipped forward and tumbled, the flock flared, and without thinking I pumped and was on another one, towering away. It felt right when I shot and I had two on the way down at once, and Hiram amid the feathers with his mouth open.

"How'd you do that?" he breathed. He hadn't made a double all day.

"I told ya, Hiram, I was *born* out here. I *know* these prairie mallards. I can do that *every time*..."

Bwana Walker's Guaranteed Sheep Hunt

Loren Tank had a plan for getting a sheep, he told me in the booth at the all-night eatery in Fairbanks when his partner, owner of their hometown's Phillips 66 station somewhere in Minnesota, left for the restroom with Bwana Walker. I only called Walker that in front of new clients because he didn't like it; it was like running the bases backwards in baseball, he said, you ought not to make a travesty of the game.

Not that unusual – a just-off-the-boat sheep hunter with a plan already. It only meant he'd read one Jack O'Connor story, or perhaps a whole book. Few hunters recognized that O'Connor's stories were in fact carrots to get them to blow their inheritance on a guided sheep hunt, and not blueprints on how to get a sheep.

"Good," I said. "Let's hear it." Loren was probably the most unworldly sheep hunter I'd ever seen, a 35-year-old baker's helper still living at home on the farm with Mom and Dad.

"I have put a lot of thought into it and decided my best chance is to put myself totally in your hands and do exactly whatever you say."

I was almost speechless. "Well, Loren," I said, "you didn't get *that* idea reading between the lines of a Jack O'Connor story." O'Connor was famous, if one could believe his stories, for wresting control of the hunting part of the hunt from the real guide, and letting him tag along and watch the master operate. It gave a lot of less-experienced readers the wrong idea. Estimating distances accurately, for instance, can be a much different kettle of fish in the mountains than on the Minnesota prairie.

"If every hunter I ever took out followed that plan, I'd be 100% on sheep."

"Really?"

"You bet. There's no such thing as a guaranteed sheep in the country we hunt, but that plan will pretty near guarantee you at least a good shot at one. Seriously." This guy, I thought to myself, is starting out like the best hunter ever. As usual, I was right.

Bwana Walker and Randy Randall returned from the men's room in an expansive mood. "And as I was saying," Walker said grandiloquently, sliding his bony rump onto the Naugahyde booth seat beside me and looking around in vain for his cheeseburger basket, "the hunt comes with an absolute guarantee."

"We're guaranteed our sheep?" Randall said incredulously.

"Oh no," Walker said, "you're guaranteed that when you see Fairbanks the next time, you'll have a great appetite and your feet'll be clean."

Which meant we'd spend the last two days of the hunt wading down the creek in the Brooks Range we'd spent the first two days wading up. All Walker's clients were instructed to bring tennis shoes for these four amphibious days, which he wore himself. I wore jungle boots from Vietnam, which had a harder vibram-type sole to protect from punji sticks. If I came out under a packful of meat, I felt every rock in the creek bed through my Converse All-Stars, the one and only time I wore them.

Bwana Walker's very brief tenure in the armed services never afforded him the opportunity to conduct that type of inspection which we in the Marines aptly termed "junk-on-the-bunk." So he did one back at the motel on every poor hunter we ever took out. It was his favorite part of hunting. Especially when he got to do his Katharine Hepburn *African Queen* impression and pour Randy Randall's Old Grand-dad down the toilet, with the stock admonishment, "Ya wanted to drink, ya coulda stayed home." Loren liked that part pretty well himself, probably having seen his partner in his cups a time or two.

In five minutes, the pile of clothes and other "contraband" Walker had flung into the corner of the room was larger than the pile left on Randall's bed. Other than the dozen pair of clean socks, all the spare clothing got vetoed. "Ain't any honky-tonks out there to dress up and go to."

Loren's niggardly pile of belongings was a big disappointment.

"This is *it?*" Walker exclaimed.

"Well, you sent us that list of what we should bring."

"Yeh, but nobody ever... what's this? *Brand new* backpack and camera?"

"My old ones weren't the kind you recommended. So I bought new."

Walker was stunned, idly working the new zipper pulls on the pack and twisting the focus ring on the 35mm lens. "Loren," he finally said, "if it turns out there's only one legal ram left in the whole Brooks Range when we get there, you get it. I'll sit on Randy here while you shoot it. That's a promise."

The plane ride in was a tad bumpy, but Walker assured everyone he had a surefire cure for airsickness. We no sooner had our feet on the ground than he had our packs on us and led us diagonally upstream across a larger river than our clients had ever fished in. "A little good cold river water running through the cracks of your asses and you'll forget that plane ride before you know it." We did, too.

After that, it was in the creek, out of the creek, in the creek, out of the creek. We stopped three times the first mile for Loren to get his new camera out and snap our picture at midstream. His concern for slowing us down caused him, finally, to just leave it out, dangling vulnerably from his neck. Which looked a little unwise to me, but one of the hardest parts of guiding is not sounding like some grown man's nursemaid, so I held my tongue. My first mistake of the trip, other than working for Bwana at all. The camera lasted about a half hour before a slick underwater rock brought Loren to his hands and knees in two feet of water and the camera to its at least temporary end. I felt as bad as he did.

"Loren," I said as he packed it away for the last time, "you did the right thing – you kept your rifle scope out of the creek. You don't need a dern camera to kill a sheep. I've hauled mine up and down this damn creek a dozen times to make sure we'd have pictures, so any time you need a camera, use mine. That's why I pack a rifle. I ain't shooting any sheep out here. It's for you if you booger your own."

Walker had it in his head that our best chance was to walk right through our usual best country on Day Two and camp on the near edge of that part of his area we termed "Outer Slobbovia," after a country in the Li'l Abner comic strip. Which meant putting the creek and lake behind us, those two spots where, after the sheep meat was hung in game bags in the willows, I could unlimber my fifteen feet of 6 lb. test monofilament and Woolly Worm, fastened to any available stick, and catch modest-sized grayling for my skillet. That was always my favorite part of the hunt, signalling as it did that the pressure was off and every step between me and the airstrip was downhill.

The weather was mild to the point of being what I'd call hot, which meant all day in my T-shirt. As soon as we stopped the second evening to camp, Loren got out his down jacket and put it on. Not a hot day in Minnesota.

"You know," he said, "I ordered this jacket out of the Cabela's catalog for this trip, but it's almost too nice to hunt in. I think, if I can keep it clean up here, I'll wear it for good when I get home. My mom says it's the nicest jacket I've ever had."

I set up my rinky-dink sheep-hunting tripod after the tent was pitched, mounted my good Redfield spotting scope and had a look around. Lambs and ewes. There was dead willow aplenty nearby for a cookfire, which we always used when the opportunity arose. The two one-burner gas stoves were our fallback heat source if the weather turned bad and the wood stayed wet. Two of our three daily meals depended on boiling water – instant oatmeal for breakfast and freeze-dried entrées for supper: Turkey Tetrazzini, Chicken à la King, and Chili Mac. We packed ten of these apiece, one per day. Walker's one and only extravagance was ignoring the instructions ("Provides two servings") and let everyone eat a whole one.

Randy Randall, the oldest of us at forty and barely under Walker's "No sheep hunters over forty" ceiling, was holding up well, though puzzled.

"I can't figure out," he said, unlacing his boots outside Walker's tent, which was ten feet from mine, "why last night, on that rock pile, I slept twice as good as at home on my waterbed."

"Sound sleep," pontificated Walker, "comes only to those pure in thought and deed. It's why Hewitt always looks so tired."

Next morning, after coffee, oatmeal and more coffee, we made our first climb, spending an hour and a half getting to the top of Forty-five Minute Ridge. Walker was taking it easy on Randy. Halfway up I was down to my T-shirt again.

In the saddle atop the ridge, Walker was champing at the bit to get on over the hump and inspect the precipices and meadows of Outer Slobbovia. The trouble with shooting a sheep there was, you had to pack the meat *up* hill before starting back *down* to camp. I preferred to exhaust other alternatives first, and set up the scope again, aimed down the valley we'd walked through the day previous.

"Well, well, well," I said, almost immediately. "Here's an old boy nobody's going to mistake for the Chadwick Ram, but he's either full curl or a little over, not broomed, and very nice bases. All alone."

Loren looked, then Walker.

"Now, where'd he come from?" Walker asked. "If he'd been right there yesterday we'd have had ribs for supper instead of Tetrazzini. What do you think, Loren?"

"He just looks huge to me. If I were close enough and you were sure he was okay, legal, I mean, I'd shoot him in a minute."

"If you pass him up, there's maybe a 50 percent chance we'll locate something bigger for you, with six days to look. But there's also a 10 percent chance that, if nothing bigger comes along, we won't find another this big before we have to haul out of here. It's your call."

"What would you two do if it was you?" Loren wanted to know.

"I'd wait," Walker said. "There's a couple of bigger ones in here if we could only find 'em."

"I'd shoot him and eat sheep meat while the less fortunate

scramble around these ridges looking for another one. I know where there's some fish not too far from where he's standing, and I got what it takes to catch them in my pack."

"Okay. You guys have no idea what it'd be like for us, going home without sheep. The whole *town* knows we're up here. So let's John and I try a stalk, and if we goof it up, there's always five other days to find him again and start over."

And the die was cast. I picked our stalk route after he lay down, halfway down to the lake from the mountaintop he must've come over. On the good side, we would be in defilade the whole time, screened from him by intervening terrain features, and could make a gentlemen's stalk (standing up) to within 250 yards, *and* approach from above, always preferred.

On the bad side, while he wouldn't see us the whole time, neither would we see him, and thus have no warning when or if he moved. If we finished our stalk, peeked over, and he was gone, we'd have to ad lib something, unless he'd moved uphill, seen us and left the country.

"We got a fighting chance here, Loren," I said, "but we better keep our fingers crossed all the way across this valley and up the hill behind him. We'll have to play the wind by ear once we're over there. This'll take at least three hours. It's going to be one of those deals where it's better to be lucky than good. One horsefly nail him between now and lunch and we've had the biscuit."

"I just can't believe we found such a nice one, so soon."

Walker and Randall disappeared into Slobbovia while we traversed the valley floor, and with them any chance of a warning should our sheep move. Then, once on the sheep's mountain, things tended to start looking all the same, and Loren got justifiably nervous over where the sheep was, in relation to us.

"This," I whispered to him, finally, "is where being good is good enough. You see that white rock in the water, sticking up fifty feet out from our shore? He's right exactly straight up from that, unless he's moved. And you see this sheep trail we just crossed, that goes back around the mountain as far as you can see? He's about three hundred yards below it. So, we're going to very quietly ease down to that gray knob yonder and peek over, and there he ought to be."

And he was, still sound asleep. I got into my pack and took out my own down vest, rolled up in a wool shirt, and slid it onto the top of the knob for a rifle rest. Then I pointed to my wrist watch face, to the number five minutes ahead of the minute hand, a conservative settling-down period, and mouthed the words, "Check your barrel." He did and it was clear. I checked my own scope and the round I always carry in the chamber. If he missed by a lot with his first shot, I'd already explained, he'd get my rifle with the safety off for his second shot. The ram would be confused and run, if at all, uphill, which would put him closer.

But Loren was a regular trap shooter at home in Minnesota, and I have run into few trap shooters who are not also pretty fair rifle shots. The smart money was on sheep for supper.

"Any time," I finally whispered, and he slid the barrel and forend onto the jacket, raised his head just far enough to spy the sleeping ram, shook his head slightly in disbelief that he was really still there, licked his lips once, settled in behind the scope and nudged his safety off with his right thumb.

The report was incredibly loud, or seemed so after two and a half days of nothing louder than water running over rocks. I half stood to observe the sheep. His legs were still folded beneath him. Even to the naked eye, the red patch high behind his near front shoulder grew. Loren stayed behind the scope a long time. He'd chambered a new round immediately, and his finger was still on the trigger. Finally, he drew the bolt back, shoved the live round back down into the magazine, and closed the bolt on the empty chamber.

When he rolled over to face me, his lower lip was in a full quiver, and tears were rolling down both cheeks. He tried to grin but wasn't able to manage it and dragged his index finger across his nose.

"I, uh, don't guess you ever seen anyone cry before that just shot their sheep." I was looking at the ram through my binoculars. The bases were even better than I'd thought.

"Actually, no. But when he got his Stone sheep down in B.C., I heard from his wife that Walker did."

John Hewitt

Bobwhites, Doctors, and Hunts Remembered

Uncle Joe and Clyde were walking quite close together. They'd seen the covey put down, and the safest way for both of them to flush the birds was to walk straight in. It was in the hardwoods along the creek behind Joe's barn, reasonably open, and someone was going to get a shot.

Since it was the year before I got my own shotgun, I'd have been nine. My job was the same as my twin's: stay to one side of the hunters, walk the thickets while they walk the edges, mark down dead birds, and be still. We had no dog.

Joe was my best uncle, the oldest of thirteen children on my mother's side. He was the only uncle I had who hunted – it had been behind his barn on a previous farm in another state that Clyde had brought down his first pheasant.

I remember his gun. It was an ancient autoloader of the old hump-backed Browning design, devoid of bluing from use, but true and dependable as Clyde's pump. At some point, the stock had been broken off, and refastened at the pistol grip with copper wire and friction tape. Both guns were choked full, products (like their owners) of a duck-hunting era revelling in the novelty of choke-boring of any kind.

The flush remains in my mind in all the minute detail of an Audubon print; I was watching the two hunters closely. In later years, after I had a shotgun of my own and focused on the birds themselves, I'd never again pay such close attention to the other hunters at the moment of the flush.

This time, we'd walked just past the birds before they went, behind us and a little to Uncle Joe's side. It was his shot. They broke back the way we'd come, scattering among the open woods, presenting the sort of shot that quail hunters hope for and grouse hunters never get.

Joe spun, and the old wired-together Browning leapt partway to his shoulder, even as he dropped to one knee.

"Take 'em, Clyde!" he said.

If you'd known him, you'd know how basic the impulse to give up the shot was in his makeup. If you didn't, you might reason that he'd given up the shot because he could hunt quail any day he pleased, while Clyde had only a few weekends a year to devote to them. But he'd have done the same thing for whoever he was with… any of his sons, who had more opportunity than he to hunt, or a neighbor, or whatever friend shared the day. It was a kind of humility or generosity that went deeper than explanation, to somewhere beyond what another might call sportsmanship. Uncle Joe was a gentleman by instinct.

Dad's reflex, already begun, carried through as his own recoil pad touched his shoulder. His barrel swung with a bird on my side. It was good, clean shooting, two shots and two dead birds, one for Tom and one for me to bring back to the two men. Clyde pushed fresh loads into the magazine of his Winchester, and Joe, still on one knee, grinned and complimented him on his shooting, puzzling aloud at how four of us had walked through so nice a covey.

Joe eventually sold the farm and moved to town, to a place he could nearly pay taxes on, nearer his children and grandchildren and the doctors he and his wife would one day need.

Clyde and I, Mary and Mom stopped in to see him and Aunt Goldie, en route across the state to our pheasant hunt some years ago. He'd suffered a stroke, and was in the hospital. Goldie had told Mom on the telephone that he'd only recently come out of his coma, and, though he was conscious, had lost the power of speech. Neither she, nor their kids nor the doctors knew how much, if anything, he remembered. There had been no communication since the stroke, no sign that he knew who or where he was, or what had happened, or who his wife and children were. His only activity thus far with the good side of his body had been an attempt to pull out the catheter and intravenous feeding tubes. I didn't look forward to seeing him like that.

In the hospital parking lot, Clyde opened the back of the truck and rummaged in his duffel bag. Finally, he unearthed his old Jones-style hunting cap and older canvas shell vest, and put them on. Mom regarded him quizzically, and led us inside.

There were other relatives in the hall outside his room, sons of his I couldn't remember, middle-aged now, and their wives, in church clothes. Mom hadn't seen some of them for years, and fell on them with all the enthusiasm her side of the family reserves for such reunions.

A nurse showed us in, and we all looked at Uncle Joe, spectral and white-haired on his tilted bed. The relatives talked about him and his progress, or lack of it, through the last week. I wondered if he could hear them, or understand, and if it embarrassed him as it would have me. It was impossible to tell. He lay still, and looked at his guests only occasionally. The old animation was gone from his face, the spark gone from his eye, and he seemed among strangers.

Eventually, the room emptied. Mom said we should go, so he could rest. He was staring at his hands, folded in his lap, and looked worn out. Clyde, who had stayed behind near the door, himself only a few years younger than Joe, stepped to the bed, took the one good hand in his own, and shook it.

Uncle Joe's eyes lifted, up Clyde's arm, and fell on the ratty old vest with its canvas shell loops. There were two shells there, left over from the year before. He looked Clyde in the eye, then. Clyde grinned, winked, squeezed his hand and laid it back in his lap.

Slowly, the good hand raised back off the sheet, the old fingers curled around the wired-together stock of the shotgun he'd given to one of his boys twenty years before, and his high cheekbone canted on to the comb. His trigger finger tightened on the trigger, the barest ghost of a smile flickered at the corners of his mouth, and his eyes filled with tears.

"He remembers," Mom whispered.

Outside, walking toward the truck, Mary, who had never known Joe in better times, broke the silence.

"I'll bet he was a fine man to hunt with."

"As good as there was," Clyde said. "As good as there was."

Walker Among the Musk Ox

Alaskans do not choose their careers rationally, the way junior high school counselors would like. Rather, we begin by embracing the most exciting and unrealistic options, often in rapid succession, and fail magnificently at each. Our first marriages are often casualties of these intemperate career choices. Finally, we settle into occupations so unattractive it is impossible to fail, because no one else can be found to do the work. Such as hanging sheet rock or taking photographs of wild animals. Walker is a prime example.

Walker got a head start by failing at a couple of things before he even thought of coming to Alaska. Here, as John McPhee said of the southerner with a dozen derelict automobiles and an oak tree in his yard, and a V-8 engine hanging from one oak limb, dripping oil onto the dirt, was an Alaskan who just hadn't left for the North yet.

First, there was baseball. His father, according to the Walker family myth, could've played in the big leagues if he hadn't had to go to work with *his* father, as a plasterer in the old lath-and-plaster days. Walker's timing was very poor; he tried to break in a year or two before batting helmets became common. In the process of showing everyone *he* wouldn't be moved off the plate by inside pitching, he took one for the team. In the left temple. When he woke up some days later, he discovered he needed lenses as thick as coke bottles to get anything into focus.

Which narrowed his options a little. The obvious next choice was bull riding. He enjoyed some success in *that* uncrowded vocation for a summer or maybe two, until his neck got used for a landing gear once too often, and lost its elasticity.

The draft got him next, and the neck which wouldn't bend like everyone else's provided him with the military bearing necessary to promotion there. But he gave that up after one tour for the more exciting fields of marriage and taxidermy. The Army got him to Alaska, though.

Since wives rarely throw their unsatisfactory husbands twenty feet into the air, to land on their heads, he had a harder time determining he wasn't making a go of marriage either, but something wasn't working out so he gave up taxidermy for guiding.

Guiding, to those who have never tried it, may seem the ultimate in excitement and adventure. In fact, it was so much more miserable than anything else Walker had tried that he had to hire someone to share the misery. Namely, me.

If he had chosen someone normal for a partner, the guiding enterprise would've folded in one season. But I had once been a Marine. That is, the worse it got, the better I liked it. If we finished the season broke but still alive, I thought it a huge success.

The guiding and marriage both unraveled about the same time, leaving him with one skill, of no value except in possible future courtship rituals: the ability to sneak up close to large, sometimes dangerous animals without getting attacked. So he turned to photography.

That was close to twenty years ago, before everybody and his brother had a drawerful of musk ox transparencies, so Walker determined that fame and fortune lay in the form of fifty-eight musk oxen known to reside in the Arctic National Wildlife Refuge.

How I figured into this folly was, he needed to travel light. One luxury we both insist on in grizzly country is a pump shotgun. So he took me along to carry the shotgun, plus, my pack being otherwise empty, the tent, stove fuel, cooking utensils, all the food and a subsistence kit. The subsistence kit consisted of ten Winchester AA Heavy Handicap #7 ½ trap loads (for ptarmigan in case we faced actual starvation) (I lobbied for their use from the second day onward but was vetoed...) and an Orvis four-piece pack rod I had recently bought for Mary. And a few flies.

The bush pilot deposited us, one at a time, beside a river about as roily as the Mississippi at Vicksburg, and in my spare moments I wet a line. Two weeks later, I still had not unpacked my skillet. Walker embarks on these death marches as skinny as the rodeo cowboy he formerly was, and after two weeks of freeze-dried rations, his belt buckle clanks on his backbone when he walks.

Then it snowed. By itself, the July 1st snow wouldn't have been so bad, but the wind blew a hundred miles an hour and Walker decided we should take a day off. In thirty-six hours in my two-man tent with him, I only went outside three times: twice to pee, and once to drive the shotgun barrel into the tundra when the stakes started pulling out. Guying the tent to the barrel took the pressure off the stakes, I explained. Grizzlies wouldn't be out in such weather, anyway.

Walker was not amused. The shotgun was mostly mine, but we'd put his barrel on it in Fairbanks, as his was eight inches shorter than either of mine, and eight inches of 12-gauge barrel weighs as much as three Snickers bars.

"Hell's bells," I said, "it doesn't have any choke in it anyhow. What could it hurt?"

"Here," he said, handing me two pages torn out of a paperback copy of *Lady Chatterley's Lover*, "you got behind while you were out there." I slid back into my sleeping bag, read a page and stacked it carefully in the corner.

"According to this book," I said, "it's no wonder our marriages fizzled out. We were approaching our wives from the wrong direction."

"I don't think this was supposed to be a 'how-to' book," Tom said. "How come you're saving those pages after you read them?" He tore another page out and handed it to me.

"Well, if we ever meet those two Fish & Wildlife girls you claim are wandering around up here, I thought a small gift, such as a book of high literary merit, might be in order."

"Hewitt," he said, "subtle you are not. If this storm doesn't blow us clear to Hudson's Bay, I think we'll head for the coast and set up camp on that little clearwater stream you've been whining about. I need to check out the barrier islands for snowy owls, and you'll be close enough to the girls' base camp to set up an ambush and get us invited to dinner. The pilot overflew them on the way in and they got a pile of food the size of your cabin under a blue tarp, unless the bears got to it."

"Why would they *possibly* want *us* for company? We ain't had a bath for two weeks."

"When I talked to them last winter, they said there's grayling the size of pumpernickel loaves in that creek, but they can't catch 'em. All you have to do is offer to catch a mess and fry them for anyone and we're in like Flynn. They'll volunteer to cook everything else."

"Easy for you to say."

"You're the fisherman. You said so yourself."

Once in awhile, God gets bored or inattentive, and things come off practically as planned. Or so I was thinking several days later as I scaled the last of the eleven grayling which had fallen to a #8 McGinty older than I was, fished deep. Marcia and Martha had been so keen to act immediately on my suggestion of a grayling dinner that I suspected some kind of trap, but when they mentioned the possibility of individual loaves of fresh cornbread, canned peas and homemade cheesecake, I decided there were worse things than being trapped.

A little before suppertime we raised the wall tent and blue tarp over the tundra horizon. Our pace picked up noticeably. The pile of food under the tarp, while not the size of my cabin, was still larger than the wall tent.

"Walker," I inquired, "does all of a sudden your feet feel like you've got wings on 'em?"

"You've been carrying that hundred-pound Kelty too long," he said. "It always feels like this when you take your pack off."

Soon I was sitting cross-legged on the floor of the wall tent, attending to four grayling sputtering in the girls' skillet, which was bigger than ours.

"So," Walker said for openers, "you girls have a gun with you?" My trusty 870 was standing in the corner, keeping us all from harm with four one-ounce slugs in its plugless magazine.

"Well, you know," Martha replied, "there was a lot of talk among the other field techs on that topic when we first came out three years ago." Martha seemed to be the leader. "And the men insisted we bring a rifle. Want to see it?"

"Sure," Walker said. Both girls burrowed into one corner of the cluttered tent like parka squirrels and exhumed a cheap soft gun case from beneath an assortment of duffels and other paraphernalia. They took the rifle out and handed it to me. I laid down my cooking fork, accepted the rifle and automatically opened the bolt. What I saw gave me goose bumps.

"It's...it's empty!"

"Well, sure," Martha said. The girls glanced at each other and, a little nervously, at my shotgun. "You mean...yours is loaded?"

"Say," Walker said, "if it's not too much trouble, slide those four fish onto this plate. I'm a little hungry."

After we'd all eaten one grayling apiece, some peas and cornbread, and I'd divided the next four grayling two ways as the girls had had enough, he couldn't stand it anymore and asked.

"Uh, where do you guys keep the ammunition for the rifle?" We'd put the rifle itself away.

"Oh, out under the tarp with the food. Say, are you okay? Did you get a bone in your throat?" Walker was having a coughing fit. He took a large swig of coffee and attempted without success to compose himself.

"You mean," he said, "if a bear comes around and gets into your food cache you've got to run clear out yonder in your pajamas and ask him to move so you can get some cartridges out from under the bacon to shoot him with?"

"In a nutshell," Martha said. "But it's okay. They showed us how to load the rifle."

"Oh, well then," Walker said politely, "no problem, I guess."

"Besides," Marcia reassured us, "there aren't any bears. This is our third summer and none has ever come around."

The grayling were huge, I was stuffed, and there were three more in the skillet. I took one and Walker took one. Then, he deftly lifted half the meat off the last one, leaving me with the other half, plus the bones.

"Aren't you guys going to eat your cornbread?" he asked. The girls had only eaten half of one loaf.

"We're full," they said.

"You, uh, mind if we clean it up?" he asked.

"Not at all," Martha replied.

I'd forgotten the cheesecake entirely. Walker had not. When the last shred of grayling disappeared into his mouth and he dabbed at the grease in his beard with his bandana, he looked around expectantly.

"Oh, the cheesecake," Martha remembered, and they retrieved it from behind the tent. There were cherries all over the top. "We're too full, you two go ahead and finish it off," she added.

Walker divided it precisely in half. I knew I could get my half down, but keeping it down was feeling iffy. Walker studied his half carefully and began like he hadn't eaten for a week.

The tent had no furniture, so when I finished the cheesecake I groaned softly and stretched out on my back beside the cookstove like a dead bull too long in the sun in a Kansas pasture. This, I was thinking, must be what a boa constrictor feels like after it swallows a pig.

"What's in the pot on the stove?" Walker asked, reached over me and picked it up. It was the juice the peas had been canned in.

"Pea juice!" he exclaimed. "Split it with you." He poured half in my canteen cup and guzzled his half right out of the pot. I sipped mine until it was gone and wondered if anyone would be hurt when I exploded.

"Think I'll go for a little walk," Walker said, pushing himself to his feet.

"Us, too," the girls said, and they set off in different directions. I went to sleep. No bear arrived to slay the fatted calf.

After we'd said our thank-yous and bestowed D.H. Lawrence's once-controversial novel on our hostesses, tied back together with a broken bootlace, I shouldered the shotgun and we strode manfully off, still in considerable distress.

"Matter of time," Walker finally said.

"Before what?"

"Before a bear gets them or their groceries. I seen one only a mile over the hill this morning. Matter of time, mark my words."

"Actually, all this has left me feeling a lot like John Wayne. I'm the one who has to carry this cannon," I said. "I hope you're wrong. I kind of like those two. Even if they did try to kill us with all that food."

"What a way to go," Walker said, cheerfully.

Although the Super Cub scheduled to pick us up a week hence pancaked in, one stop before our tundra strip, we survived three extra days on a diet of straight grayling and backhauled to Deadhorse and Fairbanks uneventfully. Three weeks later I got a postcard from Walker, on which he had penned, "I told you so." He must have been referring to the mother that a grizzly got, hiking gunless with her husband and two kids in the valley we'd vacated. Marcia and Martha finished their third and last summer cataloging what and how much the musk ox were eating, and never had a moment's difficulty that I heard of, unless I got the pages of the book out of order when I tied it up.

Stanley Goes with the Flow

I wasn't thinking so much about fishing as about the logjam still ahead of me and how I'd need a few more rocks in front of the bow seat to get me over the narrow riffle there, when the deep hole appeared beneath the canoe. I throttled the outboard back, and eased to the inside of the bend. Plenty of rocks right there – I could kill two birds with one stone.

There were no footprints on the sand part of the bar where I strung up my fly rod and tied on a size 12 Mosquito, which was the advantage of being 130-odd miles from where I'd left the car. It sat at the end of the road beside a dead slough four days, a dozen pike fillets and innumerable fried grayling behind me. The only disadvantage was that, in the event I committed any one of a host of everyday errors, I had no one to turn to for help.

Bears were also a consideration. But they were never anything a 12 gauge pump with seven slugs, such as the one tied to the thwart nearest the stern of the canoe, couldn't handle. In theory, when questioned, as one frequently is, as to whether I'm "scared" of bears on such trips, my honest answer has always been, "Scared? When I'm the one with the gun?"

And yet. Stanley was supposed to have had his .338 along when the bear got him the year before, below the logjam. I had heard four versions of the story, trusting only Russ's, which was the least melodramatic. Russ was always fastidiously accurate in recounting such incidents. Most people, for reasons of their own, try to make bear encounters sound worse than they are. Russ figured that since other people draw conclusions and base specific future actions of their own on these stories, you owe it to everyone not to stray from the facts. That had been part of Stanley's problem, Russ claimed; he'd had a lot of advice on bear behavior, some good, some not so good, and in the process of finding out which was which, he got chomped.

"When you see Stanley," Russ had insisted the day before, "don't forget to mention how grizzlies can't climb trees."

There was a leaning spruce, not right at the edge but set back a few feet from the edge of the high cutbank opposite the canoe, and the deepest part of the pool lay under it. In the time it took me to set up the rod, the waves from the wake had lain down and the rises I'd seen from the moving canoe had started again. One of the Arctic grayling's nicest character traits is its willingness to forgive the less-than- stealthy approach.

It was early enough in the summer, May, that salmon were not in the river yet, nor salmon eggs. But late enough that some hatches were occurring, and at least a few grayling were watching their respective one square foot of surface for passing entrées. Judging from the stomach contents of the bottom-feeding grayling I've cleaned, that form of foraging must be the underwater equivalent of rooting through urban grocery store dumpsters for spoiled fruit or outdated dairy products. Not that mosquitoes are that appetizing, but grasshoppers aren't bad.

There was a take on my first good float, and in half an hour I had the four keepers I wanted on a stringer; a half-dozen smaller ones were probably back at some other feeding station. In Alaska, the notion that catching grayling on flies, at least during a decent hatch, is more sporting than other methods is laughed at; the *last* guy you want to see on your favorite grayling water is a guy with a fly rod and no respect for the limit.

After soaking a gunnysack, I whacked each fish, wrapped the sack around them, and stowed them under the front seat. The rod, broken down, went back in its tube, the vagaries of wilderness river travel being what they are, and I got my old De-Liar out, with its built-in tape measure. The day-old grizzly track in the sand beside the canoe, at seven inches, was wider than my smallest released grayling had been long.

Ice going out, or something, had gouged out a deeper channel past the logjam, and the prop on the 15-horse never bumped bottom.

You never expected to sneak up on Stanley; he'd hear an outboard coming, or his dogs would, an hour before his cabin hove into view as you rounded the last bend downstream. He'd be standing out on the edge of the bank, shading his eyes, watching.

But Stanley had had an unusually good marten catch, and had been seduced by a rototiller catalog. Helen saw me coming, though, and met me at water's edge.

"Godfrey," I said after I killed the outboard and stepped out into the clear, shallow water, "So much for the silence of the North…"

Helen, small, trim, dark hair pulled tightly back into a single braid, and not as heavily Boston-accented as Stanley, laughed as she made the bow line fast to a drift log root, and nodded at the racket emanating from beyond the dead slough behind the cabin.

"Stanley," she said, "is into agriculture. Two acres' worth."

"Good," I said, fishing two large cans of Elberta freestone peaches, ragged chunks in heavy syrup, out of my grub box. "Let's hide one can of these and let him catch us finishing the other one without saving him any. There hasn't been anything to talk about on the river since the nurse jilted Tom Fogg." Stanley loved canned peaches, but didn't have the surplus cash to buy any of his own.

Eventually the rototiller engine died and Stanley appeared at the cabin door, his ponytail half undone, and unslung his rifle. He blinked several times in the dim interior before recognizing me as I spooned the last peach chunk into my mouth.

"Oh, hi, John," he said, "I thought you were Russ."

Helen, struggling to keep a straight face, peered into the empty can like she was looking down an empty well, and said, "Gee, Stanley… John brought some really good peaches but they're all gone. You want the juice?"

"No, no," he replied, without rancor, "you guys go ahead. Wow. You think next week is too late to still plant potatoes, John?"

"In a perfect world, Stanley, you'd have had 'em in last week like everyone else, but they'll still make it if you don't get 'em in even till June 10; they'll just be smaller." I didn't mention that, while my two rows of Kennebecs had been in the ground two weeks, I'd got them there with Ron Rau's father's discarded 20-year-old front-tine Montgomery Ward tiller, or that Stanley's purchase of an 8 h.p. Troybilt, the Purdey of rototillers, had pretty much upstaged me forever. My share of the money Russ and Mary and I'd made trapping full-time two other winters wouldn't have bought Stanley's Troybilt. Inexplicably to me, life had dealt Stanley the tiller I was supposed to get, and I'd gotten his.

But his rifle demanded examination. Not for the long tooth gouge in the buttstock, or the piece bitten clear out of the heel, but for the magazine. It looked, if not like an M-14, then at least like a Mosin-Nagant or Mannlicher-Carcano, or maybe a Lee-Enfield.

"Say," I said, picking it up, "*nice* magazine. How many's it hold?"

"Six," Stanley said.

"Make it yourself?" This was a rhetorical question. The soldered seams, the rivets homemade from sawed-off, rusty nails, the multitude of tiny ballpeen hammer dents, all spoke of Stanley's particular mix of bush ingenuity, resourcefulness, and stubbornness. Helen kept me up-to-date on the latter. I opened the bolt, ejecting the round in the chamber, and cycled the other six through. With my index finger, I depressed the follower as far as I could and released it. It sprang back without binding.

"Well, yeh," Stanley answered. "Everyone said they'd never heard of anyone making a seven-shot Model 70." 'Everyone' meant Russ Wood and Tom Fogg and, maybe, Bill Fliris.

"What's it made out of?"

"Two springs riveted together, the old follower, and metal from an army 30-caliber ammunition box. I made the first two out of barrel metal, oil barrels, but I never got them to work right. You know, work *every* time. They worked most of the time, but now and then they'd jam."

"This one works?"

"So far."

"But, Stanley, the four rounds *my* .338 holds has been three more than enough, up to now. From now on you're just going to spray this thing like a fire hose?"

He laughed. "Whatever it takes. Russ told you about me and the bear?"

"Sort of."

"Well, there were really three."

"Ah."

"And they were 400 yards downstream when I first spotted them. Those two-year-old cubs are hard to tell from Mama at that distance, particularly if she sees you the instant you see her, and here she comes."

"Dang."

"That's what I thought. My old magazine spring had rusted through and broke in half the last time I cleaned it, and I could load four, but after the first shot you had to turn it upside down to make it feed. Except then sometimes they all fell out on the ground. So actually shooting a bear that had me in her sights was not real high on my list of options."

"So up a tree you went."

"Uh-huh. You know that big spruce that leans out from the north bank over the deep hole about eight miles down?"

"Yeah… in fact, I just caught some grayling under it."

"Well, I was standing right beside it, and started up. Still had the pack frame on. Rifle in my right hand. I heard her huffing —you know that sound they make, running, every time their front feet come own — and *just* glanced down when she jumped up. So I poked the buttstock at her and she bit down on it and gave a big yank and fell out of the tree, rifle and all."

"How high were you?"

"Maybe ten feet."

"And you climbed higher?"

"I meant to. When she first bolted for me I kind of thought, 'Oh shit,' but at the same time I was also thinking, 'Hey, no problem.' I mean, I had a lot of time. Probably ought've gave her one at

50 yards, and had time to reload by hand if I had to. But what if it's only a bluff charge? And what about the other two? For all I knew they were right behind the first one. One would've been okay, but who wants a gang fight with three grizzlies when you're carrying a single-shot? Or I could've got 'way up the tree if I'd dropped the gun and climbed with both hands. I thought, 'Oh shit' again when she grabbed the rifle, but it was more like, "OH SHIT!!!"

Helen had set a cup of tea – Lipton's tea; she hoarded store-bought tea for company, and brewed horrible combinations of roots and spruce needles and tree bark the rest of the time – in front of Stanley as he picked up the peach can and sniffed the juice left in it, and read the fine print on the label.

"So you didn't climb higher?"

"Maybe an inch. She was back up there in the tree like she was on a pogo stick. You know how these guys write that you can buy time by giving bears something else to chew on? This bear never read any of that stuff. I was just reaching for the next limb when she grabbed me by the knee."

"And your life flashed before your eyes on the way down?"

"No... the bite must've hurt so much it blacked me out. I think I only hit about half on the bank and she must've relaxed her jaws when *she* hit. The cold water woke me up. My feet couldn't reach bottom, but I stuck my head up and could hear her up there on the bank ripping into my pack, so I just let the current take me."

"Stanley goes with the flow," Helen said, laughing.

"My wife the comedian," Stanley said.

"One of these days, Alice..." I said, "to the moon."

"Oh sure," she said, "pick on the girl. So Stanley hobbles the last two miles across the tundra..."

"I stayed a lo-o-o-o-o-ong way from that river."

"And everyone below the forks goes into a big panic to get him to the clinic in Russ's canoe like yours," Helen said. "You know who they send back upriver to break the bad news to poor Helen?" She was really laughing now. This was her favorite part of the story.

"Let me guess. Jack."

"Right. And Jack of course gave up partway and camped overnight, two hours after Stanley should've been home – it's only 10 miles – I *knew* what'd happened, so I took the .303 and went downstream expecting to find a bloody arm sticking out from under every bush. It got dark so I came back. What a night."

"Next day Jack shows up across the river, and you know what he says?"

"No."

"He said, 'Hey, Helen, we had a poker game and Stanley lost. I won you.' And then he came across and told me what really happened, and five days later, Stanley's back home."

"Victor Carol gave me this canvas 13-footer with an old 5-horse motor and it took me *18* gallons of gas to get home. But I built a lift for the motor and a steering extension on the motor handle I use standing in the middle of the boat, and *now* it trims up okay. Come on out and I'll show you. Helen, do we have any canned moose left for John for supper?"

"Sure," Helen said.

Stanley skimmed up and down the big hole in front of his cabin like a surfer, standing up and steering more by leaning than by manipulating the willow lashed to the outboard tiller.

"With this we can go down to the bluffs and home in half a day, unless the water comes up," he said, stepping out of it, limping just noticeably on the bad knee.

Supper was superb, although I wished I'd brought a head of let-

Stanley Goes with the Flow

Helen and Stan Zuray, 1978

tuce and some store tomatoes for Helen. The plywood for the cabin floor, which Stanley had somehow freighted in with his dog team, had left her not wanting for anything, she said, unless they had another good marten year and she could afford a motorized washing machine.

When it was time to leave, I remembered. "Oh, Stanley," I said, squeezing the fuel line pump bulb near my gas tank, "remember: Grizzlies can't climb trees."

Stanley grinned. "Russ told you to tell me, didn't he?"

"How'd you guess?"

"Tell Russ I said at least I'm not cutting myself up like a pizza to make it easier for the bears," Stanley said, referring to Russ's recent chainsaw accident.

"Okay," I said, yanking my outboard's starter cord. "He'll be glad to hear you're taking care of yourself. 'Bye, Helen."

The Dharma Goose

"Now what're we going to do?" Clyde's Depression-era pessimism was still intact, forty years after. The canoe was loaded, the shotguns stowed in their soft cases, the Bronco parked and Mary and Jessie hunkered on the center seat. Only a few miles of perfectly flat water separated us from duck camp.

"Well, first I'll get in, then you push us out and you get in. Then I start the motor and an hour from now we'll be in camp, cooking supper... if the motor starts. What's for supper, Mary?"

"All you brought besides bacon and eggs is hot dogs," Mary said.

"I can eat about four. So that's the plan."

"But it's as dark as the pit out there," Clyde observed. "I can't see my hand in front of my face. And there isn't one straight stretch in ten miles."

"Remember, we've run this piece of river a few times before. Besides, it's no darker than some of the nights you and Ted Zercher ran limb lines and trotlines on the Wakarusa, paddling boats a lot smaller than this."

"We were all drunk, too. And sometimes we sank the boat. And I was only thirty-odd then."

"And I'm only thirty-odd now, and stone sober," I said from my stern seat, swinging my end of the long canoe out with my paddle. Jessie, Mary's Golden, a year old that September, whined.

"I can taste those hot dogs already," I said. We felt the canoe tip slightly as Clyde stepped in and sat down.

"Lead on, MacDuff," he said.

The motor started on the first pull. Things went better than I expected – often I run aground once or twice navigating at night, unless the moon is up. As usual, the longer we were out, the better my night vision got, until the black horizon was always visible with the myriad constellations above it contrasting brightly. The river held no surprises.

It was a normal year for water level, neither high nor low, so when I had the little island just upstream from camp hard on the beam, I bent gradually in to shore at speed, in a long sweeping turn. Finally, our course was exactly perpendicular to the shoreline and we were still on the step when the mud bottom kicked the motor up and we slid rapidly to a halt, Clyde's end of the canoe thirty feet closer to camp than water's edge. My attempt to panic him by running ashore wide open failed – maybe he couldn't see the shoreline rushing at us the last fifty yards.

He stood up in his chest waders and life vest, the coil of nylon bow rope in one hand, and stepped out. "Lafayette, we are here," he said, in the dark. "I think you hit the nail on the head."

"It's amazing what you can do when you're sober," I replied.

Our night vision went the way of the buffalo when I fired up the Coleman lanterns, but they made the camp seem much more civilized. A flock of roosting geese on the lake across the river voiced another opinion, but soon settled back down. Jessie stood at the edge of the circle of light, her ears cocked at the geese.

The secret to staying on the path to where we pitch the tent up the hill, lacking a flashlight, is to stay close behind the dog, which I did. The new tent, the Morning Glory, was only two years old, but went up quickly while the fire down the hill flickered to life and Clyde unlimbered the Swede saw on the most-lately-fallen aspen. I was untangling the fly tie-downs when Mary arrived with an armful of sleeping pads and duffel bags.

"Lafayette, we are here?" she said.

"That's what General Pershing said when he arrived in France with the AEF in '17 – actually, it was a captain or colonel on his staff, laying a wreath on the grave of the Marquis de Lafayette. Lafayette helped us out during our Revolution, you remember. Clyde's oldest brother was with the AEF. Clyde would've been thirteen and read about it in the *Topeka Daily Capital* or the *Kansas City Star*. Didn't you read about that in History?"

"Canadian history books mostly have Canadians in them."

"Oh."

Just now it escapes me why we'd gotten such a late start for duck camp but it's not hard to figure out my reasoning; no matter how difficult the passage to camp, getting there assured us of being on the marsh at first light on the morrow, instead of on the road. The morning flight, when there is one, is often brief. Then there's the whole rest of the day to search out the whereabouts of the ducks and geese not cooperative enough to fly by in range at sunup.

Ten years previous, in the Marines, I'd learned to carry a penlight to read maps at night, so when I woke up in the tent and listened for wind, my old penlight was close at hand to illuminate my watch. Time to get up. It had clouded over, a good sign, and a small breeze had sprung up, a better one. No frost. Jessie explored camp while I built the fire back up and hung the coffee water over it, from our willow tripod. Two handfuls of coffee had gone into the cold water, and the moment it rolled to a boil, I'd set it aside to steep and give the grounds a chance to settle. Most of the myths of coffee-making I've considered but not bought into – eggshells to settle the grounds, cold water to settle the grounds – reasoning that no one ever died of ingesting a few coffee grounds, anyhow.

"Holy mackerel!" Clyde exclaimed after one taste. "You save any coffee for tomorrow?" The two world wars of his lifetime had had less effect on the way he lived than the one Depression. The permanent casualties of that great economic collapse had still camped along the creek next to the Rock Island tracks behind our house in the early Fifties, and even *they* used two handfuls of begged coffee per pot.

"We got enough coffee to last two weeks," I said.

"What sounds good for breakfast?" Mary asked, sorting through the grub box.

"Coffee's enough for me," I said.

"Think I'll make some instant oatmeal," Clyde said.

"Spoken like a true Scot," Mary teased. She assumed anyone named 'Clyde' who was close with a dollar had to have roots in Scotland (them having an actual river named Clyde), as she assumed her own people, and anyone else named 'Coote' must hail from Cootehill, Ireland. "That sounds good to me."

"In that case, I'd better have some, too," I said. "If you two fool yourselves into thinking you've had breakfast, you may want to stay out till noon, and starve me to death."

The good part about not frying one's bacon and eggs until midmorning is, even if the morning flight is a total bust, one still has something to look forward to.

As is probably the case with most marshes, there was a best place for ducks within walking distance of camp (after a short paddle across the river, and a second best place, and a third best. Since Mary and I, at our ages, were looking forward to fifty more years on the marsh, we insisted Clyde take the best spot, he being already in his mid-seventies. Mary went to the alternate spot two gun ranges north of him, and I went to the old spot I'd pioneered the first evening on that piece of marsh seven years earlier, where, if I got a shot, it'd be a mallard. Clyde's spot was a potpourri; seven years hence, Terry would kill seven ducks of seven different species in one morning.

That morning was a little slow, however. When it got light enough to see a mile, we could make out small flocks working the largest lake east of us, and trading up and down the river in front of camp, but only a few used our passage out of or into that lake system. "Only a few" is a relative description, of course. I got no shots, Mary got three and killed a nice pintail, and Clyde banged away intermittently and bagged a widgeon, a shoveller and one mallard.

"Who ever heard," he asked on the walk back to the canoe, "of trying to shoot sitting flat on your butt in the mud? Man. I hope old Terry gets up here someday. Every duck he ever shot was off a nice plank seat in a log duck blind. He needs to see how the other half lives."

After breakfast we got busy and picked our four ducks, singed and gutted them, and stored them in an empty metal ammunition box in the shade. The sun came out, and Clyde, as was his wont, stretched out in the feather pile with his feet on the picking log and was soon sound asleep beside the dog. Mary and I repaired to the tent for our own nap.

It was close to a half-mile walk back to our spot that afternoon, so neither Clyde nor Mary felt moved to log any more miles in chest waders. I was certain a two- or three-mile hike might not only yield a few jump shots at local mallards on potholes, but might move enough flight ducks off the larger lakes to improve the shooting near camp. Plus, Jessie was dancing around at the first mention of "walk," one of the favorite words in her vocabulary, and dashed off in this direction and that, to look over her shoulder expectantly.

The wind, and the small noise it made in the grass, made the walking operation possible – otherwise, we'd never have gotten in range of a resting mallard. I had to keep Jessie pretty close, at that. Three hours later, I had four mallards on the leather strap over my shoulder, and had moved several hundred more. I'd walked far enough from camp, however, that I couldn't hear Mary or Clyde's shooting, if they'd gotten any. The wind stood from me to them, so I assumed they'd heard mine. Jessie explored the tall grass eagerly, splashing most of the time in ankle-deep water.

We were almost back, within a quarter mile, when the one distant note put me down on my knees in the grass and, I figured, got Mary and Clyde pointed in the right direction. A half mile west of them and hard down on the horizon, a long, undulating line appeared. Geese! Heading down our lakes for the mud flats I'd just traversed, and Clyde and Mary right in the center of their favored route. Jessie sat nervously on command, her ears up, and whined. She could see a duck or goose as far away as any of us.

The flock, as they often do, began drifting to our right, off their line to Clyde's hiding place, and toward Mary, putting on a little altitude as they came. Still, it promised to be a thirty-yard shot.

The black barrel of her 12 gauge, still loaded with duck loads probably, lifted vertically from the grass, tracked the left end of the flock, and a goose folded before the sound reached me. Jessie was

The Dharma Goose

The author, Clyde, and 3-month old Jessie, 1977

off at a dead run, leaping repeatedly above the grass to mark the fall. The geese put on a lot more altitude, honking excitedly, but no more shots came.

The water where the goose fell was deep, so Mary stayed put. She'd been watching us approach for an hour and knew Jessie would beat her to the goose anyway. Jessie and I got to Mary's hide at about the same time, her with the goose in her mouth. Clyde beat us both and was already congratulating Mary.

She held the goose high, by the neck, and turned it this way and that, while I patted Jessie and told her what a good girl she was. Clyde was happier than if he'd gotten the goose himself. It was Mary's first goose.

"But," I finally asked, "why only shoot once? They were in perfect range. You might've gotten two or three."

"I don't know," she replied. "At the time, one seemed like enough. Do you know the Ten Precepts?"

"Of what?"

"Zen Buddhism."

"Are you kidding? I can only remember half the Ten Commandments."

"Well, one of the big ones is, 'Don't be greedy.'"

"Cripes. How do you know He wasn't talking about shooting over the limit?"

"It's hard to believe," Clyde said, "that someone who's never picked a goose already has enough sense to only shoot one a day. The last two you got, John, took us almost the whole next day to pick."

"If you two will excuse me," I said, "I'm still two birds short of my limit, and I got to go try to get them. Buddhism sounds unAmerican to me, and counter to human nature, not to mention the dog's. Try leaving the hot dogs lying around camp on the ground and see how far this 'Don't be greedy' stuff gets you in duck camp."

"Still an hour till sundown," Clyde said, starting off for his own hide. "I guess this means you're volunteering to pick any more geese we might get tonight…"

John Hewitt

Avoiding Zillich's Mortgage

Living with Mary was a lot like trying to steal a shotgun out of an unlocked pickup cab also occupied by a sleeping Chesapeake; you never knew how it was going to turn out. A few years after we met, she began exhibiting nesting behaviors familiar to any observer of waterfowl, which I succeeded in postponing with the purchase of a puppy.

Puppies are a much more forgiving medium than children to hone one's training skills on. After a dozen years, give or take a couple, they all conveniently die and wipe the slate clean. Children dog the inept parent forever, with their continuing appearances in the police blotter, the divorces and dissolutions column, and the weekly bankruptcies listing.

I had been thinking about a Chesapeake, for no other reason than that, like Everest, they were there. Training a Lab is about as challenging as learning to type. Mary had been thinking about a Golden.

On the way to town to buy the Golden, I listed all the breed's drawbacks I'd ever heard, and made up a few that sounded pretty good. It was a pleasant change from wrangling over who was going to do the dishes, which had been going on for five years.

There was no way I could lose on the puppy project. If it blew up in her face, it would further forestall starting a family – maybe forever. If Jessie turned out well, which she did, then I'd have a good dog for ten or fifteen years.

The eventual negotiations over children lasted about five minutes also, as long as it took me to make enough dire predictions to justify an "I-told-you-so" if any of the kids ever got caught with their hand in the till at the PTA cake raffle.

Life would have been so much simpler, though, if, like me, Mary had been weaned on *Field and Stream*. Her reading tastes were more eclectic, however, and between Jack Kerouac's *On the Road* and Tom Hornbein's *Everest: The West Ridge*, she was always going through some phase. The phases often overlapped.

"I absolutely did not ever," I remember telling her, "lose anything on Mount Everest," when she started making noises about hiking from Katmandu to the base camp there at 17,000 feet. This was the year before Jessie.

So she did that one by herself, and discovered a great truth about Asia: if the young gentlemen in black pajamas don't succeed in sending the visiting foreigner home in a bag after one of their quaint nocturnal hand grenade rituals, there are even more insidious things present in the water that can get the same thing done from a different direction. She was always spare at 125 pounds. The next time I saw her, at 98 pounds, she was skeletal.

She made it to the base camp, of course, intestinal parasites or not, but the hike back about got her. This interlude, which I call her Tenzing Norgay phase, occupied the briefest of gaps in her longer

Avoiding Zillich's Mortgage

"Me and Bobby McGee" phase. For a while there, she was a hitchhiking fool. Acquiring the puppy did not immediately allay that impulse, although trying to hitchhike with it eventually did.

I'd winched the engine out of the Bronco the previous year, at 145,000 miles, and completely rebuilt it, but had decided it'd made its last trip Outside. So I had no other alternatives handy when she suggested we hitchhike from Alaska to Kansas for pheasants and ducks.

The first hundred miles took two hours. The next hundred took two days. As I had predicted, a lot more people gave rides to single young redheaded girls with daypacks than to two people with monster Kelties and a puppy. And shotguns. She couldn't get over how narrow-minded travelers had gotten since the last time she'd hitchhiked that stretch of highway.

The opening of pheasant season in Kansas was approaching us a whole lot faster than we were approaching Kansas, so she agreed to throw in the towel in Edmonton and buy a car. Volvos have more latterly become associated with yuppies, but the one we acquired for $141.00 was built when most yuppies were in elementary school, and the term had not been coined. Originally blue, it had acquired what Ed Gray would have somewhat nostalgically termed "a patina of age," while Terry Coward would've called it "rust." Too many Montreal winters, with that province's ubiquitous salty slush, had corroded all of its external panels so thoroughly that there was some question as to what was still holding the fenders and hood on the chassis. The tires were as bald as Terry's father, Jesse, and as it turned out, about as dependable.

And yet. No affluent Canadian burgher rolling comfortably across the prairie in his new Lincoln Town Car or Chrysler New Yorker was half so delighted with his lot as Mary and I in our rusted, smoking Swedish derelict, with our shotguns and bedrolls in the trunk and the little Golden Retriever snoozing on the threadbare back seat, opening day but a week away.

That was Mary's fourth year with the Model 1100, thankfully the last shotgun I would ever have to buy for a girlfriend, unless you count the new trap gun I bought her last February. She had survived the cramps-between-the-shoulder-blades that had plagued her first season with the new gun, and was shooting it more confidently on both pheasants and ducks.

Jessie decided pheasants were her favorite thing, a heretical but common failing of all the retriever breeds. Terry cites this predilection of every retriever we've ever owned as further proof of their intelligence. They'd have to be stupid, he says, to prefer clamping their wet butts to a frozen sand bar in a drafty duck blind for hours at a time, and for what? For the chance to dive into ice water over their heads and swim a hundred yards in a strong current to bring back some uncooperative duck that, with a few memorable exceptions, they never get a bite of? If only Jessie could have convinced us to shoot hen pheasants, which come without spurs, life would have been as perfect for her as it was for us.

Federal wildlife poobahs in charge of managing duck futures in D.C. that decade were in a liberal mood, not insisting we leave as many for seed as before, and not only was it legal to shoot five mallards a day, but often there were enough around that we all did it.

Unless Russell Chatham is a liar, I told Mary, I bet he'd be happy to lighten our duck load a tad on the way home. We planned to pass through his corner of Montana westbound for a Thanksgiving eastern Washington chukar hunt.

Russell was taken aback twice; first, when we roared (there was a foot of exhaust pipe missing upstream of our muffler) into town offering plucked, wrapped, frozen, grain-fed Kansas mallards, and second, when we voiced our intention to drive through the night west over the mountains in a horrific snowstorm with four bald tires. We thanked him for the copies of his latest book that he signed and pressed on us, and attributed his unexpected conservatism in the area of all-night marathon drives to his advancing age. One way or another, he appeared to be close to 40.

When Mary insisted it was her turn to drive, I sensed this was about to become An Issue, crawled into the sleeping bag in the back seat, and consigned my fate to the Swedes who allegedly designed Volvos to be the most crash-worthy vehicles on the road.

All the traffic but us was eastbound, coming down the mountain. Our rear tires frequently broke loose and spun, and we'd sashay left and right before Mary regained control. Kerouac's book should have come with a warning label.

She finally really lost it. "Ohhh, John!" was all she said. The headlights of the oncoming cars and tractor-trailers shone through our front, side, back, other-side, and front windows in rapid succession as we spun up the road once, twice, thrice, and I braced myself for the crash.

The snowbank on our side of the road was soft and deep, stopping us with zero damage, and the snow shovel I'd bought in Billings paid for itself. At that, we'd have been there until May 15th (as we say in Alaska) but for the typical kindness of a Montana stranger with a large pickup, who snatched us right out. I drove thereafter. Very carefully. I have always pretty much *enjoyed* life, but the rest of that night I *savored* it, all the way over the Rockies with Mary and Jessie snoring peacefully on the back seat.

The hood blew off at an inopportune time...nothing was open to buy the requisite cheap drill and bit, two dozen fat, short sheet metal screws, screwdriver and two huge barn door hinges to fix it with. It could be tied back on with rope, and was.

John Zillich, a boyhood pal of Rau's, was at a somewhat different stage in his life than us. He had a brick home on a nice street in Kennewick, two Labs, a wife, one small boy, five fruit trees, two working automobiles, a steady job, a much-used 16-gauge Browning auto of the old design, and the tiniest shotshell reloading press in the history of the world. I had known him before he started his family, when he had been fairly normal, but after his blessed event he had gone off the deep end on the subject of children. As if any new dad has any idea what he might be in for. Mary was all ears.

Thanksgiving dinner, which they may have held an hour or two for us, was great, though my efforts at keeping the conversation on retrievers and chukars largely failed, with three-fourths of the diners wanting to talk about babies.

We had a good hunt, though. The expression "good chukar hunt" is redundant, however, particularly in cool, wool-shirt November weather, due to the nature of the country chukars inhabit. Mary and Jessie loved it. We may have killed a bird or two, also, although I wouldn't swear to it. I used my time climbing out to rimrock and back to canyon floors productively, marshalling my arguments against children any time soon, for us.

Mary, though Canadian, was as true a product of the Bobby Kennedy era as I was of the Eisenhower years, as her reason for a starting a family revealed: "Why not?"

"Well, look," I explained, recently showered and shaved and tucked into our bed in the relatively palatial downstairs bedroom that the baby squalling overhead would one day boot me out of, "Just look at this poor bastard Zillich. You *know* he has to have a mortgage the size of the National Debt on a joint like this. Mary, he can't even afford to buy factory shotgun shells to hunt *chukars* with! Cripes, we'll have birds scattered out for half a mile down the rimrock and he's screwing around looking for lost empties. You call that a *life?*"

Apparently she did, because she got up early, threw her sleeping bag, shotgun, and pup in what was technically her car, and headed north. I still had chukars to hunt and enough money in my billfold to get me home via an airport or two.

Being an advocate of the truth, I have to admit I missed the puppy more than her that day – it had been showing a world of promise. John rooted me out of bed the following midnight to take a phone call. She'd had the new tires that I'd given her the money for put on in Spokane, but the temperature in B.C. had been dropping steadily and was down to -40°F where she was trying to recross the Rockies at Crowsnest Pass. The Volvo was only barely running.

I told her to put a bottle of gas line de-icer in the gas tank, and went back to sleep. It cured the little problem, but not the big one.

Consequently, that summer I found myself cornered in a Fairbanks café booth by Russ Wood's wife, Ann, her upriver neighbor, Maria, (both only recently married), and Mary. "So why," Ann more or less demanded, "don't you guys just go ahead and get married?"

I invoked two of Terry Coward's Rules to Live Your Life By: (1) Stay out of kicking fights with mules, and (2) Never argue with anyone about anything while you're trying to eat dinner.

"Okay," I said, washing down a mouthful of BLT sandwich with hot coffee, "let's get married Friday." This was Monday. The pause in the conversation threatened to last through dessert.

"Why Friday?"

Girls aren't the only ones who can echo Bobby Kennedy at opportune moments. "Why not?" I said. "It's my mom's birthday. Why go to the trouble of having to learn to remember a whole new date when it's just as easy to use one I already know?"

"That's what's so nice about men," Ann said. "They're so romantic."

Our anniversary falls on Saturday this year. Terrific. I think I'll go fishing. Every morning for a week I've been finding the table covered with old atlases and old *Mileposts*, the standard travel directory for the Alaska Highway. Two of the girls, the oldest, seem to have inherited their mother's Kerouacian genes and have the road gleam in their eyes. Katharine figures they can make Vancouver in four driving days if she does half the driving. There is a pile of tentage and sleeping bags and a stack of fishing rods in one corner of the basement. Tom has to be in Tacoma the morning of our anniversary for some excellent Boy Scout seagoing adventure.

Which will leave me at home alone, August being the peak of the building season. Maybe they'll leave the Chesapeake or the setter. I had better slip downstairs and hide my fly rod, lest, in their enthusiasm, they include it in their trip paraphernalia.

Rose, our second-oldest daughter, leadoff hitter and shortstop on one of the two softball teams I coach, started a double play with Russ and Ann's second-oldest daughter, Heidi, turning the pivot at second, and Heidi scored Rose from first on an opposite-field long ball for the winning run in the second game last week.

Zillich, who is two dogs into a German Shorthair phase, and ten years into coaching youth soccer, called out of the blue last week also, for the first time in sixteen years, to invite me chukar hunting in November. I think I'll go. If I have time after fishing on this year's anniversary, maybe I'll crank out some chukar loads on the reloading press in the cabin…

The author with Jessie, southeast Washington, 1979 – photo by John Zillich